Great Sea Battles

Oliver Warner

Great Sea Battles

SPRING BOOKS

London · New York · Sydney · Toronto

Originally published 1963 by
George Weidenfeld & Nicolson Ltd
© 1963 by Oliver Warner

This edition published 1968 by
The Hamlyn Publishing Group Ltd
London · New York · Sydney · Toronto
Hamlyn House, Feltham, Middlesex, England

3rd Impression 1971

Printed in Italy by
Arnoldo Mondadori Editore Officine Grafiche, Verona

ISBN 0 600 01650 1

To Christopher Lloyd

Contents

CONTENTS

On the maps the symbol ⚓ marks the site of the battle

Introduction

SEA-BATTLES HAVE HAD as diverse causes as war itself, and they have provided as many surprises. Few who have survived one have been enthusiastic for another, though there have been exceptions, the elder Tromp perhaps, Monck, Hawke, Suffren, Nelson and a handful more. Sometimes sea-battles have been conducted with skill such as to amount to high art – Howard in the Channel, Tromp off the Downs, Suffren off the coasts of India, Hawke at Quiberon Bay, Nelson at the Nile, Togo at Tsushima – but as it is one in which suffering and often protracted horror plays a major part, the truest gallery illustrating the theme would have beauty only as an incidental, almost accidental, ingredient.

Fortunately, the artist has seen battles at one remove, though again there have been exceptions such as the two Dutch masters, the van de Veldes, and the Englishman Nicholas Pocock. In general the painter's aim has been to produce from rough sketches and other immediate records works representing ships in action which will at once commemorate and please. And for centuries the artist had in the sailing ship a subject of infinite variety and wonder, a creation of man's hand which came to its perfection during the course of the nineteenth century, the earlier decades of which saw the golden age of the ship of the line.

At a time when her glory was at last in decline, when steam had already been applied to maritime war, Ruskin wrote in *The Harbours of England* (1856): 'It will always be said of us, with unabated reverence: THEY BUILT SHIPS OF THE LINE. Take it all in all, a ship of the line is the most honourable thing that man, as a gregarious animal, has ever produced. By himself, unhelped, he can do better things than ships of the line; he can make poems and pictures, and other such concentrations of what is best in him. But as a being living in flocks, and hammering out, with alternate strokes and mutual agreement, what is necessary for him in these flocks to get or produce, the ship of the line is his first work. Into that he has put as much of his human patience, common sense, forethought, experimental philosophy, self-control, habits of order and obedience, thoroughly wrought handwork, defiance of brute elements, careless courage, careful patriotism, and calm expectation of the judgment of God, as can well be put into a space of 300 feet long by 80 broad. And I am thankful to have lived in an age when I could see this thing so done.'

We have moved on. We have exchanged Ruskin's advantage for others; yet the artists he so admired, not least his beloved Turner, captured the beauty of the ship of the line in all her ramification, and in whatever country she was built, for the benefit of posterity. They have salvaged beauty from destruction, and it is as fresh today as when it was first looked upon, sometimes with highly critical eyes, by those for whom it was commissioned.

When the sea-battle became swifter, its representation became poorer, even when it lost little in purely factual value. The artistic distance between Navarino, the last battle fought wholly under sail, and the weird duel of thirty-five years later between the *Monitor* and the *Merri-*

Suffering and protracted horror play a major part in sea battles. ABOVE: *Ludolf Bakhuizen's painting of a boat action during a battle of the Anglo-Dutch wars provides a shockingly vivid picture of hand-to-hand fighting in the seventeenth century.* BELOW: *The appalling devastation wreaked by twentieth-century air attack on the Japanese heavy cruiser* Mikuma *was recorded by a photographer just before she sank after the Battle of Midway in 1942*

mac in Hampton Roads, is so great as to seem to belong to another world. Presently, with increasing use of the camera, it would be still greater. Photographs showing the battered Russian ships after Tsushima convey a sharp though not a lovely notion of the effect of shell-fire, and there is an appallingly timed photograph of the battle-cruiser *Invincible* at the moment of her destruction at Jutland. Such items add to the technical though scarcely to the pictorial record of sea battle. They commemorate indeed, but such response as they engender differs widely

from that appertaining to, let us say, Pocock's martial but still gracious version of the fight between the *Brunswick* and *Le Vengeur* at the Glorious First of June: and yet Pocock was realistic enough – he was there in person.

In the end, the formal battle-piece tends to disappear altogether. Distances grow so great that battles are won not by ships but by aircraft launched from them, and when that happens, the best that the recorder can do is to show the sort of machine by which the day was won.

Yet when all is said, and whatever the means employed

INTRODUCTION

– galleys, ships of the line, ironclads, dreadnoughts, air-craft and their carriers – it is men who win and lose battles, and it is in the portraiture of the sea-commander, from Don John of Austria, through Drake, de Ruyter, Howe, Perry, Farragut, Graf von Spee, Nimitz and many another, that a principal aspect of success or failure is recorded – in these leaders, and in the officers and men they led. These are the people who braved danger for their country; their story must be the chief subject of any such book as this.

Sailors, whatever their personal qualities, have particular problems to resolve: they relate to the sea itself and the winds which disturb its surface; in war, the way in which to get the better of the enemy visible or not yet in sight. Moreover in a naval encounter, every man faces the same danger at the same time. The admiral who errs, himself pays the penalty, which is not always true of land warfare, though modern generals are apt to be found as near the forward positions as they were at Waterloo.

The chase, the mêlée, the stratagem, the surprise, the combination, the assault, these are a few of the innumerable aspects of maritime warfare, and if any lesson may be drawn from a series of great actions, from Lepanto to Leyte Gulf, it is that the day does not necessarily go to the stronger nor even to the better equipped, and that the admiral who inspires as well as commands, the man who refuses to let his resolution weaken in adversity, above all the man who makes shrewd use of his intelligence, may pluck advantage from loss, even from near-disaster, and may turn that advantage into triumph.

BOTTOM: *The most famous British ship of the line and the fastest sailing three-decker in the navy of her time, the Victory, painted by Monamy Swaine in 1792, when she was Lord Hood's flagship.*

Willem van de Velde the Younger in the seventeenth century and Nicholas Pocock in the eighteenth were two 'war artists' who were actually present at the battles they painted. RIGHT TOP: *In van de Velde's painting of the Battle of the Texel, 11 August 1673, de Ruyter's flagship is on the left.* RIGHT CENTRE: *A French two-decker of de Grasse's fleet in the foreground breaking off the engagement at the Battle of Frigate Bay, 26 January 1782, painted by Pocock.* RIGHT BOTTOM: *Norman Wilkinson's painting of a German air attack on the Malta Convoy, 9–14 August 1942, points the contrast between the differing conduct of sea battles and the different styles of representing them under sail and under steam*

The Speed of Ships, 1570–1942

This diagram shows how the improvements in ship design and, later, the change from sail to power enabled a Second World War aircraft carrier to sail, under the best possible conditions, almost six times as far in twenty-four hours as a Spanish galleon at the time of the Armada.

It can be seen also that, in speed (as in design and in the conduct of naval warfare), there was little change from the middle of the seventeenth to the middle of the nineteenth century.

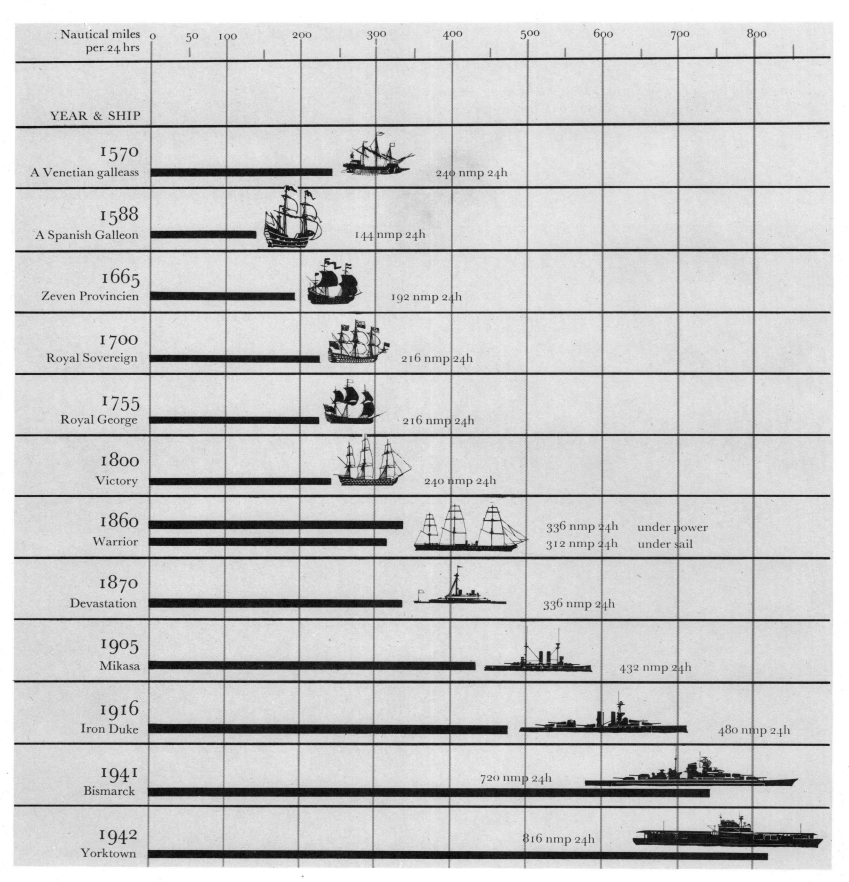

Nautical miles per 24 hrs — 0   50   100   200   300   400   500   600   700   800

YEAR & SHIP

1570 — A Venetian galleass — 240 nmp 24h

1588 — A Spanish Galleon — 144 nmp 24h

1665 — Zeven Provincien — 192 nmp 24h

1700 — Royal Sovereign — 216 nmp 24h

1755 — Royal George — 216 nmp 24h

1800 — Victory — 240 nmp 24h

1860 — Warrior — 336 nmp 24h   under power
312 nmp 24h   under sail

1870 — Devastation — 336 nmp 24h

1905 — Mikasa — 432 nmp 24h

1916 — Iron Duke — 480 nmp 24h

1941 — Bismarck — 720 nmp 24h

1942 — Yorktown — 816 nmp 24h

The Range of Guns, 1570–1942

From this diagram it can be seen that the big guns of a Second World War battleship had a range almost twenty times as great as a galleass cannon of the time of Lepanto. The diagram shows that, as with the speed of ships, there was very little change from the middle of the sixteenth to the middle of the nineteenth century, during which time battles were decided by the broadside, delivered at almost point-blank range. Greater speed and improved manoeuvrability brought new tactics, which required longer-ranged guns.

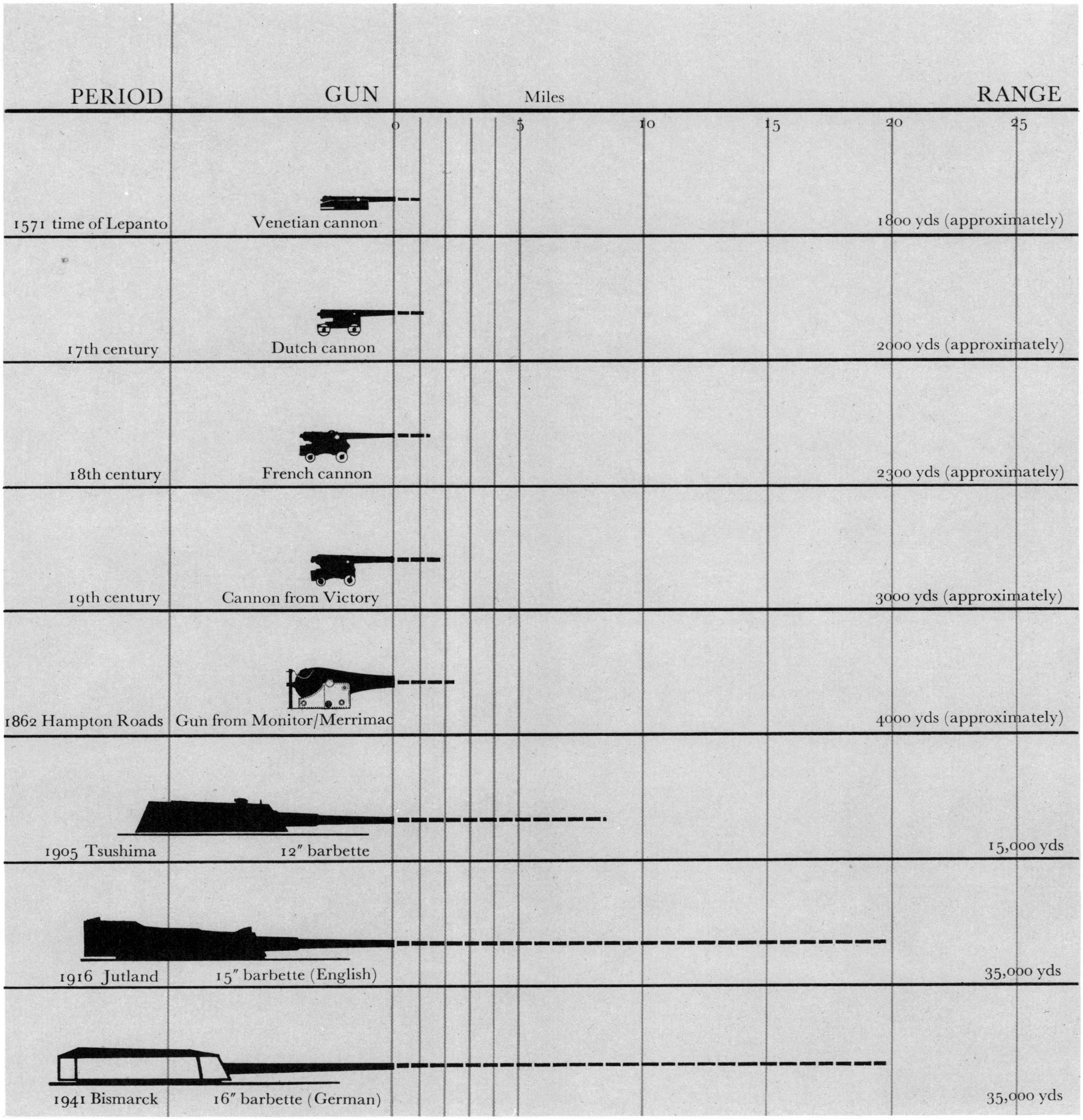

PERIOD	GUN	Miles	RANGE
		0 5 10 15 20 25	
1571 time of Lepanto	Venetian cannon		1800 yds (approximately)
17th century	Dutch cannon		2000 yds (approximately)
18th century	French cannon		2300 yds (approximately)
19th century	Cannon from Victory		3000 yds (approximately)
1862 Hampton Roads	Gun from Monitor/Merrimac		4000 yds (approximately)
1905 Tsushima	12″ barbette		15,000 yds
1916 Jutland	15″ barbette (English)		35,000 yds
1941 Bismarck	16″ barbette (German)		35,000 yds

Lepanto

1571

A crushing defeat of a massive Turkish fleet by the forces of Don John of Austria, representing Spain, Venice, Genoa, Malta and the Papal States

SEA-BATTLES MAY BE GREAT IN showing the seaman-fighter at his most skilful or resolute: they may be tame and even indecisive as encounters yet important in their effect: or they may be both. Lepanto, the earliest sea-battle of the western world to be celebrated by artists of renown, was great in every sense of the word. It was a milestone in the grim and protracted struggle between the forces of Christendom and those of Mahomet.

It was fought on 7 October 1571 in the waters which divide Thessaly and the Morea, and it marked a turning point in the history of Europe. A fleet, made up of the forces of the Triple Alliance or Holy League of Spain, the Dominions of the Pope, and the Republic of Venice, all under the command of Don John of Austria, defeated the principal fleet of the Turks under Ali Pasha. On the victor's side, notable leaders were the Marquis de Santa Cruz, a Spaniard, Andrea Doria, leading a Genoese squadron, and Marco Antonio Colonna, who commanded the forces of Pius V. It was, in fact as in name, a company drawn from most of Catholic Europe, France excepted.

Lepanto, coming as it did after the repulse which the Turks had met with at the siege of Malta six years earlier, made it certain that the Mediterranean would not become a Moslem Lake. Henceforward, no Sultan would in fact exercise paramount sea-power, and

although this result was slow to make itself apparent, the only further Moslem expansion into the Europe which they had invaded with such success would be at the expense of Poland and Russia. It would be by land. By sea, Spaniards and Italians, with the example before them of the island Knights of Malta, had shown that with leadership, courage, and the help of a new weapon, in this case the heavily-gunned galleass, they could defeat the ancient method of battle solely with oared galleys, manned by slaves.

Don John of Austria, who in the year of Lepanto was not yet twenty-five, though he had already served with distinction against the Moors in Granada, was the natural son of the Emperor Charles V by a Bavarian, Barbara Blomberg. He was thus half-brother to Philip II of Spain, one of the pillars of the Alliance, and he had long been, in name at least, the principal Spanish admiral. Fair-haired, eager for fame, Don John proved a good leader for a mixed and quarrelsome fleet.

Among the Italian forces, the Venetians, led by Augustino Barbarigo and the veteran Sebastian Veniero, were smarting under the recent loss of most of Cyprus to the Turks, and they bore no love towards the Genoese, their ancient rivals at sea, led by Giovanni Andrea Doria, nephew of one of Genoa's greatest men. In Doria's squadron, a Spanish volunteer was serving whose fame was destined to outshine even that of the commanders. He was Miguel de Cervantes, later to become the author of *Don Quixote*.

15

The Alliance had been formed in May 1571, through the tireless efforts of Pius V. Its purpose was to check the advance of the Turks by sea, and to curb the depradations of the African 'Barbary' states of Algiers, Tunis and Tripoli, by the operations of a joint Fleet. The first rendezvous was to be at Messina. When he arrived there, Don John found himself in charge of over three hundred ships, two-thirds of them known as royal galleys, each with a nominal complement of a hundred soldiers in addition to the rowers who supplied the motive power.

The Spanish contingent was the largest: eighty galleys, twenty-two other vessels, and no less than 21,000 fighting men. The Venetians contributed over a hundred vessels, but they were poorly manned, and their heavily armed galleasses, designed by the constructor Francesco Bressano, were in fact the Republic's most important asset. These galleasses, which were towed into action by lighter vessels, were commanded by patricians who took an oath never to refuse combat to less than twenty-five opponents. Broader in the beam than the galley, the additional depth of the galleass allowed the erection, forward, of a structure, fitted with swivel guns, which anticipated the modern armoured turret.

In the galleass, the usual ornamental stem of the galley was replaced by a formidable point, while lower down was a solid cutwater, which the heavy displacement of the vessel made effective against anything of smaller size which could not get out of the way. Sides and stern were also heavily armed, while the rowers were protected by a deck which served as a platform for the fighting men. In battle the rowers were yoked in both directions, some pulling and some pushing at the 50-foot oars. The galleass oar differed from that of the galley in that it had slots into which the men could insert their fists, the oar itself being too large to grasp entire.

The Pope himself fitted out twelve galleys, hired many more, and supplied the necessary troops. No less than 80,000 men assembled at Messina with his official blessing. Of these, some 50,000 volunteers, pressed men, and slaves, laboured at the oars. The rest were soldiers, and it was to representatives of the fighting men that Don John, with the aid of a black-board, explained his methods. He gave his captains detailed information as to how he would meet the most likely tactical contingencies, and he arranged appropriate signals.

While the admiral was surveying and ordering his fleet, he had news that the Turks, who were believed to have massed about 300 ships, were roving the Ionian Sea, and

Don John of Austria, whose qualities of leadership succeeded in uniting the disparate and quarrelsome members of the Triple Alliance

were attacking islands therein. On 16 September, the Christians put to sea, and the first precise news of the enemy came before the end of the month, when Don John anchored off Corfu. There he learnt that Ali Pasha had recently landed, burnt some churches, failed to subdue the island's fortress, and had then retreated to the anchorage of Lepanto which was far up the eighty-mile stretch of water now known as the Corinthian Gulf.

At a Council of War, characterized like many such Councils by acrimony and dispute, those who were for instant attack carried the day. They included Colonna, Barbarigo, Santa Cruz and Don John himself. The season was growing late, and the differences between the Allies, never far from the surface, were increasing. Spaniards and Venetians had already come to blows, largely due to the fact that Spaniards had to be drafted into the Venetian ships to bring them up to strength.

Off Cephalonia, on 6 October, a ship from Crete brought news of the fall of Famagusta, the last stronghold in Cyprus, and of the torture and death of its noble Venetian defenders. A wave of horror spread through the Allies, and an immediate advance was ordered into waters where the enemy was known to be waiting. One further item of news was not altogether cheering. It appeared that Ali Pasha had been reinforced by the ships of the Algerian corsair Uluch Ali, once a Calabrian fisherman, who was known, at least by reputation, to many in the Christian fleet.

At Lepanto, as at most earlier naval battles, the fleets met like armies. Their formation was rigid; the commands were military; and tactics were based upon experience by land. The sailors got the ships where they were wanted: the 'generals' and their soldiers fought it out.

During the night of 6 October, the Turks, with a favouring wind, advanced westward towards the Christians. At dawn on 7 October the most powerful forces which had ever met at sea came within sight of one another at the entrance to what is now called the Gulf of Patras, which is west of the larger Gulf of Corinth.

Before he drew up his formal line of battle, Don John gave two orders. The first was to remove the iron beaks which protruded ten or fifteen feet from the bows of certain of the fighting ships. The second was that no one should fire 'until near enough to be splashed with the blood of an enemy'. Both directions were wise. The battle would be won not by ramming, but by close fighting, in which the armour worn by the Spaniards, allied to their arquebuses, might prove a decisive advantage.

Barbarigo and his Venetians were placed on the left wing, Barbarigo himself sailing as close as he dared to the inshore rocks and shoals, hoping that his flank could not be turned. Andrea Doria was on the right, Papal galleys being mingled with the Genoese. In the centre was the

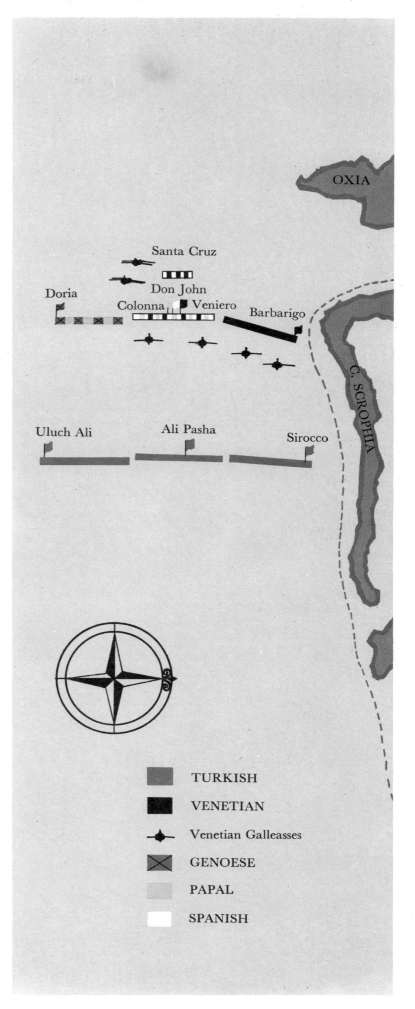

TURKISH

VENETIAN

Venetian Galleasses

GENOESE

PAPAL

SPANISH

flagship of Don John, conspicuous by its high carved poop and triple stern lanterns, its green pendant at the fore-peak and its Holy Standard at the main-top. Near him were Veniero and Colonna. In reserve were thirty-five Spanish and Venetian galleys under Santa Cruz, ready to apply their strength where it was most needed.

As the fleets neared one another, the spearhead of the Christian attack, six Venetian galleasses, were towed into position. Two, in line ahead, were placed in front of each main squadron. When every preparation had been made, Don John boarded a fast vessel and sailed along and behind the three-mile front across which his forces extended, heartening his men, and in his turn, being

LEFT TOP: *Giovanni Andrea Doria, leader of the Genoese contingent. He fought on the right wing of the Christian fleet and suffered heavy losses at the hands of Uluch Ali*

LEFT CENTRE: *A portrait of Pius V, who was responsible for the formation of the Triple Alliance to unite the forces of Christendom against the 'infidel' Turk. He himself contributed a large number of galleys and troops to the forces at Lepanto*

LEFT BOTTOM: *Uluch Ali, who had experience as an Algerian corsair and whose ships severely damaged the right wing of the Christian forces. At the end of the battle he fought a last desperate encounter with Don Juan of Cardona*

RIGHT: *The scene on board Turkish galleys during the battle*

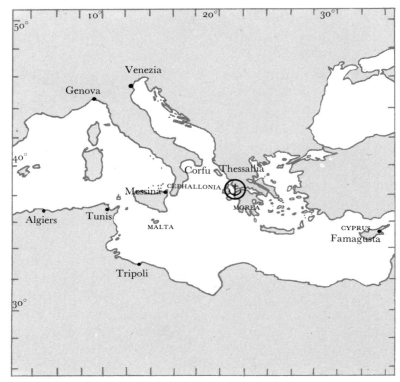

A further section from the Vicentino fresco. The Lion of St Mark can be seen flying at the stern of the nearest Venetian galley

cheered. The Allies were at least united in respect for their commander, and their trust was justified.

By the time Don John had returned to his galley, the wind had changed in his favour. He was now able to see that Ali Pasha had his fleet arrayed in the form of a huge crescent, but this was altered, almost at once, to conform to his own dispositions. There were many Christian galley-slaves in the Turkish fleet. To them Ali Pasha said: 'If I win the battle, I promise you your liberty. If the day is yours, then God has given it to you'.

First blood was drawn by the galleasses of the Allied centre. Their guns, heavier than anything the Turks possessed, were used with such effect that no enemy could close with them. They did their execution at long range, sinking several Turkish galleys even before the main forces were in contact. Partly as a result of this initial set-back, the left and right wings of the Moslems separated from the centre. Uluch Ali made a wide sweep towards the southern shore, in an attempt to outflank Andrea Doria, while Mahomet Sirocco held a similar

course towards Barbarigo. Ali Pasha's centre squadron, eluding the powerful galleasses as best it could, drove on to meet that of Don John.

By midday, or shortly after, the Turkish flagship and that of Don John were locked together, crossbow and arquebus being exchanged for sword and scimitar, the decks slippery with blood from close fighting: and by that time, all three squadrons were at grips.

On the Christian left, Mahomet Sirocco's manoeuvre succeeded. His knowledge of the shore-line enabled him to sail even closer to it than Barbarigo, and to surround him. The Venetian admiral was attacked by eight galleys, and he himself was killed by an arrow. Twice the Venetian flagship was stormed; twice it was re-taken. At last, when help came from Canale and others, Mahomet Sirocco's own ship was sunk and he himself was thrown into the water. Although by then badly wounded, he was rescued, but only to be beheaded on the spot by his captors.

On the Christian right the battle had at first gone

A typical representation by an unknown artist of the Battle of Lepanto, which was recorded and embroidered upon by every nation in Christendom. This painting emphasizes the dangers of the coastal waters in which the action was fought

equally badly. Although Uluch Ali had not been able to outflank Andrea Doria, he had at once doubled back to a gap which had opened in the Allied line, and had taken part of Don John's squadron in the rear. Among the ships attacked was the *Capitana* of Malta, commanded by Giustiniani, Prior of the Order of St John. The Prior fell with five arrows in his body, and the *Capitana* was made prize. At the most critical time Santa Cruz, seeing the Maltese in tow of the enemy, moved to the rescue, and Uluch Ali, relinquishing his capture, made haste to retreat.

The issue was decided in the centre. Here, from the first, the virtue of Don John's order to dismantle the iron beaks had been clear. The forepeak of the Turkish flagship, unshorn of its long spur, towered over the rowing benches of his adversary, but his forecastle guns fired into the air. Those of Don John, placed at a lower level, riddled the Turkish galley with shot just below her water-line, and the admiral could manoeuvre and close more easily than his opponent. The bulwarks were well

protected by boarding nets, and the armoured Spanish arquebusiers soon decimated the Turkish ranks. Not for nothing were the Spaniards reckoned the steadiest soldiers of their time.

The climax came when Don John gave the order to board; once, twice, parties were driven back, but at last they carried the Turkish poop. There Ali Pasha, already wounded in the head by a ball from an arquebus, tried to buy his life with a promise of treasure. It was in vain. Even his protective talisman, the right canine of Mahomet contained in a crystal ball, did not avail him. A soldier cut him down, hacked off his head, and carried it to Don John. The admiral, recoiling in horror, ordered the man to throw the grisly trophy into the sea; but he was disobeyed. The Spaniard mounted it on a pike, which was then held aloft on the prow of the Turkish flagship. Consternation spread among the Moslems, and, within a few moments, resistance was over. The Ottoman standard, a sacred emblem inscribed with the name of Allah twenty-nine thousand times and never before lost

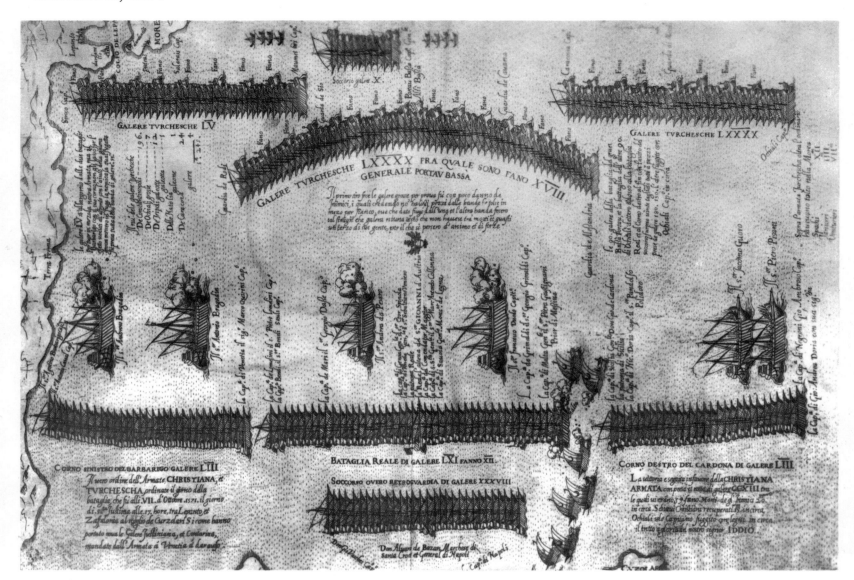

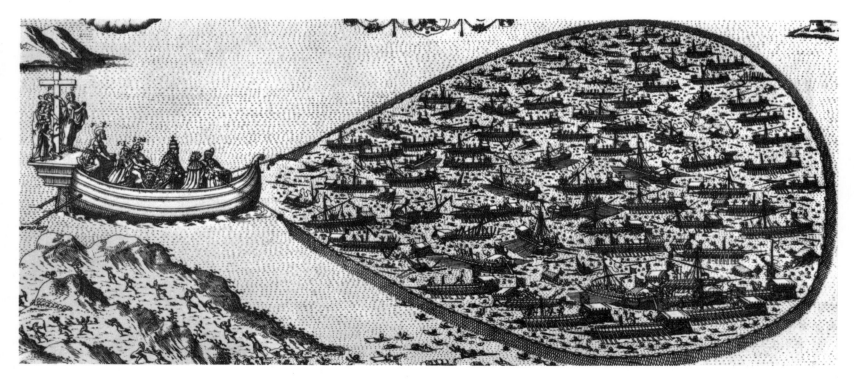

TOP: *A contemporary engraving showing the disposition of the Turkish and Christian fleets, the number of ships involved and the names of the commanders.* BOTTOM: *An allegorical engraving of 1572 showing God and his saints uniting the forces of Christendom against the 'infidel' Turk*

in battle, was lowered from the maintop. All attempts at relief were repulsed either by Don John or by the vigilant Santa Cruz, now returned from the rescue of the *Capitana*. Don John was then able to turn his attention to his right wing, where all was not well with Andrea Doria, who, for a time at least, was believed to have been the prisoner of one Occhiali.

No less than five of Doria's galleys had been stricken. The *San Giovanni* and the *Piamontesa* of Savoy were ships of the dead. The *Doncella* was in not much better case, while in the *Florence*, only the captain and seventeen seamen survived out of two hundred. The *Marquesa* was also hard pressed. It was in this ship that Cervantes was serving. He had been ill with fever before the battle, but he had risen from his sick-bed and had volunteered for a place of danger. There he remained throughout the battle, one of the wounds he received disabling his left hand for life.

Uluch Ali, whose Algerians had done most of the damage on the Christian right, retreated to the shelter of the forts of Lepanto where he learnt of the death of Ali Pasha, but sixteen of his galleys doubled back upon their pursuers, and fought one of the bloodiest encounters of the entire day with Don Juan of Cardona, whose forces they outnumbered two to one. Of Cardona's five hundred Sicilian soldiers, only fifty emerged unharmed, Cardona himself being fatally wounded before the enemy were driven off. Veniero and Colonna, Don John's companions of the centre, each fought nobly, and as the four-hour fight came to a close, with the enemy centre and right almost totally destroyed, and the left in gradual retreat, Don John at last had time to survey the action as a whole and to begin to reckon his gain and loss.

Nearly 8,000 of the flower of Spanish and Italian chivalry had perished: double that number were wounded. The Turks and Algerians lost at least three times as many killed, and some twelve thousand Christian slaves were rescued from their galleys. Never again did the Sultan contrive to assemble so powerful a fleet. Christians and Turks had been roughly equal in numbers, and they fought with equal courage. Victory went to the side with better weapons and better leadership, and in this respect the galleass, and the person of Don John, proved decisive.

Lepanto was Don John's first and last major sea battle. He died in the Low Countries at the age of thirty-one, a man of one success and many disappointments. Like the galleys he commanded, he belonged to an old order of sea warfare, one whose history went back to the days of Actium, Salamis and beyond. The future was with sail, with the broadsides of the future ships of the line.

RIGHT: *The Ottoman Standard, captured at Lepanto, which can still be seen at the Doge's Palace in Venice*

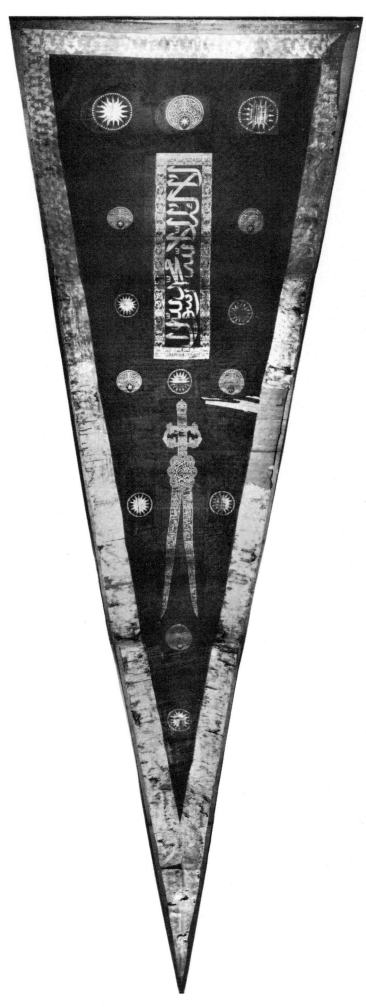

The Spanish Armada
1588

Philip II of Spain resolved to strike a decisive blow at Protestantism by conquering the England of Elizabeth I. His venture proved a great disaster

THE IMAGE OF PHILIP II OF SPAIN appeared as one of the victors on many of the medals which were struck in honour of Lepanto. He could indeed claim not only that his subjects had taken a leading part in the victory over the Turks, but that a member of his family had won the highest glory on that occasion. Seventeen years later, for his great 'Enterprise' against the England of Elizabeth I, he could command the services neither of Don John nor of Santa Cruz, for both were dead, and he himself, older if not wiser, had known constant disappointment even in that maritime sphere where he could summon the most powerful forces of his age.

The Spanish Armada, which sailed from Spain in 1588, was the culminating, though not the final episode in a war between England and Spain which had been maintained, both covertly and officially, over many years, off the southern coasts of Europe, and in Spanish territory on the far side of the Atlantic. Philip's hope was that his great fleet, transporting an army from his lands in Flanders, would be the means of subjugating England,

re-establishing Catholicism therein, and securing his overseas possessions from the depredations of such bold rovers as Francis Drake.

So large-scale had been Philip's preparations against England, so slowly were his forces assembled, that he gave his enemies every chance to delay him. They had been taken avidly. At Cadiz, in April 1587, Drake had made havoc in the inner and outer harbours, 'singeing the King of Spain's beard' to some purpose, burning the ship designed to carry the flag of his principal admiral. Then he had moved to the Azores, where he had captured the *San Filipe*, the largest prize that ever fell to him. Yet as he said, in words which have since become famous: 'There must be a beginning to any great matter, but the continuing unto the end until it be thoroughly finished yields the true glory'. That final day could not come until the Armada, ordered and assembled, was beaten at sea.

By May 1588 the Spaniards were at last ready, and command was given to the Duke of Medina Sidonia. His experience and ability could not compare with that of Santa Cruz, but he was the King's cousin, his courage was unquestioned, and everyone would obey him. His one hundred and thirty ships were divided into principal squadrons: of Portugal, Biscay, Guipuzcoa, Castille, Andalusia and the Levant. The men-of-war were to protect transports carrying the troops which were to join with those of the Duke of Parma in the Low Countries. Together, the army would be irresistible, a force against

LEFT: *Charles Howard, First Earl of Nottingham (1536–1624), Lord Admiral. He was known at the time of the Armada as Lord Howard of Effingham. A portrait painted in 1619 in Garter robes by Daniel Mytens (1590–1648)*

OVERLEAF: *The Spanish Armada enters the English Channel on 19 July 1588. An engraving by John Pine of one of the tapestries commemorating the victory*

25

The Ark Royal, *built in 1587, from a woodcut. She was Howard's flagship during the Armada fighting, and had been laid down for Sir Walter Raleigh*

which the fleet and men of Elizabeth would, on Philip's reckoning, prove impotent.

Medina Sidonia's hope was to anchor in the Downs, and then to concert with Parma how best to launch an invasion up the Thames, with London as his goal. In the event of bad weather, the admiral had orders to seize the Isle of Wight, as a move preliminary to the main campaign.

Drake held the view (one with which every strategist has since agreed) that the struggle should be begun as far as possible from the English coast, preferably off, and even inside, the enemy's own harbours. 'With fifty sail of shipping we shall do more good upon their own coast than a great many more will do here at home', he wrote. As it fell out, his ideas did not at once gain acceptance, nor was Drake himself given chief command in the English fleet. Lord Howard of Effingham, who held the office of High Admiral, was ordered to embark in person. Queen Elizabeth, like Philip her opponent, considered that only a nobleman, with the prestige of state office, could wield the necessary authority over such diverse

personalities as Drake, Hawkins and Frobisher. Without a doubt she was right.

Howard flew his flag in the new galleon *Ark Royal*, recently sold to the Crown by Sir Walter Raleigh, who had originally named her after himself. Drake was appointed Vice-Admiral at Plymouth. By 23 May 1588 the main force was assembled off the west country port. Drake sailed out with thirty ships to meet Howard, 'making a brave show of his skill and diligence'. Salutes were fired, trumpets sounded, men cheered. Howard sent a Vice-Admiral's flag from his own ship as a gift to Drake, and all went well thereafter. Drake, so said a contemporary, 'showed always of one mind and thought with the senior admiral, although there were those who had thought, or maybe feared, a different outcome'.

Elizabeth's fleet consisted of a hundred and two ships, ranging in size from Frobisher's *Triumph*, match for any Spaniard, to scouting pinnaces. Famous names were among them, the *Lion*, the *Tiger*, the *Dreadnought*, the *Victory*, flagship of Hawkins, the *Revenge*, which flew Drake's flag as Vice-Admiral, and which was to win further renown later, under Sir Richard Grenville. There were thirty-five royal ships, and fifty-three others of size, belonging to private owners, most of them well supplied with artillery. Supply was difficult. There was no great reserve of powder and shot at any of the ports, and there was a general shortage of victuals. 'I know not', Howard complained, 'which way to deal with the mariners to make them rest contented with sour beer'. Even so, he added cheerfully, he believed he was in charge of 'the gallantest company of captains, soldiers and mariners that I think were ever seen in England'.

On 30 May, Howard followed Drake's plan, and put to sea in the hope of intercepting the enemy. He was out of luck. The gales of a wild summer drove the English back to Plymouth, while the Spaniards put into Corunna. Twice more did Howard venture into the Bay of Biscay, but he never met a hostile ship. On the second sortie, the strong south wind which drove him homewards enabled the Armada to leave harbour for its final stage to the Channel.

On Friday 19 July, when the Spaniards came in sight off the Lizard, the English were in port at Plymouth. With the wind westerly, they were awkwardly placed to get to grips with an enemy who, far from having been damaged off his own coasts, was advancing with military discipline in what might have seemed an overwhelming progress. The legend that Drake was playing bowls when the news came that the enemy was upon him, and that he said, 'Play out the game: there's time for that and to beat the Spanish after', has no contemporary basis. In fact, every moment was vital if the English were to beat out of Plymouth Sound against the wind, and not a moment was lost. Some of Drake's ships, using local knowledge and keeping well inshore, soon managed to get to windward of Medina Sidonia, and by the morning of 21 July the English and Spanish were in the relative positions which they would keep, with variations, for the vital days to come.

At first Howard had his ships in no regular order, but lay astern and to windward of the slowly moving mass of his opponents, of whom he said, 'All the world never saw such a force'. He had led his main body across the enemy front on the night of 20 July, then tacked, past the Eddystone Rock, to join the inshore forces which were already on Medina Sidonia's trail. To have the 'wind-gage', in days of sail, meant that an admiral could attack an opponent when he wished, for the wind would bear

RIGHT TOP: *A contemporary copy of a letter from Sir Francis Drake to John Foxe, author of the* Book of Martyrs, *describing his action at Cadiz in April 1587*

RIGHT BOTTOM: *The secret order sent by Philip II of Spain to his Commander-in-Chief, Medina Sidonia, before the sailing of the Armada*

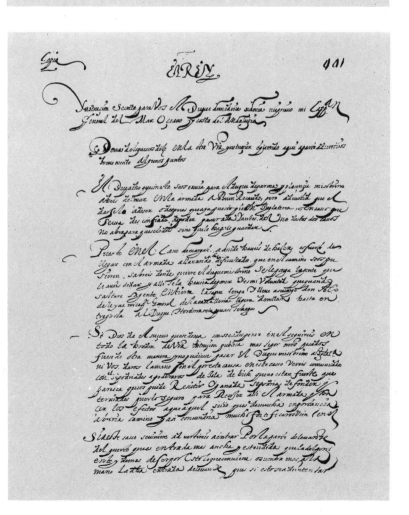

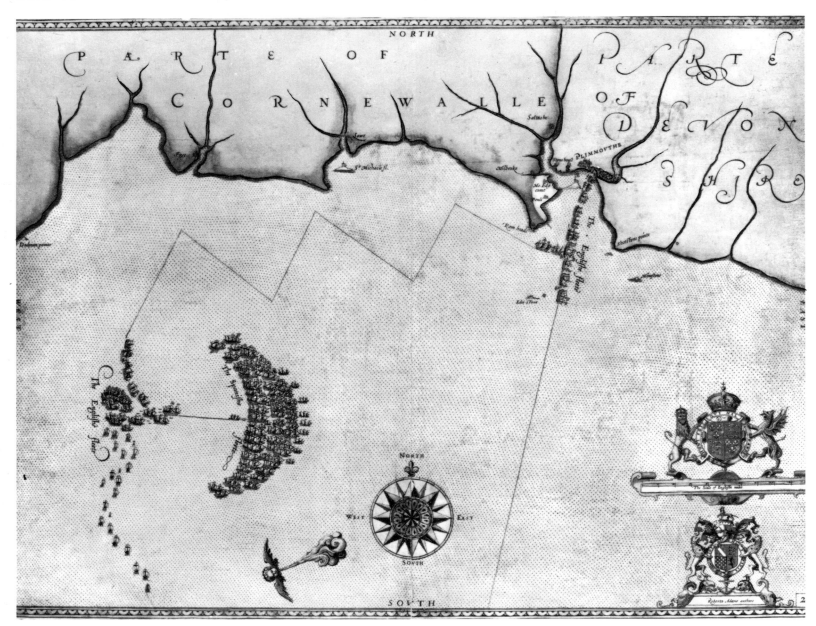

The Spanish Armada off Plymouth on 21 July 1588, with the English fleet approaching to attack the enemy from the rear. One of the set of Armada charts engraved in 1590 by Augustine Ryther

him down at any time he chose. This was an obvious gain to an aggressive leader, and before a shot had been exchanged, Howard and Drake had in fact won a tactical advantage.

A sea-battle on an extended scale was no part of the Spanish plan. If one were to be forced upon them, they would have chosen, with their tall ships and well disciplined soldiers, to have engaged closely, as Don John had done at Lepanto. The English knew this perfectly well, and they intended to use their handy ships to keep their distance, firing their guns at their longest effective range. Closing would have been stupid. 'The Spanish shipps are of wonderfull strength', came a report from sea, 'and so lyned with tow, wooll, pitch and other things, that noe shott of ours under cannon-shott can pierce them'. Cannon would be the weapons with which to engage.

'You should see that your squadrons do not break their

battle formations', wrote Philip to his commander-in-chief, 'and that the captains, moved by greed, do not pursue the enemy and take prizes.' Medina Sidonia, inexperienced as he was, held faithfully to these instructions, and the way in which he kept his fleet together, during its progress up-Channel, was a matter for general admiration. As the Spaniards did not separate, the English could only harry them, which they did by night and day. At first they attacked in no regular order, though Howard and Drake were always to the fore, but by the time he had reached the Isle of Wight, Howard had formed his ships into four divisions, respectively under himself, Hawkins, Frobisher and Drake.

Typically, Drake had one of the first strokes of luck. As early as the night of Sunday 21 July, when he was leading the fleet, he caught sight of a galleon looming up ahead, her bowsprit and foremast gone, obviously in trouble,

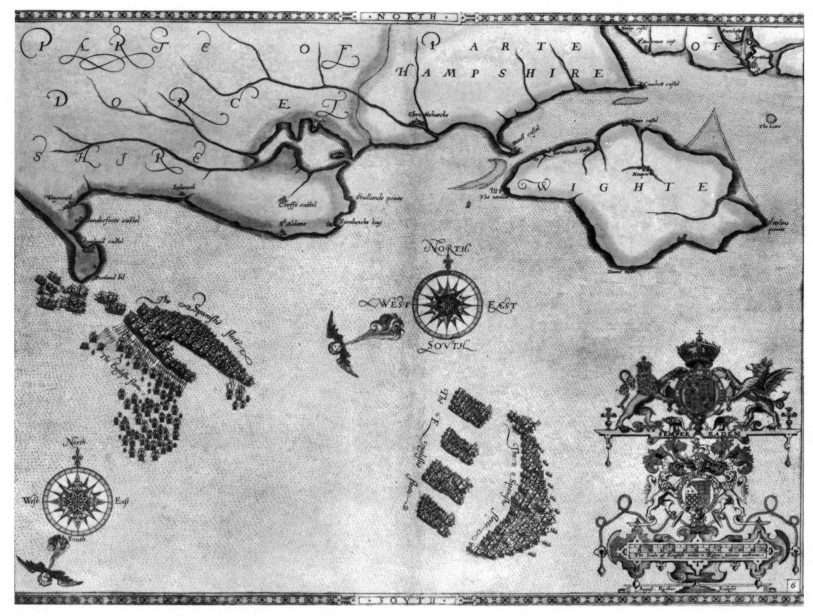

The Armada has just passed Weymouth on Tuesday, 23 July. On the following day the English fleet continued its pursuit. Ryther's charts were made from drawings by Robert Adams who died in 1595

separated from the rest of the Armada. The ship was the *Nuestra Senora del Rosario*, flagship of the Andalusians, and her captain, Don Pedro de Valdes, was one of the best seamen Medina Sidonia had with him. He had collided with another ship the day before, and had been unable to keep up with the rest of the fleet. Summoned to surrender just before dawn by Drake in person, de Valdes gave in without fighting. Drake took him on board the *Revenge*, and for some exciting days became his courteous host. The *Rosario* was sent into Dartmouth with a prize crew, and she was, in fact, the only capture made during the battle, except for the *San Salvadore*, which was towed into Weymouth after an internal explosion.

By the time the fleets were off Portland, the wind had dropped. Although fighting had been intermittent since the 21st, with more sustained action on the 23rd when a shift of wind favoured the Spaniards, who seized the

chance to maul the *Triumph*, no decisive action had yet been fought, and by Friday 26th the sea was so calm and the enemy so passive that Howard was able to summon his captains to the flagship. There, exercising his delegated right, he conferred a knighthood on John Hawkins (whose son, Richard, was also with the Fleet), on Martin Frobisher and on others, including Beeston of the *Dreadnought*, all of whom had shown prowess in action on 23 and 25 July. The intervening day had been spent mainly in storing Howard's ships.

On 27 July, towards evening, the wind freshened, and the Spaniards, going 'allways before the English like sheep', steered towards Calais, where Medina Sidonia brought the Armada to anchor. He had been thwarted in any hope he may have had of seizing the Isle of Wight, and his immediate purpose was to get in touch with Parma, who was then at Bruges.

31

Next day, Howard was reinforced by a detachment from the Thames, under Lord Henry Seymour and Sir William Winter, and he knew that he was never likely to have a better chance of taking the Spaniards at a disadvantage. Medina Sidonia must be driven from his anchorage before Parma knew where he was, and the way to do it was by fire-ships. Eight of these destructive vessels, guns shotted, sails set, rudders secured and crews removed, were ranged so that they came down with the wind and the night tide towards the compact mass of Spanish shipping, 'spurting fire, and their ordnance shooting, which was a horror to see', as a contemporary noted. Instantly, all was confusion. Nothing was dreaded more than fire in days of sail, and it was soon every ship for herself, even with the disciplined men-of-war who, up to that time, had kept so strictly together. Cables were cut, anchors lost, hulls and rigging damaged as the vessels staggered out to what they hoped was the safety of the open sea. One great vessel, the *San Lorenzo*, drifted on to Calais Bar, where Howard himself rifled her, setting an example which, had other galleons been involved, might have been unfortunate.

By dawn on Monday 29 July, the state of the entire Armada was parlous. It was without formation, its whole purpose had been frustrated beyond remedy, and Medina Sidonia's immediate hope was the inglorious one of saving his squadrons from complete destruction.

At first, his chances did not seem bright. His ships were by this time strung out along the coast between Gravelines and Dunkirk. From their base at Flushing, Dutch rebels prevented any chance of the Spaniards reaching the shelter of Antwerp. Return down Channel was impossible, and a freshening wind was driving them towards a shelving shore. By this time many ships were leaking from battle damage; food and water were getting low, for Medina Sidonia, unlike Howard, had not been able to re-victual in the intervals of fighting. Above all, a tenacious enemy were still at grips, and they were in waters with which they were thoroughly familiar. Led by Howard and Drake, the English harried the Spaniards during eight hours of continuous action. They even closed the range, though they never gave the Spanish soldiers the opportunity to board.

LEFT: *Philip II of Spain (1556–98), a portrait painted about 1560 by an unknown artist. The King is wearing pieces of the Rosenblatt armour, made for Ferdinand I*

BELOW: *A navigating instrument made by Humphrey Cole in 1569, and known as 'Drake's Dial', but the evidence that it belonged to Drake is uncertain*

Sir John Hawkins (1532–93), by an unknown artist. At the time of the Armada he was Treasurer and Comptroller of the Navy

Sir Francis Drake (1540–96), a portrait painted by an unknown artist in 1592. Drake's plan for the battle was followed by Howard

On 30 July the Spaniards had their one stroke of good fortune, and to them it seemed miraculous. The wind changed from west-north-west to west-south-west, and this enabled them to steer for the open sea, leaving half-a-dozen wrecks behind them on the Banks of Zealand. 'We have them before us,' wrote Drake to Walsingham in London, 'and mind with the Grace of God to wrestle a fall with them. There never was anything pleased me better than seeing the enemy flying to the northwards. God grant you have a good eye to the Duke of Parma, for with the Grace of God, if we live, I doubt not so to handle the matter with the Duke of Sidonia as he shall wish himself . . . among his orange-trees.'

By the time the opposing forces were in the latitude of Newcastle-on-Tyne, Howard had to give up the chase. His

LEFT: *Engravings made by John Pine of tapestries formerly in the House of Lords. These were commissioned from Cornelius Vroom (1566–1646) by the Lord Admiral after the Armada campaign. The upper picture shows the capture of the* San Salvadore *on 22 July; the lower picture shows the Armada off Calais six days later when the Spanish fleet was dislodged by fireships*

supplies were now short, his powder was spent, and the victuallers could not hope to keep up with the fighting ships, which were about to enter Scottish waters. Disease – typhus, dysentery and scurvy – was beginning to show itself among the crews, and it was becoming essential to return to port at the first moment possible.

Medina Sidonia, so gallant and so unhappy, ordered his remaining ships to make their way homeward round the north of Scotland. It was a long and stormy route, but at least it was safer than attempting to return by the way they had come. He was shadowed as far as the Orkneys, but when the scouting vessels saw the Armada turn into the teeth of a westerly gale, they knew what its fate must be. There were wrecks in the Outer Hebrides and on the rocky coast of Donegal, Connaught and Galway, while one unlucky galleon was later driven so far east that she went ashore off Bolt Head in Devonshire. Some twenty-five vessels perished in this scattered way, the total loss to the Armada in July and August being sixty-four ships and at least ten thousand men.

'The troubles and miseries we have suffered cannot be described to your Majesty,' wrote Medina Sidonia to King Philip. 'They have been greater than have ever

35

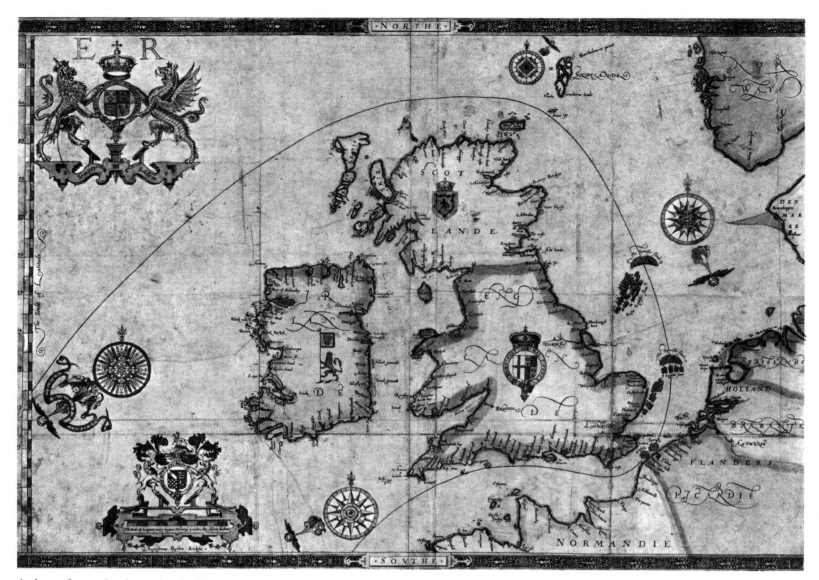

A chart of 1590 by Augustine Ryther showing the track of the Spanish fleet in its disastrous progress round the British Isles. Many of King Philip's ships were destroyed off the coasts of Scotland and Ireland

been seen in any voyage before.' The words were nothing less than the truth.

> He made the wynds and waters rise
> To scatter all myne enemies . . .

So wrote Queen Elizabeth in a *Songe of Thanksgiving* which was echoed by all her subjects.

Winds and waters had proved good allies, but it was Howard's management of the fleet, and the nimble way in which his ships could manoeuvre which ensured that England would not be successfully invaded. While the Queen had leaders of skill, and sailors of resolution, her realm would remain inviolate.

LEFT: *A medal struck in commemoration of the Armada; the Latin inscription reads 'God blew and they were scattered 1588'*

RIGHT: *Queen Elizabeth I (1533–1603). A portrait by an unknown artist, painted shortly before the Armada campaign*

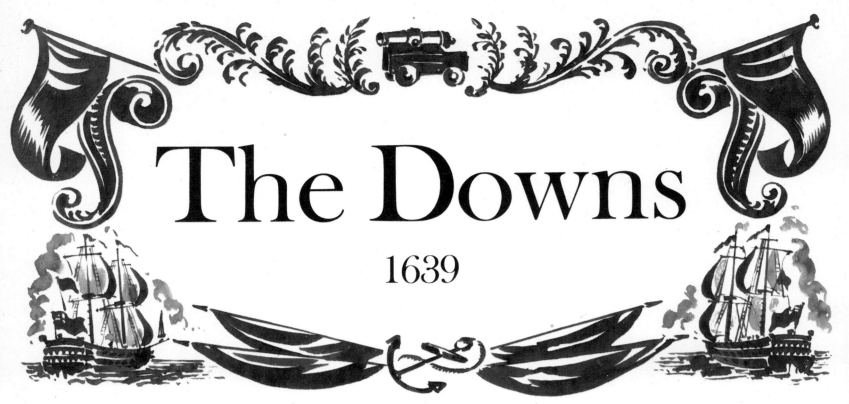

The Downs
1639

Marten Tromp, the great Dutch admiral, defeated a Spanish squadron in the English Channel, in an engagement in which an anchored force was annihilated

TOWARDS THE END OF HIS LIFE, Philip II of Spain, who was slow to learn, planned another Armada. A successful raid on Cadiz, in which twenty-four Dutch ships fought alongside the English under Howard, nipped the idea in the bud. For her part Holland had begun at Cadiz that series of successes which gave her, for the time, the leading place among maritime nations. Her stature grew from trade, but it was because she knew how to protect and expand her trade by means of her fleet that she won respect from friend and enemy.

Dutch sea victories over the Spaniards extended for more than forty years. In 1602, in the last year of the reign of Elizabeth I, Federigo Spinola, a Spaniard who still believed, against all reason, in the efficacy of galleys, even in northern waters, entered the Channel. Sir Robert Mansel and the Dutch Admiral Obdam encountered him off the coast of Flanders, and only Spinola's own galley succeeded in reaching Dunkirk. Spinola was killed in the following year, after which galleys disappeared for ever from Spain's first-line equipment except in the Mediterranean.

A generation later, when war was renewed, Piet Hein ravaged Spanish possessions and captured treasure in the West Indies and elsewhere. Nearer home, although Count William of Nassau failed disastrously in an attack on Antwerp, Marten Tromp surprised a Spanish squadron near Gravelines, destroyed it completely, and then blockaded Dunkirk, whence the enemy had come. It was the first in a series of exploits which made Tromp's a

resounding name in Dutch history. He was then in his maturity, and for some two years had held the title of Lieutenant-Admiral of Holland.

Now that there was no menace from the English shore of the Channel, the Spaniards made their most serious attempt, not only to gain supremacy at sea, but to relieve Dunkirk. To that end, they assembled a fleet of seventy-seven ships, Spanish and Portuguese, under Admiral d'Oquendo. He was to convoy 24,000 soldiers in fifty transports, nine of them hired from England, for the reinforcement of the army engaged under the Cardinal Infante.

The operation assumed that, in spite of French hostility, d'Oquendo would have a clear run up the Channel and that, with his numerical strength, he would be able to sweep aside Tromp's blockaders. Tromp, who was as aware of the danger from Spain as Drake had been in the previous century, had a scouting force constantly employed between Dunkirk and the western entrance to the Channel. On 16 September 1639, just over fifty years after Philip's Armada had been sighted off the coast of Cornwall, d'Oquendo came in view off Selsey Bill, his fleet ordered with at least something of the precision which had been admired in Medina Sidonia.

At the time of the first clash, Tromp had only seventeen ships with him, the greater part of his force being en-

RIGHT: *Admiral d'Oquendo's flagship, the* Santiago, *in action against the Dutch, painted by H. van Antonissen*

gaged off Dunkirk. He did not hesitate. Believing in the quality of his ships and his men, believing in gaining and keeping the initiative, he attacked d'Oquendo with energy and fury. D'Oquendo, with a favouring wind and vast preponderance of force, at first stood up boldly to Tromp and at one time had the Dutch almost encircled near the mouth of the Somme. But the *Santiago*, d'Oquendo's flagship, received damage, he himself had disdained to give any tactical instructions to his captains, and when the wind changed he tamely retreated across Channel, seeking refuge off Dover, realizing that he could not hope to reach Dunkirk without fighting a major battle.

D'Oquendo anchored his fleet close to an English squadron commanded by Sir John Pennington, a man who had learnt his business under Sir Robert Mansel, the last English commander to have fought at sea alongside Tromp's predecessors. Pennington promptly had the Spaniards transferred out of the English hired transports.

Diplomatically, the matter was now delicate. There were three fleets, two of them at war and the third neutral, the largest among them anchored in what was virtually the territorial waters of one of the neutral countries, whose admiral refused to allow either of the contestants to fly their flags, to their extreme annoyance. English sympathies were divided. People and seamen were for the Dutch, but the Court of Charles I inclined to the Spaniards. There was, however, no thought of immediate interference, so while d'Oquendo sent ashore for water and supplies (for which he was charged exorbitantly), Tromp kept vigilant watch to seaward. It was a situation which could not last, and a bolder admiral than d'Oquendo would have ended it quickly: but as the days went by, and circumstances did not change in his favour, he became paralysed with indecision. His dilemma arose partly because so many of his ships were transports. They carried men armed and trained for war, but, alas, equipped for land fighting. The lesson of 1588 had not been learnt. Each transport should have been given ordnance fit to counter more distant attack. As it was, a few of them got away, singly and in the night, to ports in Flanders.

Tromp was soon joined by seventeen more ships, bringing his numbers up to thirty. Even so, d'Oquendo still had great superiority. Having paused to reason, he should have pushed on according to his orders, for while Tromp might expect reinforcements, he could not look for them.

Weeks passed, and d'Oquendo did nothing. He even refused to move when Tromp offered him five hundred barrels of gun-powder to fight it out. Humiliation could

scarcely go further. For his part, Tromp sent urgent messages to Holland asking the Prince of Orange and the various Dutch Admiralties to strain every nerve to get him as many ships as possible. The response was enthusiastic. Work went on night and day in all the dockyards of Holland, and in less than a month Tromp had built up such strength that he found himself with over a hundred sail, including fire-ships. For the most part they were smaller than d'Oquendo's, but size in itself was nothing, and Tromp believed he had more than enough for annihilation. So confident was he of the result of an attack, that he told an Englishman that King Charles would soon have all the Spaniards' guns, his countrymen their ships, and the devil their men.

On 21 October, a day which was to become notable in the annals of sail warfare, since it was the day on which Trafalgar was fought, Tromp first detached Admiral Witte de With for special duties. He was given a squadron of thirty ships, and told to watch Pennington, in case the English tried to interfere. Tromp himself then bore down with the wind upon d'Oquendo's fleet, the Dutch tricolour flying at his main top-mast-head.

Rarely has a victory been more complete. D'Oquendo's paralysis continued to the last, and although his Spaniards fought stubbornly, as always, they still had no tactical plan. They relied for safety on their mere position, which helped them not at all, and they went like sheep to the slaughter before the brilliant, determined, ever-active Tromp. Almost the whole Armada was burnt, run ashore, or captured. Some 7,000 men are known to have perished, many of them in the great ship *San Theresa*, which was destroyed by fire. The Dutch loss was

LEFT: The Amelia, *Tromp's flagship at the Battle of the Downs*

LEFT: *Marten Tromp (1598–1653), Lieutenant-Admiral of the United Netherlands, whose victory at the Downs was one of a series of successful exploits against the Spaniards.* RIGHT: *Sir John Pennington, who commanded the English fleet, which was present, though not in action, at the Downs.* BELOW: *A Dutch medal commemorating their victory at the Downs, showing the destruction of the Spanish fleet*

only a handful of killed and wounded. Tromp, at one stroke, had ruined Spanish power in northern waters. At the time of the 'Enterprise of England' Philip II had been humbled. His successor was disgraced.

'In gold rather than steel lies the strength of Spain,' ran the inscription on a medal commemorating the taking of a treasure fleet by Hein a few years earlier. 'Take his gold, and the Iberian's steel will not prevail.' Tromp proved it, and the legend that he carried a broom at his mast-head, symbolical of how he swept the seas, was never more applicable than to the days following the Battle of the Downs. He himself, in the *Amelia*, engaged d'Oquendo in the *Santiago*. The Spanish admiral, though an unfortunate leader, was personally brave, and if he could not save his fleet, he did not allow his flagship to be taken. He managed to escape under cover of mist, and the port he made for was Dunkirk, from which the Dutch

RIGHT: *Fireships of the time of the Battle of the Downs, taken from a contemporary ship-building manual*

I. Cuniculus sub tabulato nauis. I. Velum praegrande subter mediam nauem alligatum, et à cursu fluminis inflatum tractumq, ac nauem pertrahens.

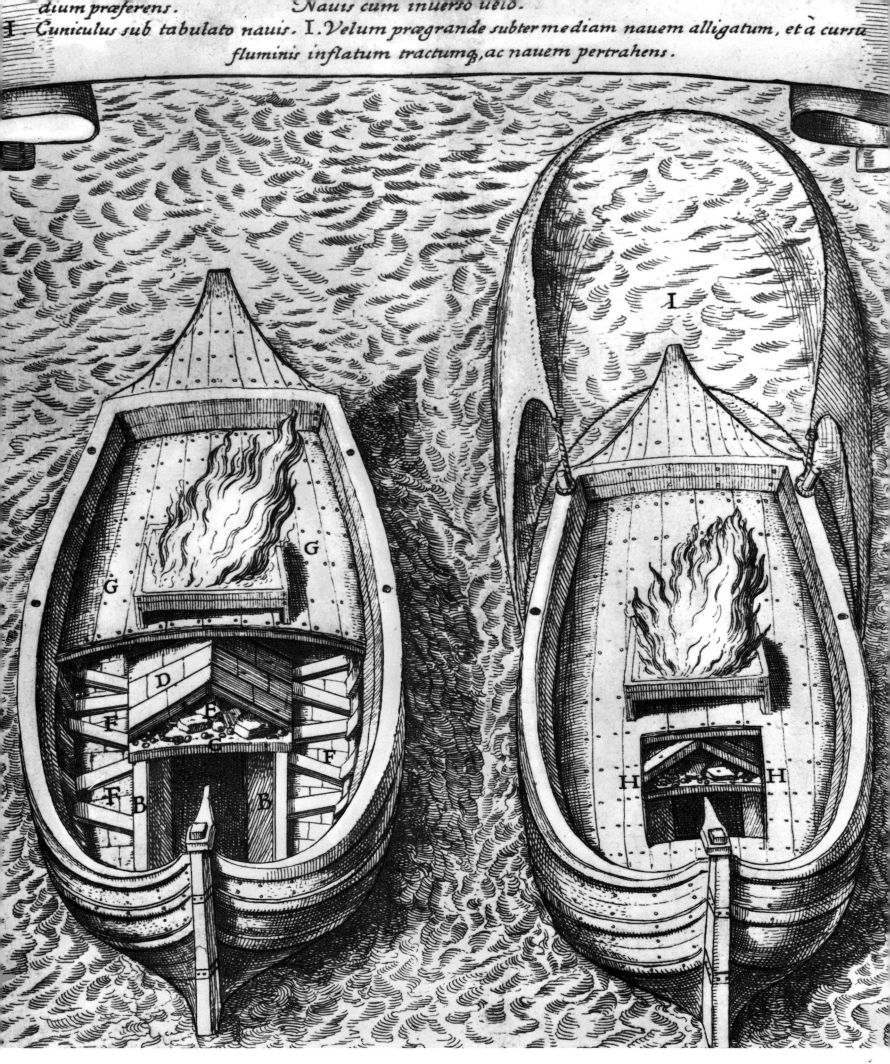

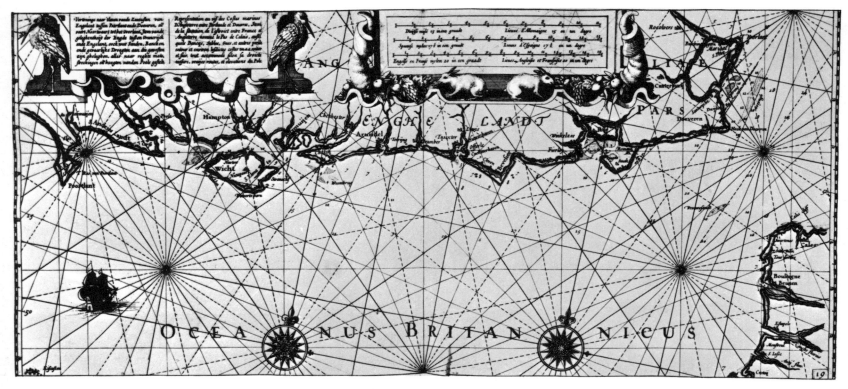

TOP: *A map showing the scene of the movements in the Channel before and during the Battle of the Downs, taken from Janszoon Blaen's atlas* The Light of Navigation *published in 1620.* BOTTOM: *A Dutch galleon of 1629*

The Battle of the Downs by Cornelisz Verbeeck: the Amelia *engaged with the Spanish Vice-Admiral (right) and Jan Evertsen and d'Oquendo (left)*

blockading force had temporarily been withdrawn. Only thirteen ships were with him, and his *Santiago*, with seventeen hundred shot holes, was like a colander. Before the winter was over he returned to Spain, a broken man, as his father had been after the earlier Armada.

The battle had an odd but important sequel. Charles I, who was jealous of his sovereignty over English waters, was furious on learning that the fleet of a friendly power had been destroyed under the eyes of one of his own admirals. But he was also irritated that d'Oquendo had anchored for so long without his knowledge or permission, so when the Dutch Stadholder, Frederick Henry of Orange, sent an emissary to London to try to smooth matters over, the King listened. Indeed Aerssons, the man in question, fulfilled his mission with such success that Charles even agreed, in the following year, to the betrothal of the Princess Royal to the Stadholder's only son.

Charles was soon to be engaged in a protracted war with his Parliament, and the son of the marriage, who in the course of time came to the English throne as William III, played a principal part in the final exile of the Stuart House. More immediately, Holland gained immensely in prestige by the match, for the House of Orange became allied in blood with the royal families of England and France.

The Battle of the Downs not only ensured the fame of Marten Tromp, it made Holland dominant in northern waters. It was some years before her position could be challenged, and, with England engaged in civil war, it was the chance for Holland to extend her power and wealth. Yet her position as the principal European carrier, together with her dependence on other countries for so large a proportion of her own needs, created difficulties as well as bringing her advantages. It involved her in a series of wars in many parts of the world.

45

The Sound

1658

The Sound, the narrow channel leading from the Cattegat to the Baltic, was the scene of a defeat of the Swedes by the Dutch, allies of Denmark

FOR NEARLY TWENTY YEARS AFTER Tromp's victory off the Downs, Dutch resources at sea were employed otherwise than against Spain. England, France and Portugal in turn provided matters for dispute which did not always stop short of war: but even Holland's protracted struggle with Portugal, which involved interests as far apart as Brazil and Macassar, were of less importance than the war in the Baltic in which she found herself embroiled.

The matter began when, in 1654, Charles X Gustavus succeeded to the throne of Sweden. The King became fired with an ambition to make his country supreme in the north by the subjugation of Poland and Denmark. Two years after his accession he had laid siege to Danzig. This was an act which affected Holland closely, for her Baltic trade was immense, and Danzig was the centre of the corn-carrying business. Under pressure from the Amsterdam merchants, a fleet of forty-two ships under Obdam – the second admiral of his house to win celebrity – was sent through the Sound, and in due course raised the siege. Thus checked, Charles X Gustavus renewed relations with Holland, and Danzig was declared a neutral port.

Holland had won the first round, but her statesmen were not deceived as to the ambition and abilities of the Swedish King. He might bide his time, but his determination to achieve domination in the Baltic remained, and the best chance for the Dutch to establish and extend what they had gained, so they argued, was to invoke the defensive alliance which had already been made with Denmark, so making it clear beyond all doubt that Holland was hostile to Swedish pretensions.

The Swedes continued to meet with difficulties on land, and when they were at length driven out of Poland altogether, King Frederick III of Denmark seized the moment to declare war on his neighbour. His timing was unfortunate. Charles X Gustavus had indeed suffered reverses, but his army was strong and well disciplined, and although it was the depth of winter, he lost no time in attacking the Danes. His success was such that by September 1658 he was able to make terms as a conqueror. Denmark virtually became a Swedish dependency, and she undertook to close the Sound, and hence the trade of Copenhagen, to all foreign ships. Had this agreement taken effect, it would have been an even more severe blow to Holland than the closure of Danzig.

Van Beuningen, the Dutch representative in Denmark, urged Frederick to rely on his alliance and repudiate the Treaty. Although he was successful in his plea, the Swedish King reacted as strongly as before: he invaded Denmark, drove Frederick's fleet from the sea, placed garrisons at Elsinore and Kronborg, and laid siege to Copenhagen.

Van Beuningen had told the Danes that 'the oaken

Cornelisz Witte de With (1599–1658), Vice-Admiral of the Maze, commanded the Dutch van and was killed in action in the Brederode

Jacob van Wassenaer, Lord of Obdam, (1610–65), Lieutenant-Admiral of the United Netherlands, commanded the Dutch fleet at the battle

A Dutch medal celebrating their victory at the Battle of the Sound

keys of the Sound lie in the docks of Amsterdam'. His boast was not empty. In October 1658 a force of thirty-five ships under Obdam, carrying 4,000 troops, sailed for Denmark with orders to destroy the Swedish fleet, and to relieve the Danish capital.

On 29 October Obdam encountered the main fleet of Sweden at the entrance to the Sound. Wrangel, the Swedish commander-in-chief, was stronger numerically, and the battle, as might have been foretold, was fierce and bloody. The Dutch fleet was divided into three squadrons, the van under Vice-Admiral de With, the centre under Obdam, the rear under Floriszoon. The Swedes were in four squadrons, the commander-in-chief, K. G. Wrangel, having as his subordinates admirals Sjohjelm, Bjelkenstjernn and Gustav Wrangel. A Danish division was ready to support the Dutch, but head winds did not allow the admiral to leave Copenhagen in time to take part in the action.

The encounter began about nine o'clock in the morning, the Dutch, with the advantage of the wind, advancing without much order, as was their way. With two resolute adversaries, a mêlée was inevitable, and action

Stockholm shortly after the Battle of the Sound, showing the principal buildings and the dockyards which supplied and maintained the Swedish fleet

quickly developed into a series of ship to ship encounters, in which signals and general directions from flag-officers played little part. De With, in the *Brederode* of 59 guns, at once made bold to attack the Swedish commander-in-chief in the far superior *Victoria*, but, on the arrival of Obdam in the *Eendracht* he drew off and engaged the *Drake* and the *Leopard*, ships nearer his own weight of metal. The *Leopard* was driven off so badly damaged that she had to be put ashore at Hven and burnt. Soon afterwards both the *Drake* and the *Brederode* went ashore together on the Danish side of the Sound. The *Drake* got off, but the *Brederode* remained fast, and was attacked by the *Wismar* of 44 guns. After two hours raking fire the Swedes boarded. The gallant de With was killed and his flagship taken, but almost immediately afterwards she slipped into deeper water and sank.

Meanwhile the *Drake* had gone to relieve the *Victoria* which was being hard-pressed by the *Eendracht* and other Dutch ships. The *Victoria* was, in fact, so much damaged that when at last she had shaken off her enemies, Wrangel had to take her out of action to Helsingor, where, together with the *Drake*, she anchored for repairs.

It was now the turn of Obdam to find himself surrounded by enemies. The *Eendracht* was soon at grips with the *Cesar*, *Pelikan*, *Morgenstjernan* and *Johannes*, the *Cesar* having previously beaten off the *Joshua* killing Admiral Floriszoon in the process. Obdam was not left unsupported by his captains, for the *Wapen van Rotterdam, Dordrecht*, and *Halve Maan* soon came to his rescue. The captain of the *Cesar* was wounded and his ship driven off, the *Pelikan* was captured, and the *Morgenstjernan* also struck, only to sink almost immediately afterwards. In further duels between ships or groups of ships, the advantage lay with the Dutch. Two other Swedes were captured, and although Obdam at one time lost the *Breda* of 28 guns,

OVERLEAF: *The Battle of the Sound by Willem van de Velde the Elder (1611–93): the large Swedish ship seen sinking is the* Morgenstjernan, *and the Dutch ships which can be identified include those of Captain D. Verveau, acting Rear-Admiral of the Dutch centre; Captain H. Bruynsvelt, Rear-Admiral of the Dutch rear squadron; the* Halve Maan *and the* Eendracht

A portrait of Captain Aucke Stellingwerf, who commanded the Dutch ship t'Prinsen Wapen, *at the Battle of the Sound, by Lodewyck van der Helst*

the enemy abandoned her when fire broke out, and she was recovered.

About two o'clock in the afternoon, with the wind freshening, the Dutch fleet got clear of the Swedes and ran down to Copenhagen, very few of Wrangel's ships being in any condition to follow. The Swedes actually claimed a victory on the score of a Dutch retreat, but since Obdam's first object was to reach and to reinforce the Danish capital, it is hard to find justification for the assertion. The Dutch losses had certainly been less than their opponents – the *Brederode* had been captured and sunk, together with a few vessels not large enough to lie in the line. The Swedes, on the other hand, had lost five

major units – three captured, one captured and sunk, one run ashore and burnt.

The war itself did not end until the following year, when Michel de Ruyter, who shares with Marten Tromp the leading place in Dutch naval history, sailed north with a large fleet and 12,000 troops to reinforce the initial advantage gained by Obdam. Henceforward, Charles X Gustavus found himself powerless to carry out his ambition of a northern hegemony. He died, disappointed, early in 1660, and although the peace which was signed at Copenhagen was on the whole favourable to Sweden, the Dutch secured their right of passage through the Sound.

The Swedish admiral Wrangel in the Victoria *(left) in action with the Dutch admiral Wassenaer in the* Eendracht; *their portraits (Wassenaer left, Wrangel right) appear above*

The battle between Wrangel and Obdam, typical of many stern fights which have taken place between the fleets of the northern races of Europe, was also significant of the length to which the maritime powers were prepared to go to maintain free access to the Baltic. For centuries a primary source of naval stores, the Baltic was as essential to the economy of northern Europe as was the Mediterranean to that of the south. Apart from wood, the materials used to equip a man-of-war of the sailing era included hemp, canvas, iron, pitch, tar, tallow, resin, oil and brimstone. These essentials came wholly or in part from the Baltic, and for some of them the Baltic countries were the only accessible suppliers. Baltic timber was itself particularly important to Holland, a land without great forests, while the importance of her carrying trade to the ports of the northern countries justified the risks and expense she incurred to safeguard her interests.

The danger to Holland and indeed to other trading countries of the closure of the Baltic by power such as might have been wielded by Charles X Gustavus did not cease with the demise of that ambitious sovereign. It was indeed fortunate that, over the course of history, the countries of Scandinavia could never consistently agree to combine to make the Baltic a sea over which they could exercise undisputed control. Had they done so, they could have held much of Europe to ransom.

The Four-Days' Battle
1666

*The second war between the Dutch and the English was notable for a fierce engagement
in the Channel in which the Dutch hammered Monck and Prince Rupert*

IT WAS PERHAPS INEVITABLE THAT, during the course of the seventeenth century, Dutch and English should fight at sea. Small, dynamic, expanding, Protestant, seafaring though both countries were, and united against Spain, they were close to each other geographically, their interest in increasing trade overseas was identical, and they bred a resolute breed of seamen, many of whom soon became experienced in war.

The first of a series of Anglo-Dutch maritime struggles took place in the years 1652-54, when England was under the rule of Oliver Cromwell. Just over ten years later, with Charles II on the throne, the two navies were once more engaged, and in a Four-Days' Battle, which was fought mainly in Channel waters between 1 and 4 June 1666, the two principal admirals, de Ruyter on the Dutch side and George Monck, Duke of Albemarle, on the English, were fairly matched in skill.

By the terms of an earlier treaty, Louis XIV had promised French help to the Dutch, and the London Government made the mistake of dividing the Fleet, Prince Rupert being sent down Channel with a squadron of twenty-four ships to intercept a force which was believed – wrongly as it proved – to be on its way to reinforce de Ruyter. 'Nothing to be heard among the seamen but complaints about the dividing of the Fleet, and the sending away of Prince Rupert,' wrote Thomas Clifford to Lord Arlington at Whitehall. The seamen had the right of it, for by disregarding the principle of concentration, Charles II risked defeat in detail. Had the English

admirals been lesser men, that defeat could have meant disaster.

George Monck, upon whom the burden would fall, was at that time close upon sixty, and his life had been spent mainly as a professional soldier. He had fought with the Dutch against Spain; he had served Charles I in Ireland and in England, and after the King's death he had been one of the principal 'Generals at Sea' in the first maritime war. It was he who, after Cromwell's death, had the principal part in the restoration of the monarchy, and Charles was thankful to find him willing to serve once more at sea, jointly with a companion-in-arms of his youth, Rupert, Prince Palatine.

De Ruyter, since the death of Marten Tromp off Scheveningen in the Cromwellian war, when he had also been engaged against Monck, had been the outstanding Dutch leader. He was much the same age as his rival, was almost his equal in general experience, and his superior purely as a sea commander. He had recently returned from an expedition against English settlements and factories on the Guinea Coast, and he was thirsting to avenge a reverse which his compatriot, Obdam, had sustained at the hands of the Duke of York the year before. The division of the English fleet offered him a golden

RIGHT: *Detail from a painting by van de Velde the Younger (1633–1707), showing an episode on the fourth day of the Four-Days' Battle, when the maintopmast of Prince Rupert's flagship, the* Royal James, *followed the mizzen over the side*

Left to right: the Defiance, *Holmes' flagship; the* Zeven Provincien, *de Ruyter's flagship; the* Royal Charles, *Albemarle's flagship; the* Gouda (*Sweers*); *and the* Royal Oak (*Jordan*). *A painting by Pieter Cornelis Soest* (fl *1665*)

opportunity, for he had ninety ships with which to oppose less than fifty, and he was never shy of fighting.

The Dutch sailed for the English coast with a fair easterly wind, but it changed later to south-west, with thick weather, so de Ruyter, in order to avoid being driven back, anchored between Dunkirk and the Downs. When Monck sighted them, it was from a windward position, and in spite of his known inferiority in numbers, he decided to attack. 'The General call'd immediately a Councill of Flag Officers,' so runs a narrative written the day after the battle from Monck's flagship the *Royal Charles*, 'which being done, the sign was put out to fall into the line of battle.'

The words are important, since it indicated Monck's intention to form line quickly, and to attack as a unified body before de Ruyter could get his ships into order. It was as bold a decision as was ever made, and with a lesser opponent it might have led to the scattering of the Dutch and even to a spectacular victory against heavy odds.

At first, all went well for the English. Monck led his whole force upon the squadron of Cornelis Tromp, Marten's son, which was in the van of the Dutch fleet. Tromp cut his cables, and English and Dutch engaged in a running fight towards the French coast, the sea at that time being so high that Monck could not use his lower tiers of guns. De Ruyter, with his main body, also cut his cables and followed Tromp's movements. Being to leeward, it was some time before he could come into action, except at long range, and he could not prevent the loss of one of his larger ships.

As Monck drew near Dunkirk, where the coast shelved, he went about, and on his returning course he was roughly handled by ships which had not hitherto been engaged. Two English flagships, Berkeley's and Harman's, were cut off. Their fates were very different. Sir William Berkeley in the *Swiftsure*, a young man of twenty-seven, with a ship which had been launched eighteen years before he was born, was boarded on both sides. He would accept no quarter, and at last, being wounded in the throat by a musket ball, he retired to his cabin, where he was found dying, stretched out upon a table almost covered with his own blood. The ship surrendered.

RIGHT: *Detail from a painting by Abraham Storck* (*1644–c 1705*) *which, like nearly all paintings of this action, incorporates incidents from all four days: the capture of Berkeley's* Swiftsure (*left*), *de Ruyter's* Zeven Provincien *in action* (*centre*), *and Prince Rupert's* Royal James *losing her maintopmast* (*right*)

56

A portrait after Sir Peter Lely of Prince Rupert, the joint commander of the English fleet

RIGHT: *The attack on the first day of the battle, 1 June 1666*

LEFT TOP: *The state-portrait of Michel Andriaenszoon de Ruyter (1607–76), Lieutenant Admiral-General, painted after the Four-Days' Battle by Ferdinand Bol (1613–81). De Ruyter wears the gold-hilted hanger presented to him by the Admiralty of Amsterdam*

LEFT BOTTOM: *George Monck, First Duke of Albemarle (1608–70), one of the 'flagmen' portraits commissioned from Sir Peter Lely by the Duke of York after the Battle of Lowestoft in 1665*

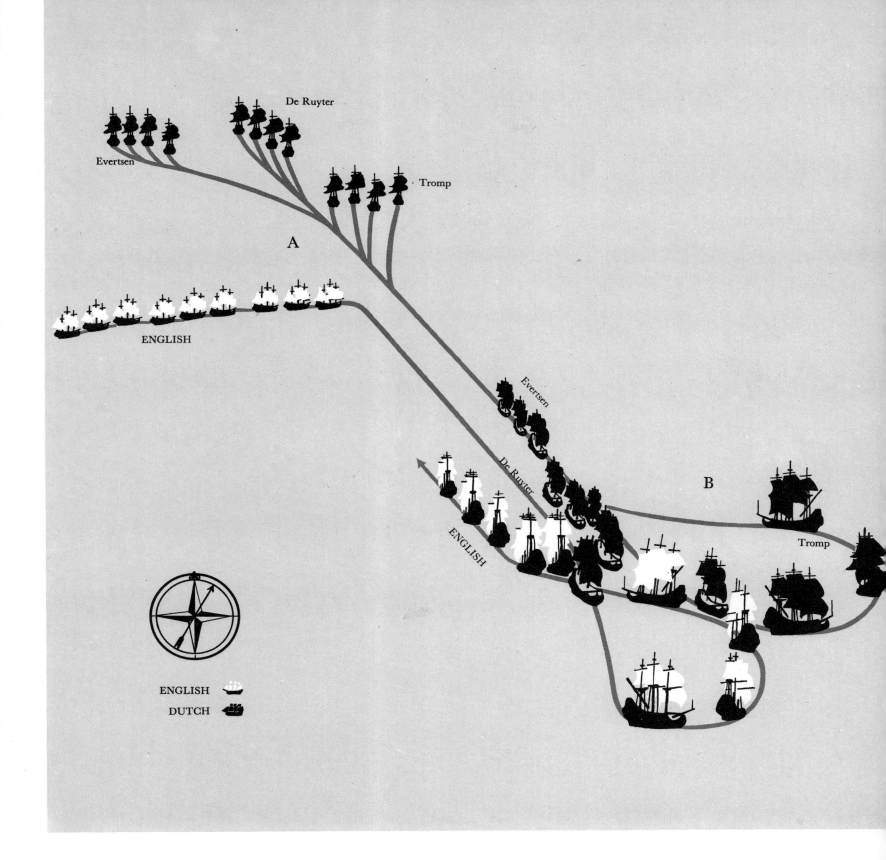

In Harman's case, the *Henry*, which was even older than the *Swiftsure*, was grappled by a fire-ship. By heroic exertions a lieutenant managed to cast off the grappling irons. Then a second fire-ship, approaching on the other side, set the sails alight, an incident which so terrified the crew that a number jumped overboard. Harman ran among the rest with his sword drawn, forcing them to get the fire under control. Then one of the top-sail yards fell from aloft, pinned Harman to the deck, and broke his leg.

Soon afterwards, a third fire-ship tried to grapple, but she was sunk by the *Henry*'s broadside before she could achieve her aim. At this stage Evertzoon, the Dutch second-in-command, bore down and offered Harman quarter. The reply came swiftly: 'No, no, it is not come to that yet!', and Harman, with another broadside, drove the Dutch to a respectful distance, saving his ship.

Monck's bold opening had failed, chiefly because of the difficulty his ships met with in keeping together, which was due in part to stress of weather. Yet for a commander

inferior in strength, he had not done badly. He had lost
one flagship, and many other ships had suffered damage,
but he had inflicted loss. More than one Dutch ship had
been forced to return home, two had been sunk outright,
while the moral effect of his tactics was immense. 'Nothing equals the beautiful order of the English at sea,'
wrote a French observer in de Ruyter's fleet. 'They bring
all their fire to bear upon those who draw near them' –
mutual support was the paramount virtue of a 'line' in
battle. 'They fight like cavalry which is handled according to rule . . . whereas the Dutch advance like cavalry
whose squadrons leave their ranks and come separately
to the charge.'

Night ended the first phase of the encounter, and
Monck knew that his sternest test would come next day.
Once again he decided that the best form of defence was
attack. 'We engaged again about 7 of the clock,' said the
writer from the *Royal Charles*, 'and our General did all
that man could doe, both by his conduct and valour, in
exposing himself to obtain a victory : but seeinge many of
ours gone away, and those that were left much torne, he
prudently resolved to make a retreat.'

In his attack, Monck once again had Cornelis Tromp
at a disadvantage, and might have captured him but for
de Ruyter's move in hauling up to his rescue. Shortly
afterwards, Tromp went on board de Ruyter's flagship.
The seamen cheered, but de Ruyter said gravely: 'This

RIGHT: *The captured English ship* Swiftsure *arriving at Hellevoetsluis
on 14 June 1666, some days after the fighting ended, as seen by Willem
van de Velde the Younger*

is no time for rejoicing, but rather for tears.' What he meant was that he had been forced to alter his dispositions to come to Tromp's aid, that his squadrons were disordered, and that the English, had they not been crippled, might have pressed their advantage.

But Monck was in a bad state, and although his rearmost ship was able to damage the Dutch commander-in-chief to such a degree that she had, for a time, to withdraw, his own immediate object was to retire in good order, shepherding his most damaged ships, and showing a brave front with the rest. Fighting became intermittent, the English slowly retreating towards their own coast. Next day this retreat continued, Monck giving orders to burn three disabled ships.

The Royal Charles (*formerly the* Naseby) *sketched by van de Velde the Elder when she was sent to Holland in 1660 to bring back the restored King Charles II*

LEFT: *Officers proceeding to a Council of war aboard de Ruyter's flagship, the* Zeven Provincien, *before the Four-Days' Battle, by van de Velde the Elder*

Unfortunately, one of the finest ships in the English fleet, the *Royal Prince*, ran ashore on the Galloper Sand, and was captured by Tromp, though Monck's line was so steady that he was otherwise unmolested. Sir George Ayscue's surrender affected him only personally, for to Tromp's disgust the *Prince* had to be burnt to prevent her recapture, and it was the admiral alone who was borne off to Holland.

At one time Monck's own flagship went aground, and there was a danger that she might share the fate of Ayscue's. John Sheffield, a young man who was later to become a duke and a notable patron of men of letters, was serving in the *Royal Charles* as a volunteer. He recalled later that, before the ship had been got off, he 'spied the General charging a little pistol and putting it in his pocket'. As Monck had been heard to say that he would never allow himself to be taken prisoner, the pistol was obviously intended to blow up the magazine as a last resource: 'and therefore,' said Sheffield, 'Mr Savill and I in a laughing way most mutinously resolved to throw him overboard in case we should ever catch him going down to the powder room.'

If one thing more than another could have been calculated to put Prince Rupert into a frenzy, it would have been the thought of taking his twenty-four ships on a wild goose chase, leaving his fellow commander-in-chief, for whom he felt affection and respect, to fight it out at a disadvantage with the Dutch admiral.

In point of fact, as soon as it was known that Monck was likely to become engaged, the Admiralty signed an order for Rupert's recall and sent it to Arlington, expecting that he would at once countersign and despatch it. But Arlington happened to be in bed, and nobody dared wake him, so the order never went. Fortunately, the sound of distant firing reached Rupert's squadron. Guessing what had happened, he reversed course on his own responsibility and made his way back at his best speed to join his colleague. The swaying struggle in which Monck and de Ruyter had been engaged since 1 June, over a wide expanse of sea, gave Rupert just the necessary time to make the junction, and it was not a moment too soon. 'About one o'clock Sunday (3 June) in the afternoon we discovered the Prince's squadron standing with us,' reported the observer in the *Royal Charles*. 'The shouts of joy that went from our ships at the sight so disordered the Dutch, that those ships of theirs that were almost come within shot of us, shortened sail and fell back again into the main body of their Fleet.'

Prince Rupert, as he arrived at the scene of action, must have seen in a moment how hard Monck was pressed. Ayscue had just surrendered, the Dutch had the advantage of the wind, and their numbers were at last beginning to tell. Soon after nightfall on 3 June, the

One of the many medals celebrating the Four-Days' Battle

Lely's portrait of Cornelius Tromp (1629–91), Lieutenant-Admiral of the United Provinces, painted when Tromp was on a visit to England

The surrender of the Royal Prince, *when aground on the Galloper Sand, by van de Velde the Younger; on her port bow is Cornelis Tromp in Sweers' ship, the* Gouda, *and astern of her is the artist's own galliot*

English joint commanders were able to confer, and to decide how to conduct the final phase of the action. It could scarcely last much longer. The crews were nearing exhaustion; powder and shot were beginning to run low and, on both sides, ships were being forced in increasing numbers to return to port for repair.

With two men of the calibre of Monck and Rupert, it was almost inevitable that the decision should be to continue to attack, in the hope of wearing down the enemy by continual mêlées. If Monck's ships were battered, Rupert's were fresh, and as always, the Prince was eager for a fight.

Five times, during the course of the last day, English and Dutch engaged in close action. Rupert had his fill. His flagship, the *Royal James*, was soon in the thick of it, losing her main yard and main top, and by the evening the *Royal Charles* was so damaged aloft that 'neither the Prince nor the General could work their ships, or lead on the Fleet'. De Ruyter had also had enough. 'In the night,' said the observer in the *Royal Charles*, 'we mended our rigging, but the General's squadron having spent almost all their powder and shot it was impossible to engage again. The Dutch left us in the night, being as unfit to fight as we, and their loss doubtless at least as great as ours.'

So ended the Four-Days' Battle, with great damage to both sides, but greater to the English, who had one flag-officer killed in action, another taken prisoner, and a third, Sir Christopher Myngs, mortally wounded. Myngs, who was in the van of the English fleet in the last fighting, was the subject of a touching incident, recorded by Samuel Pepys from direct observation. Myng's body was brought home, and he was buried in London. Pepys was there, in an Admiralty coach, when

about a dozen able, lusty proper men came to the coach-side with tears in their eyes, and one of them spoke for the rest . . . 'We are here a dozen of us that have long known and served our dead commander . . . and have now done the last office of laying him in the ground. We would be glad we had any other to offer after him, and in revenge of him. All we have is our lives; if you will please to get His Royal Highness to give us a fire-ship among us all, here is a dozen of us, out of all which choose you one to be commander, and the rest of us, whoever he is, will serve him; and if possible, do that shall show our memory of the dead commander, and our revenge!'

Such were the heights of devotion in the fleet after this extraordinary battle, without doubt a defeat for the English, but a costly triumph for their opponents. Monck and Rupert lost five thousand killed, three thousand prisoners and seventeen ships, eight sunk and nine in Dutch hands. Yet within seven weeks they were ready for sea again, and on St James's Day, 25 July, off Orfordness, they had their revenge, causing de Ruyter the loss of twenty ships for a single ship of their own. Following up the victory, Sir Robert Holmes destroyed a hundred and fifty ships in the Vlie, and burnt the storehouses of Brandaris.

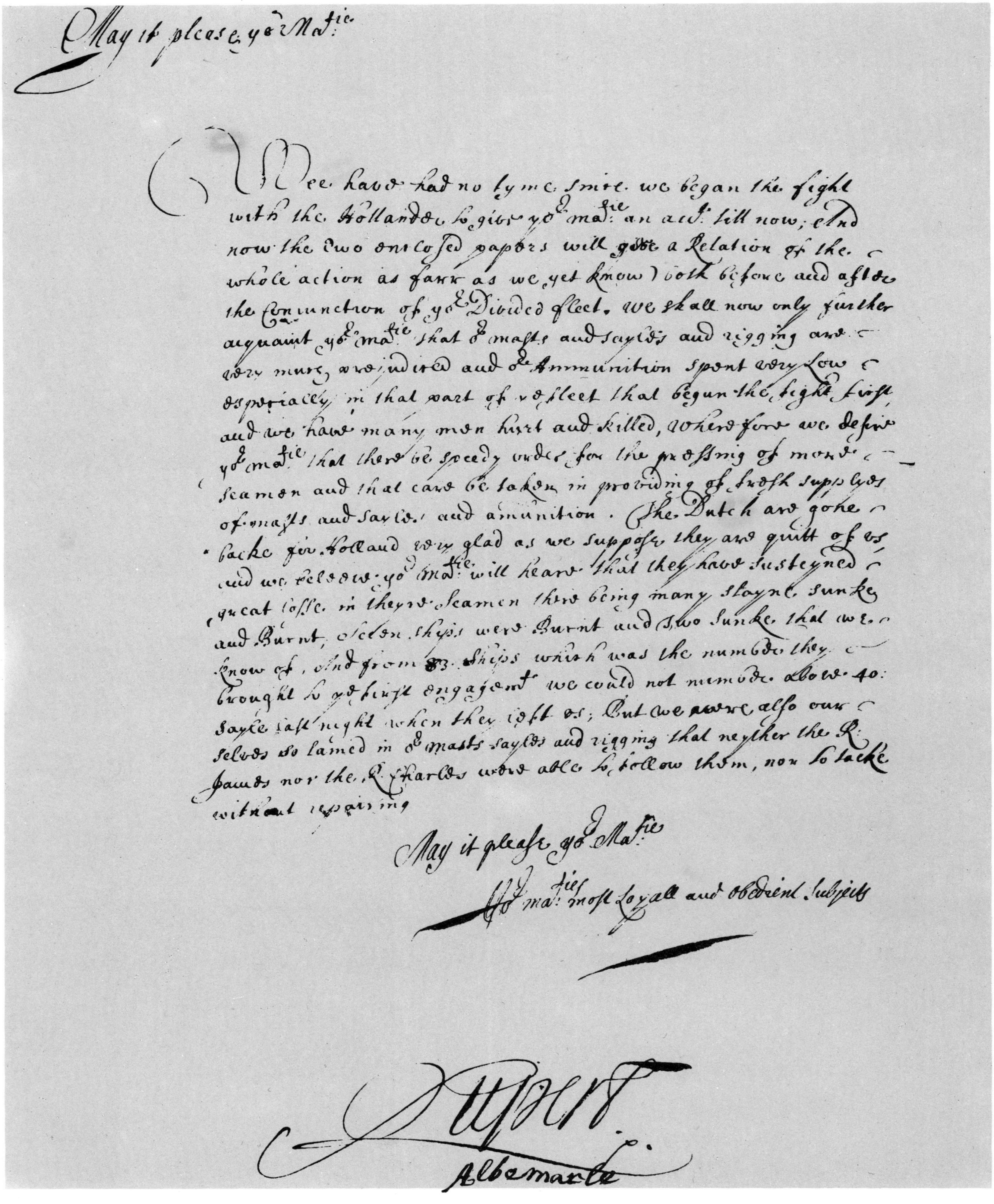

May it please yo.r Ma.tie

Wee have had no tyme since we began the fight with the Hollander to give yo.r ma.tie an acc.t till now, And now the two enclosed papers will give a Relation of the whole action as farr as we yet know both before and after the Conjunction of yo.r Divided fleet. we shall now only further acquaint yo.r ma.tie that o.r masts and sayles and rigging are very much wounded and o.r Ammunition spent very Low especially in that part of o.r fleet that began the fight first, and we have many men hurt and killed, wherefore we desire yo.r ma.tie that there be speedy order for the pressing of more seamen and that care be taken in provideing of fresh supplyes of masts and sayles and amunition. The Dutch are gone backe for Holland very glad as we suppose they are quitt of us and we beleeve yo.r ma.tie will heare that they have susteyned great losse in theyr seamen there being many slayne, sunke and Burnt, Seven ships were Burnt and two sunke that we know of, And from 83. ships which was the number they brought to yo.r first engagem.t we could not number above 40. Sayle last night when they left us; But we were also our selves so lamed in o.r masts sayles and rigging that neyther the R. James nor the R. Charles were able to follow them, nor so tacke without repairing

May it please yo.r Ma.tie

Yo.r ma.ties most Loyall and obedient subjects

Rupert

Albemarle

Splendid as the feat was, it did not altogether satisfy Rupert. After the St James's Day battle he wrote a brief despatch to his cousin the Duke of York in which the sentence occurred: 'I hope your Highness will be satisfied with our endeavours, though some gross errors have been committed by Persons, not in point of courage but want of conduct.' By 'conduct' Rupert meant strict obedience to the Admiral, a characteristic which, as signals and instructions grew more precise, would be looked for as much as valour in the sea officers of the future.

The war was not to end happily for England, since Charles II made a second blunder. Shortly after the July victory, he laid up the fleet. In June the following year the Dutch sailed up the Medway, captured the *Royal Charles*, and threw all London into a panic. Pepys heard of English voices calling from Dutch ships: 'We did heretofore fight for tickets: now we fight for dollars!' It was an ignominious moment, the result of throwing away, by short-sighted ineptitude, what had been gained by resolution. Once more it was de Ruyter, with a cruising force, who ensured the success of the operation, enabling him to end the war in a blaze of glory.

The same French observer in his flagship, the Comte de Guiche, who had seen with what discipline Monck ordered his fleet, gave posterity the best thumb-nail sketch of de Ruyter during the time of the Four-Days' Battle. It was one which may serve to typify his character throughout a long and illustrious career. 'I never saw him other than even-tempered,' he said, 'and when victory was assured, saying always that it was the good God that gives it to us. Amid the disorders of the Fleet and the appearance of loss, he seemed only to be moved by the misfortune to his country, but always submissive to the Will of God. He had something of the frankness and lack of polish of our patriarchs, and to conclude what I have to say of him, I will relate that the day after the victory I found him sweeping his own cabin and feeding his chickens.'

LEFT: *A letter to Charles II signed by Prince Rupert and the Duke of Albemarle, describing the Four-Days' Battle*

RIGHT TOP: *Sir George Ayscue (c 1615–72), Admiral of the White Squadron at the battle, who was captured in the* Royal Prince, *painted by Sir Peter Lely*

RIGHT CENTRE: *Sir William Berkeley (1639–66), Vice-Admiral of the White Squadron, who was killed in the* Swiftsure *at the Four-Days' Battle, painted by Sir Peter Lely*

RIGHT BOTTOM: *Sir John Harman (1630–73), Rear-Admiral of the White Squadron, who made a notable defence of his flagship, the* Henry, *painted by Sir Peter Lely*

Sicily

1676

The French admiral, Duquesne, defeated a combined Spanish and Dutch fleet, and de Ruyter, the great Dutch admiral, was mortally wounded during the action

HISTORY ABOUNDS IN IRONIES; not the least of them is that de Ruyter, champion at sea of the Protestant Dutch, should have met his death at the hands of a French admiral of the same religion, and in a campaign which, full of interest as it is, lay outside the main area of Dutch and French achievement.

In the summer of 1674, when the Dutch were allied with Spain and with the Austrian Empire against the France of Louis XIV, the Sicilians revolted against their Spanish rulers, and called on France for help. Louis at once responded. Thanks to the genius of his minister, Colbert, his navy had never been so strong, and by the early months of 1675 his fleet had brushed aside such local forces as Spain was able to employ, and had occupied Messina, sustaining the rebels by its presence. Spain thereupon called upon Holland for help, and de Ruyter, who was by that time sixty-eight years old, worn by incessant and arduous service, was sent to the Mediterranean with eighteen ships of the line and four fire-ships. He left Holland depressed in spirit, but with characteristic acceptance of destiny.

He reached Cadiz in September 1675. There he was delayed by the Spaniards, who in the outcome were only able to strengthen his force by one ship. The French in

Sicily had, meanwhile, taken Augusta, a port commanding the south-east coast of the island, and they had been given essential time to strengthen their whole position.

When de Ruyter finally reached the scene of operations, in January 1676, he saw that his main task must be to prevent the French from bringing supplies and forces to Messina. He was prevented by head-winds from entering the Messina Straits, so he cruised between the Lipari Islands and Sicily, in the hope of intercepting a large convoy and its protecting fleet, commanded by Abraham Duquesne, which was hourly expected. The French admiral, whom he was now to encounter for the first time, was nearly as old as his opponent, with a reputation won in the service of France and, at one stage of his career, of Sweden. It was likely that with two such leaders, warfare at sea would be both skilfully conducted and stubborn.

On 7 January the French were sighted by de Ruyter, and he perceived their force to be formidable – twenty ships of the line, most of them of Colbert's building, and, therefore, new and large, and six fire-ships. De Ruyter had the advantage of the wind, and there is not much doubt that, had he been a younger man, he would have attacked, like Monck at the outset of the Four-Days' Battle, and gained the initiative at once. On this occasion he was cautious and he spent the first day manoeuvering. During the night, the wind shifted, and daybreak gave Duquesne the chance to attack.

The Dutch, though inferior in numbers, were in a strong position, and could await events with confidence.

LEFT: *The Battle of Palermo, 12 June 1676, after Petrus Schotel. In the centre is Duquesne's* Royale Thérèse, *and on the far right the flagship of the Dutch admiral Haan, who succeeded de Ruyter*

A romantic portrait of Abraham Duquesne (1610–88), the great French admiral who successfully supported the Sicilians by sea in their revolt against Spain, by Alexandre Steuben (1814–62)

LEFT TOP: *A contemporary portrait of Michel de Ruyter (1607–76) in the heyday of his career, by H. Berckman (1629–79)*

LEFT CENTRE: *A drawing, attributed to Pierre Puget (1622–94), of a French first-rate ship of the line at the time of Duquesne, showing her making ready for action*

LEFT BOTTOM: *A model of a French first-rate,* Le Soleil Royal, *belonging to the period of the Sicilian operations; the carved stern is of particular splendour*

De Ruyter himself had incomparable battle experience; he was between the convoy and its port, and he felt he would soon have Duquesne's measure.

About nine o'clock, the French bore down obliquely, in a movement requiring skill and co-ordination. Two ships drew too far ahead. They were roughly handled, and were forced to leeward. The French line was soon in confusion, and de Ruyter, by orderly, gradual withdrawal, made their situation worse.

Action continued most of the day, Duquesne attempting, and failing, to isolate part of the Dutch fleet, de Ruyter edging away, firing at the French spars and rigging as he did so. When the battle ended, neither side had lost any major war vessels, though Duquesne, in an attempt to use his fire-ships, had had two of his number sunk. Both fleets were much damaged aloft, and de Ruyter found a use for a number of Spanish galleys, which had hovered round his squadron, to tow his more injured ships out of harm's way.

By the morning of 9 January, Duquesne, though in no condition to attack, could congratulate himself that he had saved his convoy, and that de Ruyter was unlikely to do him further harm. Both sides were now reinforced, Duquesne by ten ships from Messina, de Ruyter by six Spaniards, whom he judged to be of little value. But de Ruyter still barred his opponents' passage through the Straits, and Duquesne, after some days manoeuvering, stood away to the westward, being forced to circle the island of Sicily before he could reach Messina safely. De Ruyter had denied the town relief for many days and had shown how skilfully, in the day of battle, an admiral could use the lee-gage, even with inferior numbers. With Duquesne out of sight, de Ruyter withdrew to Palermo to refit, one of his damaged ships sinking on passage in a storm.

The Dutch admiral could regard his sparring with the French complacently, and although no further action on any large scale occurred for nearly four months, yet during that time de Ruyter established an efficient block- ade of Messina, and even threatened the French position at Augusta.

RIGHT: The French under heavy fire, as each of their divisions come into action in succession, during the engagement on 8 January 1676

OVERLEAF, LEFT: The action off Augusta in April 1676, during which de Ruyter was mortally wounded; a contemporary picture of the battle, with diagrammatic plan, published in France. RIGHT: The Battle of Palermo in June 1676. Haan had succeeded to the command of the Dutch fleet after de Ruyter's death

FRENCH

DUTCH

LA BATAILLE NAVALE
donnée prés d'Agouste le 22. Avril 1676.

L'AVIS estant venu a Messine, que les flottes d'Espagne et de Hollande commandées par le Vice-
Admiral Ruiter avoient paru aux environs d'Agouste, et sembloient avoir quelque dessein sur cette ville. Du Quesne
Lieutenant general de l'Armée navale de France, eut ordre du Maréchal de Vivonne de sortir du Fare avec toute la
flotte, et d'aller chercher les Ennemis ; Il les rencontra a trois lieües d'Agouste et les attaqua aussitost : le choc fut terrible, et Almeras qui conduisoit l'Avantgarde françoise, fut tué d'abord ; mais presque en même temps Ruiter combattant fort
vaillamment eût la cheville du pied emportée et fut mis hors de combat : La blesure de ce Capitaine, fit perdre aux Ennemis,
une partie de leur audace, et donna le temps au Chevalier de Valbelle qui avoit pris la place d'Almeras, de rasseurer l'Avantgarde des François qui s'estoit un peu ébranlée : Sur ces entrefaites Du Quesne s'estant avancé avec le corps de bataille et tout le
reste des vaisseaux, il se fit de part et d'autre un feu épouvantable : la bataille dura jusqu'à la nuit qui separa les deux armées,
l'une et l'autre à l'ordinaire s'attribuant l'avantage du combat : mais le lendemain les Ennemis se confessérent vaincus, par
la retraite qu'ils firent en diligence à la veüe de l'Armée françoise, qui les poursuivit jusques dans le port de Syracuse.
Ruiter mourut peu de jours apres de sa blesure, au grand regret des Hollandois qui se consolerent plus
aisement de la perte de la bataille que de la mort de ce Capitaine, le plus grand homme de mer
que la Hollande ait jamais produit.

LA
BATAILLE DE PALERME.

*Le Mareschal de Vivone ayant eu avis que le Vice-admiral Ruiter estoit mort—
de la blessure qu'il avoit receüe dans le dernier combat donné contre luy sur la mer mediterra-
née; songea aussitot a profiter de la consternation ou la perte d'un chef de cette importance devoit
apparement avoir jetté les ennemis. Il fait remettre a la voile, il part de Messine, et les va chercher. les deux
flottes d'Espagne et de Hollande estoit a la rade devant Palerme, occupée a reparer le dommage de leurs vaisseaux, et mal en ordre par la mesintelligence qui estoit desja entre les chefs. Le desordre augmente a la veüe
de l'armée de france qui venoit sur elles avec l'avantage du vent, et qui les attaqua brusquem. les ennemis fuyent;
les uns vont échouer sur les rivages voisins, les autres se refugient dans le port sous les murailles de Palerme;
Mais le Mareschal de Vivone les y poursuit, et les foudroye de tous costez, il fait sauter une bonne
partie de leurs vaisseaux. Les éclats tout embrasez en retombent sur la ville et y mettent le feu en plu-
sieurs endroits On n'a jamais remporté sur la mer de victoire plus complete, ni moins douteuse. Les ennemis y perdirent plus de cinq mille hommes, six Galeres et douze gros vaisseaux entre lesquels
on comptoit l'Admiral et le Vice-admiral d'Espagne. Cette bataille se donna—
le deuxieme Juin 1676.*

Oared galleys towing damaged ships out of the line, with Mount Etna in the background. From a painting by Petrus Schotel of the Battle of Augusta

It was off Augusta, on 22 April, that de Ruyter and Duquesne met once more. This time, the French had twenty-nine ships of the line, and their advantage was greater than numbers implied, for de Ruyter was not in chief command. His ships had been joined by ten Spaniards under Don Francisco de la Cerda. The Spanish commander-in-chief insisted that his own division should form the centre of the allied line. Although, in the way of formal warfare, this was the appropriate place for it, the arrangement did not meet with de Ruyter's approval, for it separated him from Haan, his Dutch Vice-Admiral, and de Ruyter knew something of the quality of the ships and men with whom he would be fighting. Had he had his way, it is certain that Dutch and Spaniards would have been intermingled, the seasoned Dutch stiffening their southern allies.

The pattern of the engagement went much as de Ruyter would have predicted. He himself commanded the van, and, having the wind, he attacked in his old style. De la Cerda did not support him. The Spaniards fought desultorily, and at long range, allowing the brunt of the action to fall on de Ruyter. In the course of the day the Dutch admiral, who during his long career of active service had never been struck by an enemy shot, received a serious wound, and was carried below. It was only to-wards evening that the allied rear under Vice-Admiral Haan, who had dutifully followed the movements of the Spaniards, was able to come into action. When he did so, Duquesne edged away to leeward, until night separated the fleets.

The next day broke in rain and mist, and there was no sign of the French. They had made for Messina. The Dutch and Spaniards put into the harbour at Syracuse, and it was there, on 29 April, that de Ruyter died of his wound, mourned by brave men of every nation. Haan, who succeeded him, was not of the same heroic cast, and it was not long before the biockade of Messina was raised, and before the French had won a signal victory off Palermo. Soon afterwards, the Dutch returned home.

Not unnaturally, the French made much of their successes. Duquesne was given a marquisate, though his elevation softened his arrogant temper not at all, and he was never a popular officer in the navy he served. Great as his services were, Duquesne was not an admiral whose distinction approached that of his opponent. De Ruyter was a thoughtful, bold and inspiring leader, a man who would have been an ornament to any country: Duquesne was brave and fortunate, but he had neither great tactical genius nor long experience of high command. Indeed it was Colbert, not a Dutchman, who said that he saw no real comparison between the head and heart of his countryman and those of Michel de Ruyter, his great opponent, and indeed it was Colbert's fine ships which, in Sicily, at length decided the issue.

LEFT: *Jean Baptiste Colbert (1619–83), whose superb organisation of Louis XIV's Navy led to the success of the Sicilian operations*

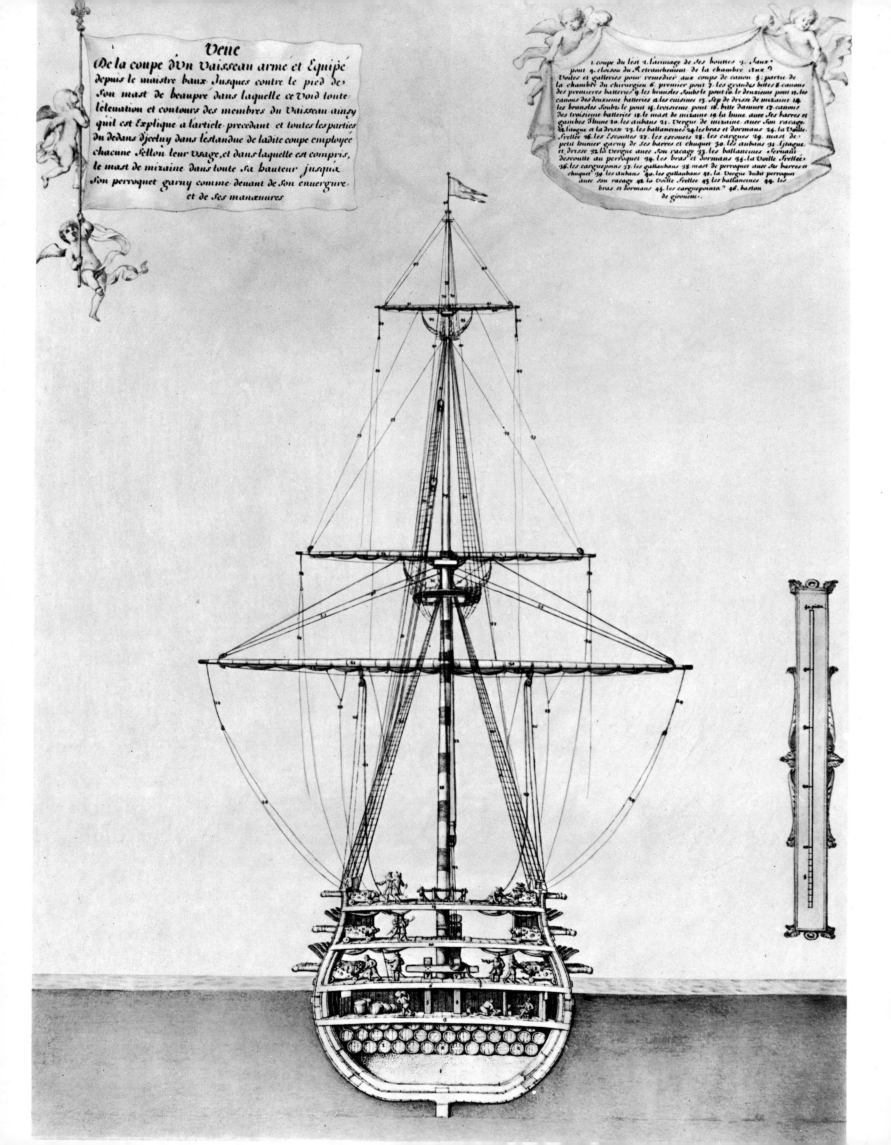

Gibraltar and Malaga
1704

A joint British and Dutch fleet under Sir George Rooke compelled the Spanish Governor to surrender the Rock. A sea battle off Malaga ensured possession

THE CAPTURE OF GIBRALTAR, an episode in Marlborough's wars against the French, was due as much to soldiers as to sailors, for the soldiers took the Rock. They were marines, and it is fitting that to this day the British Corps of Royal Marines, with a record second to none, have as their badge a globe encompassed with a laurel wreath. Their battle-honour 'Gibraltar' stands for their achievements then and later in every part of the world.

The event itself, which took place in 1704, the same year as the great land victory at Blenheim, was almost accidental, and had no part in the plans of the London government. The credit belonged mainly to Sir George Rooke, an admiral who had learnt his business in the wars of the previous century, and who had a way of making a success of secondary plans when the first went wrong.

The war of the Spanish Succession, which had opened in 1702, was fought mainly to decide, first, whether Spain and all her dominions should belong to Philip of France, to whom they had been left by the Spanish King Charles II, and then whether the powerful France of Louis XIV and the Spain of his grandson should be united. It lasted for over ten years, and was of great complexity. So far as Britain was concerned, it saw her ships fighting side by side with their old opponents, the Dutch, and it also saw

LEFT: *A section of a ship of the line, probably Dutch, showing guns run out and the stowage of powder and stores in the hold*

the use by the Allied fleet of the harbours and bases of Portugal, which were to be of infinite value in this and later times.

The war at sea opened with two failures. Off the coast of Spanish America Admiral Benbow was deserted by his captains (two of whom were later shot for cowardice) when in chase of an enemy squadron. In Spain Rooke failed to take Cadiz. But on his way home, he learnt that a Spanish treasure fleet, guarded by a French detachment, had put into Vigo Bay. The French admiral threw a boom across the inner harbour, covered by guns from sea and land. Sir John Hopsonn was ordered to break the boom, while Rooke's ships followed him in and attacked the treasure ships. All went well. Although there was much destruction, a large part of the treasure was taken, and even today fine silver coins bearing the image of Queen Anne are to be found with the word 'Vigo' below the Queen's bust. They were minted from Rooke's haul.

Two years later, an allied attack on the great French port of Toulon was agreed upon, with Marlborough's approval. It failed, as had an attempt on Barcelona, and the French were reinforced by the arrival of a strong French fleet from Brest, which compelled Rooke to withdraw to the Atlantic. Off the south west of Spain he was joined by ships under Sir Clowdesley Shovell. Rooke and Shovell, not wishing to return home empty-handed, decided, on Rooke's responsibility, to attempt Gibraltar. The fleet turned south.

Geographically, the great rock-fortress of Gibraltar oc-

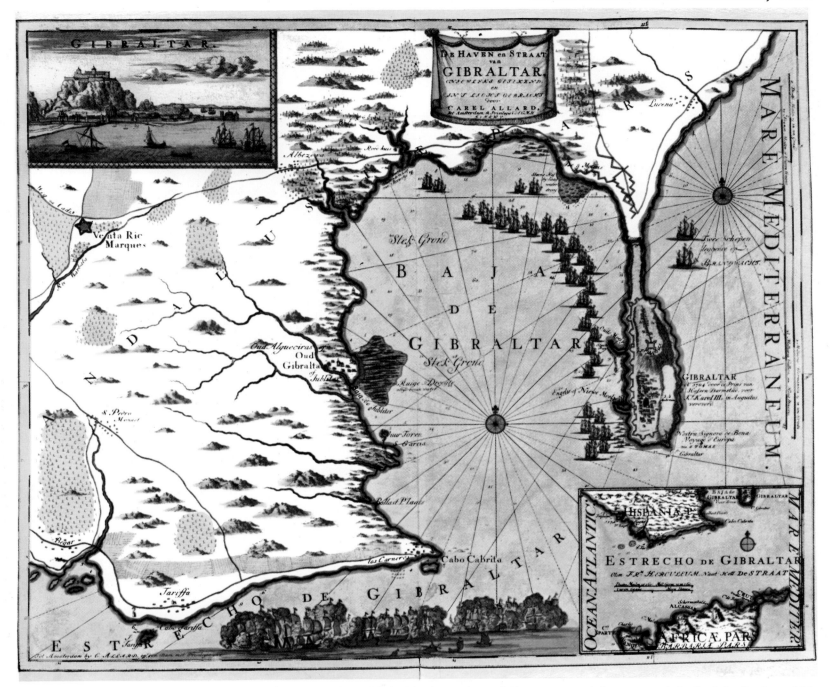

A map of Gibraltar by Carel Allard from P. Schenck's atlas published in Amsterdam within ten years of the capture of the Rock by Rooke and his Allies

LEFT: A portrait of the Comte de Toulouse, Grand Admiral de France, who took command at Malaga in 1704 and received the order of the Golden Fleece after the battle from his father and sovereign, Louis XIV, painted by an unknown artist of the school of Largillière

cupies a key position. At the entrance to the Mediterranean, it seems to thrust like a sword into the sea, which is open to the eastward. The western side of the Rock faces the bay of Algeciras. To the north a low stretch of land links it to the country to which it seems naturally to belong. The Romans called Gibraltar Mons Calpe, and it was known as one of the Pillars of Hercules, the other being Mount Abyla on the African side of the Straits. In the eighth century the Moorish conquerors of North Africa crossed the water and stormed it. It was taken by Tarik-ibn-Zeyad, and the general's name is

lastingly commemorated, for Gibraltar in fact means Gebel Tarik, 'the Mountain of Tarik'.

Tarik built a castle and a palace, which took him fourteen years, and the Moors held undisputed possession until, in 1309, it endured the first of many recorded sieges. It fell to the Spaniards under Alonzo de Guzman. But the Spaniards did not value it, and it soon became a sanctuary for criminals. Presently, the Moors returned, and then there began a series of sieges and disputed possession until at last, in the year 1462, it finally fell to Spanish power. It was garrisoned by men who owed al-

LEFT: *Sir George Rooke (1650–1709), Admiral of the Fleet, who commanded the Anglo-Dutch fleet at the Battle of Malaga and the taking of Gibraltar, by Michael Dahl (c 1649–1743).* RIGHT: *Gerard Kallenberg (1642–1722), Lieutenant Admiral of the Maze, who commanded the Dutch division at the taking of Gibraltar, after Jan Vollevens (1685–1758)*

legiance to the Duke of Medina Sidonia, forbear of the man who commanded the Armada of 1588.

When Rooke decided on his attack, Gibraltar, so formidable in its natural position, was weakly held. There were fortifications, mainly built by the Emperor Charles V, father of Philip II of Spain and of Don John of Austria, and there was a mole on the Algeciras side, where the modern harbour has been constructed: but the troops had not expected an assault, and after what was almost a token resistance the Governor signed articles of surrender.

Among Rooke's captains was Sir John Leake, who had charge of the *Prince George*, a ship named after Queen Anne's consort. Leake left a diary in which the story of Rooke's success is told tersely, and with a fine contempt for spelling and grammar.

The fight began early in the morning of Sunday 23 July 1704, when the fleet was off the harbour. 'At 5 the

ships that was appointed to cannonade the towne began to fire,' wrote Leake, 'as likewise the Bomb Vessells to heave in their bombs.' These 'bombs' resembled mortar shells and they were lobbed from close inshore. Firing continued for about four hours and then slackened. The ships could not afford to use up all their powder and shot.

By eleven o'clock those who were nearest the mole saw that the Spaniards were 'beate from their guns' and a signal was then made for boats to go in. Some had already landed on the western side, but they had made little progress. Serious business began again shortly after midday. 'Several of our boats crews haveing got ashore upon the new Mould (Mole) to take possession of the Fort,' wrote Leake, 'the Magezen of powder blew up, and destroyed several men, and wounded Capt Hicks whoo had landed with Capt Jumper upon that service.' After more setbacks, reinforcements arrived, 'the rest of the boats gitting ashore under the command of Capt

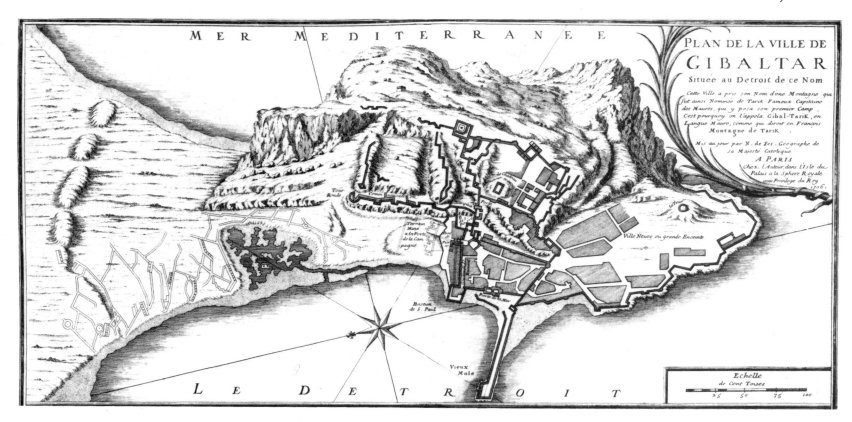

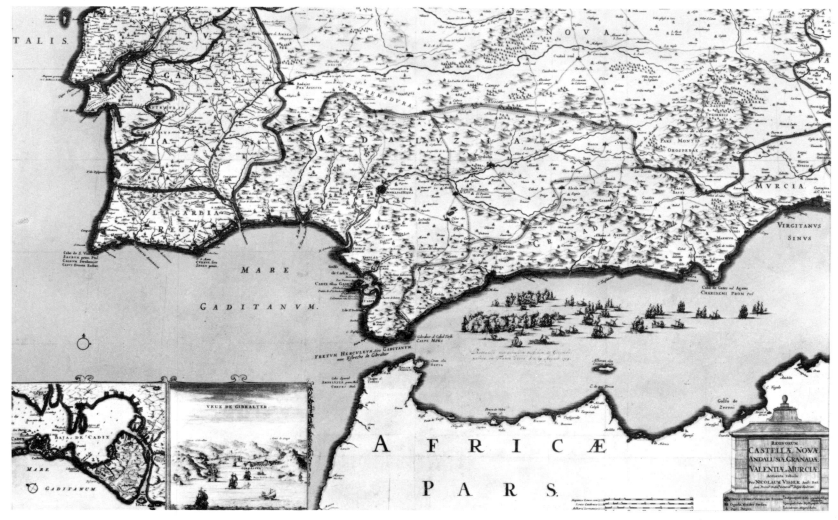

TOP: *A line-engraving of Gibraltar by A. Coquart, published in Paris in 1706, showing the defences at that time.* BOTTOM: *A line-engraving by N. Visscher, showing the area of operations of the opposing fleets at the Battle of Malaga, 1704*

Frigates & Fireships	Ships	Commanders	Men	Guns	& Division
	Somersett	Capt. Price	500	80	
	Berce	Hubbard	440	70	
	Triton	Trevor	230	50	
Charl. Galley 32	Dorsetshire	Whitaker	500	80	R.r Adm.l of the Red
Vulture Fireship	Newleigh	G. Byng Esq. — I. Cole	535	80	
	Torbay	Caldwell	500	80	
	Centurion	Herne	280	50	
	Kingston	Acton	365	60	
	St. Firme	Wilde	440	70	
Lark 40	Grafton	S. J. Leake	440	70	
Newport 24	Nassau	Dove	440	70	
Henke & Fireships	Mountague	Cleveland	365	60	
Hoffing Fireship	St. George	Jennings	680	96	
Star	Roy.l Catherine	S. G. Rooke	730	90	Adm.l of the Fleet
Peace Bombs	Eagle	L. Hamilton	440	70	
	Monmouth	Baker	440	70	
Wm. & Mary Yacht	Shrewsbury	Crow	500	80	
	Bedford	S. Tho. Hardy	440	70	
	Swallow	Haddock	280	50	
	Suffolk	Anton	440	70	
Tartar 32	Roy.l Oak	Elwin	500	76	
Lightning Fireship	Kent	Ino. Wilkes Esq. — Hanway	400	70	R.r Adm.l of the White
	Cambridge	Lestock	500	80	
	Monk	Mighells	365	60	
	Burford	Rosy	440	70	
	Warspight	Loads	440	70	
	Nottingham	Whitaker	365	60	
	Assurance	Hancock	440	66	
Roebuck 40	Defiance	Norris	440	70	
Vulcan Fireship	Barfleur	S. C. Shovell — Stuart	710	96	Adm.l of the White
Griffin Fireship	Namur	Mynne	680	96	
Firebrand Fireship	Swiftsure	Wynn	440	70	
	Tilbury	Delavall	280	50	
	Lenox	Jumper	440	70	
			5525	2420	

A model of the 6o-gun Dreadnought, *a vessel of 1704; the planks are cut away below the water-line to show the construction of the hull*

Edward Whitaker, the men rallied again and got into the fort, set up a union flagg and marcht to annother small fort nearer the towne, which was deserted by the Spaniards.'

By the late afternoon, all was under control. The Prince of Hesse, who was in command of the Dutch and German troops, who also took part in the operation, 'summoned the towne from the north gate, where the Marreins were encamped, and soone after the Admiral did the same from the south gate, where the Seamen where, and received an ansure from the Governor.'

LEFT: *A contemporary list of the ships which served under Sir George Rooke at Malaga, indicating the Admiral's order-of-battle*

The garrison had had enough. At eight o'clock next day, said the Governor, they would surrender, provided that hostages were exchanged forthwith. This was done, and Leake was able to conclude his story by recording that at four o'clock on Monday 'the articles being agreed on, the Marreins marcht in and took possession . . .'

If the actual taking of Gibraltar had been easy, the event was to produce some stiffer fighting. Although the Spaniards and the French seem not to have appreciated the great value of the fortress to their enemies, their re-action was swift. Spanish honour was affronted, and if the Dutch, Germans and English were once allowed to consolidate their gain, Gibraltar might prove to be a running sore. It must be retaken, and the first step to-wards that end was to defeat Rooke's fleet. Rooke had

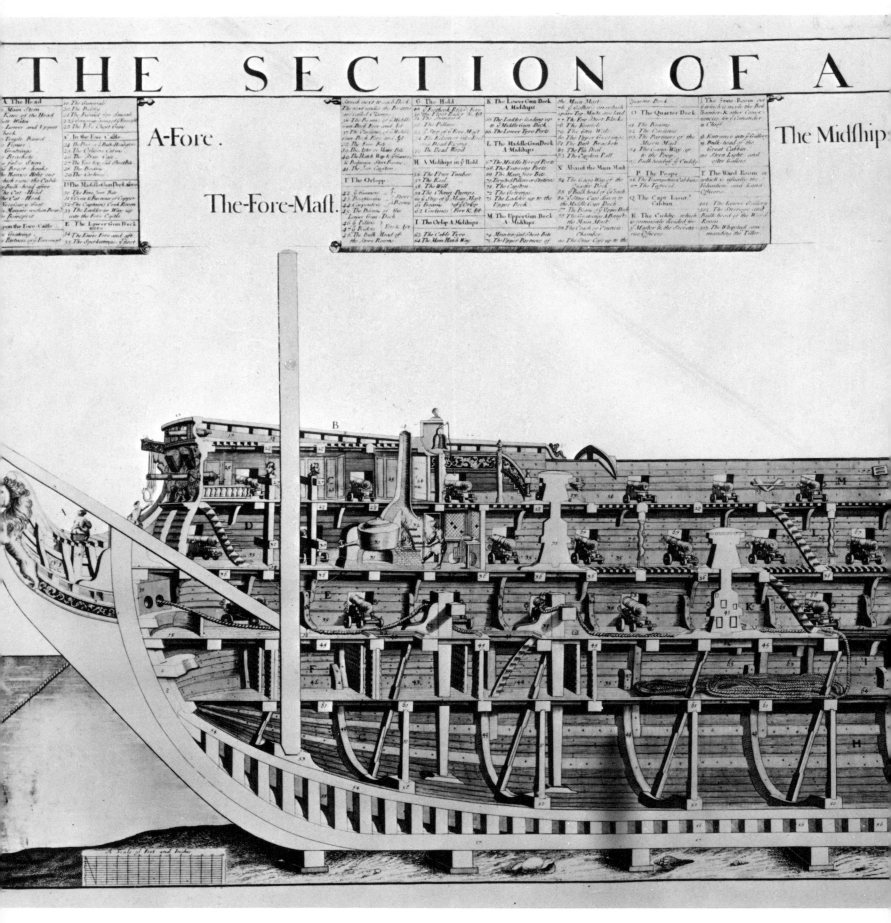

Section of a British First Rate ship of 1700. She carried an armament of 100 guns, 12-pounders on the upper deck, 29-pounders on the main deck, and 32-pounders on the lower deck. She had a crew of 850, and her best speed was about 10 knots. The length of her keel was 140 feet, her beam was 50 feet, and the depth of her hold was 20 feet

FIRST RATE SHIP.

A-Bauft.

Mifon-Maft.

ain-Maft.

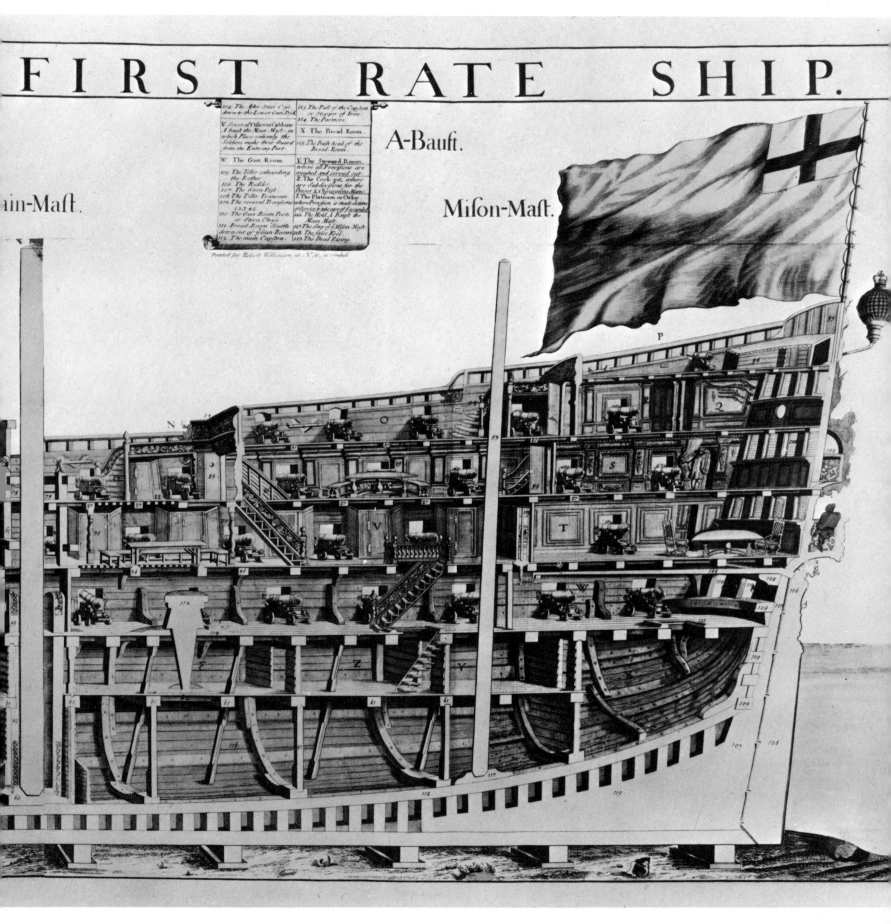

been driven once from Toulon: he should be expelled from the Mediterranean for good.

The Spaniards mounted an attack from the northern side, where Gibraltar, as Rooke discovered, was most easily defended. They also called upon Louis XIV to aid with his fleet, and the response was swift. The King gave the command to his natural son, the Comte de Toulouse, and ordered him to annihilate the Anglo-Dutch.

The fleets met on 13 August, only a few weeks after Rooke's success, off Velez Malaga, some little distance into the Mediterranean. The battle proved to be one of those stiff, unsatisfactory encounters typical of formal sea warfare. Each commander manoeuvred rigidly. Neither of them could discover a way by which to break the enemy line and so reach a decision. Shovell led the van, Rooke the centre, while the Dutch under Kallenberg brought up the rear. The fighting was hard, the casualties heavy, and the French, with their fresh fleet, should have made their advantage felt. But they fought at too long a range, and even when they saw that, in the centre of the Allied line, four ships had to be towed away when they had used up all their ammunition (15,000 shots had been fired at Gibraltar), they did not press Rooke either then or next day, when they had the advantage of the wind.

Leake, who fought in Shovell's squadron, said that on 14 August, 'wee lay expecting them but indeed in a

Dutch ships of the line under construction; a scene in a shipyard, from Van Yk's Manual of Naval Architecture, 1697.

RIGHT: *A Dutch private ship in action with French and Spanish galleys at the Battle of Malaga, 13 August 1704, by an unidentified Dutch artist*

A dramatic painting by J. S. Copley (1737–1815) of Lord Heathfield, (1717–90) and the other principal officers concerned in the long and successful defence of Gibraltar during the siege, 1779–83

shater'd condition, and several of our Fleet without Ammunition; but I believe they had enough, for they ply'd to windward: and soe keep at a Distance till the 16th at night they gave us the slip, and went to the Eastward.'

The Fleets were large. The Anglo-Dutch line consisted of no less than fifty ships. The French had one more, and they also brought with them twenty-five French and Spanish galleys. It was almost the last time that oared men-of-war, with a history stretching back as far as classical times, took part in a general engagement. They proved useless.

Both sides claimed a victory, the French and Spanish very loudly indeed, for propaganda is not a new activity. A writer in Seville claimed that sixteen enemy ships had been sunk and thirty-six captured, 'among them the flag-ships of England and Holland, and the admiral, Rooke'. This was lying on a grand scale. The account admitted the loss of four ships 'two galleys of Spain and two of

France', and concluded: 'The end of the remainder of the enemy is to be expected momentarily, the Comte de Toulouse having sent a squadron to the Straits of Gibraltar, that none of the enemy may escape.'

Velez Malaga ranks as a major sea battle for a sound reason. In itself, it was indecisive: no ship was lost on either side: but Rooke could, and did, claim a victory, for it was only necessary for him to keep his fleet in being, and near Gibraltar, to ensure that the Allies retained their conquest.

Even so, the danger to Gibraltar was not quite over. The garrison was small, and it had to be supplied, both with food and ammunition, from a fleet which was itself in sore need of replenishment. Sooner or later, Rooke would have to refit, but when he withdrew, Toulouse sent only ten ships to support the land attack, and his squadron was later destroyed. 'With this reverse,' said a French naval officer, 'there began in all French people a

A view of Gibraltar engraved by F. Hegi after a painting by Alexandre Jean Noel (1752–1834), which appears to have been painted during one of Noel's travels before the Revolutionary Wars

regrettable reaction against the navy . . . The army, more directly in contact with the nation, had all its favour, all its sympathy.'

Rooke's enterprise was not as well rewarded by the authorities in London as it deserved, for he was superseded, and his capture was so little valued by Queen Anne's successor, the first of four Hanoverian Georges, that later in the century he offered to give it up. Government and people showed more sense. Gibraltar was retained, and indeed it proved its value only four years after its capture, when it served as a stepping stone to the capture of Minorca, the most easterly of the Balearic Islands. There, at Port Mahon, was a splendid natural harbour, and an island whose supplies were so valuable that it was retained by the British for the greater part of the eighteenth century.

Gibraltar's finest hour came later, when, during the years 1780-83, it withstood its fiercest siege, the Governor

being George Eliott, Lord Heathfield, one of the most determined officers ever sent to the Mediterranean. But even Heathfield could not have held out without supplies brought to him from England under cover of the main fleet. There were three principal reliefs. The first, conducted in 1780 by Admiral Rodney, led to the capture of a valuable Spanish convoy off Cape Finisterre, and to a moonlight battle against Admiral de Langara in the latitude of Cape St Vincent, during the course of which six prizes were taken, including the enemy flagship. The second, under Admiral Darby, was less eventful in itself, though the relaxed watch on France allowed a squadron under Pierre-André Suffren to leave Brest for the Indian Ocean. The third and last was conducted by Lord Howe in the face of a superior enemy fleet, which was held off while the transports delivered their supplies. Howe's operation was considered to be the most difficult and successful he ever conducted.

A magnetic dry-card ship's compass set in a wooden bowl, dated about 1750

Quiberon Bay

1759

Fought between the British and French fleets during the Seven Years' War, the battle resulted in an overwhelming victory for Sir Edward Hawke

THE WORLD-WIDE STRUGGLE KNOWN AS the Seven Years' War (1756-1763) involved rivalry between France and Britain for supremacy overseas, France having taken the place of Spain as the leading expansionist Power. On land Austria and Prussia fought for supremacy in Germany. France, wishing to see Germany weak, took the side of Austria against Frederick the Great, and it was mainly owing to his country's continental position that Louis XV devoted more of her resources to the land struggle. Britain, on the other hand, gave her best energies to the naval and colonial war, and aided Prussia partly through the accident that George II happened also to be Elector of Hanover, and partly because by so doing she could hamper France.

The war began disastrously with Admiral John Byng's failure to relieve Minorca, and with the loss of Hanover, which was later recovered by Frederick. Events began to take a more favourable turn after William Pitt, generally known by his title of Lord Chatham, to distinguish him from his equally famous second son, was given office as Secretary-of-State. Pitt was a master of war, and the fact was shown partly in his choice of land and sea commanders. In Canada, India, Africa and upon the seas, a vigorous policy encouraged vigorous men. By 1759, in spite of the fact that the French were planning an invasion, Britain went over to the offensive, and the capture of Guadaloupe in the West Indies, General Wolfe's success at Quebec which gave his countrymen the key to Canada, and three episodes at sea, caused it to be known

as the Year of Victories.

So far as the navy was concerned, the matter may be said to have begun in July, when Sir George Rodney, destroying by bombardment the flat-bottomed boats assembled at Havre for an assault across the Channel, took the first step towards thwarting it. In August, Edward Boscawen defeated a fleet from Toulon under de la Clue off the coast of Portugal, capturing three ships and running two others ashore. In November, Sir Edward Hawke crowned his fellow-officers' achievements by a victory in a gale on a lee shore, after one of the most daring chases in history.

Quiberon Bay, on the coast of Brittany, where Hawke's engagement with Admiral Conflans took place, cliff-girt, studded with rocky islands, and a place of dangerous shoals, was a befitting place wherein to crown the professional life of a man recognized as outstanding. Hawke had been born in the reign of Queen Anne, but was nearly forty by the time he had had the chance to distinguish himself in action. When it came, he not only took it with both hands, but he never looked back. Once before, in 1747, he had chased and defeated a French squadron which was protecting a convoy from Rochelle. The success had won him a knighthood, and from the opening of the new war he had been given high command at sea. For much of the time, he had exercised a close blockade of Brest.

All through the summer of the year of his victory Hawke lay so close to the Isle of Ushant that Conflans,

Toulon, the principal French naval base, in 1775, painted by Claude Joseph Vernet the greatest French marine artist of this period

commanding the French fleet in Brest, could not stir without the certainty of having to fight. The army of invasion, which had been assembled at Vannes, in the country facing Quiberon Bay, lay idle, waiting for Conflans to embark it, and carry it across the sea.

The season grew late, and Conflans remained penned in at Brest: but it was also late for the British fleet to be on watch, day by day, in a season of gales. On 9 November the wind blew from the west in such strength that Hawke was forced to take shelter in Torbay. Less than a week later he was out again, but Conflans had seized his chance. Reinforced by a squadron under Bompart, which had gained Brest in Hawke's absence, he put to sea the very day that Hawke left Torbay. It was a perfect illustration of the weakness both of the system of blockade, and of Brest as a port. Strong westerly winds could temporarily drive the watchers away from Ushant, but unhappily for France, Brest harbour was so situated that no fleet under sail could beat up the narrow Goulet while

the westerlies lasted. The danger point came when the wind's direction changed. A wind which would bring the English back released their opponents, and if they were ready, they could get clean away before the British had made good their return. It was so now. Seizing the moment, Conflans came out, making south east for Quiberon, to pick up the army of invasion.

Wild weather, with changeable winds, now affected both fleets, but by 20 November Conflans was near his destination, where he found Captain Duff, with a squadron of frigates, watching the transports. Conflans gave chase, but soon broke off. His look-outs reported sails from the west, and they were Hawke's. The admiral had learnt by chance from some store-ships returning to England that the French were at sea in strength, and his captains knew their duty.

RIGHT: *The* Royal George, *Hawke's flagship at Quiberon Bay, painted by Dominic Serres*

92

The launching of the Duc de Bourgogne *at Rochefort on 20 October 1751, showing the elaborate and curious ceremonies used at that time*

Conflans, who had local pilots, made inshore, while Hawke, who had chosen the word *Strike* for his motto, flew the signal: 'Form as you chase'. It was the opportunity of a lifetime.

The dark November afternoon was advanced, with an increasing north-westerly gale, before Conflans' leading ships had passed between the Four Shoal to starboard, and the rocky cluster of the Cardinals to port, into waters where he could consider himself safe. His opponent had no local pilots, but where Conflans led, Hawke could follow. With darkness not many hours away, with a rising sea and off a lee shore, a more prudent man would have stood away while he still had sea-room, and seen what next day would bring forth. Had mere defeat of invasion been Hawke's aim, this would have been enough. No invasion force, with vulnerable transports, would put to sea with enemy ships in the offing. But Hawke's purpose was more positive. It was nothing less than the destruction of the French fleet.

His line was led by the *Magnanime*, a French-built ship taken as a prize eleven years before, commanded by Lord Howe. The *Magnanime* was followed closely by the *Torbay*, *Dorsetshire*, *Resolution*, *Warspite*, and the admiral's flagship, the *Royal George*. Gunfire from both fleets soon roared out amid the steadier thunder of breakers. Conflans was leading his own fleet, and when he knew Hawke's intention he tried to head out to sea again. The gesture was useless. He was soon encountered by the *Royal George*, and he recoiled, anchoring his ship, the great *Soleil Royal*, off Le Croisic.

The first loss was the French *Thésée*, a new 74-gun ship which was in action with the *Torbay* (Captain Keppel). The *Thésée* was laid on her beam ends by a sudden squall, and as her lee ports were open to enable her guns to fire, she instantly filled and sank, carrying with her Captain Kersaint de Coetnempren, who was considered to be Conflans' best officer, and six hundred men. The *Torbay* hoisted out her boats to save as many as she could, but there were only twenty-two survivors. Next to strike was the *Héros*; she surrendered to Howe after she had sustained a loss of four hundred killed or wounded. She anchored, 'but it blowing hard,' said Hawke in his despatch, 'no boat could be sent on board her'. Later she ran ashore.

Soon after four o'clock, after exchanges with the *Soleil Royal* and other ships, the *Royal George* poured two broadsides into the *Superbe*. The Frenchman had already been roughly handled, and she foundered almost at once. The *Royal George* could give no help to the wretches struggling in the water, for the sea was by now too high for boatwork. Hawke's chaplain noted that although the men gave a cheer, 'it was a faint one: the honest sailors were touched at the fate of so many hundreds of poor creatures'. Before darkness added to the mounting noise and confusion, another French ship, the *Formidable*, struck and was made prize. 'Night was now come,' wrote Hawke, 'and being on a part of the coast of which we were totally ignorant . . . and blowing hard on a lee shore, I made the signal to anchor.'

'I had no reason to believe,' wrote Conflans afterwards, 'that if I went in first with my ships the enemy would dare to follow, in spite of his superiority, which must anyway constrict his movements in so confined a space.' With the rival fleets anchored in the darkness, the night was made alarming by the sound of signal guns from ships aground or in distress. Conflans, in home waters as he was, could not have awaited the morning light with any confidence. The situation was in fact unique in warfare, and its pattern was not to be repeated for nearly forty years until Nelson (who had been a pupil of one of Hawke's captains) found himself in a similar situation near the Rosetta mouth of the Nile.

When dawn came, Conflans found the *Soleil Royal* within range of Hawke's guns. He made no attempt to fight it out, but in his efforts to escape he ran upon the Rouelle Shoal, ordered his ship to be burnt, and escaped ashore with the crew. A boarding party just had time to dismantle and carry off as a trophy the golden-rayed figure-head which graced her bows. They could not save any of her splendid green-bronze guns, made of old bells, red Swedish copper, yellow copper and pure tin.

The British fleet also had their troubles. During the hours of darkness both the *Essex* and the *Resolution* drove ashore, and as they could not be got off, they were burnt where they lay, the crews being saved.

Most of the French ships managed to beat out of the confined waters during the course of 21 November, but out of a less fortunate group, which jettisoned guns and gear and contrived to work their way over the bar at the mouth of the River Vilaine, one, the *Inflexible*, broke her back and never re-emerged, and the others were immobilized for the better part of a year. The 70-gun *Juste*

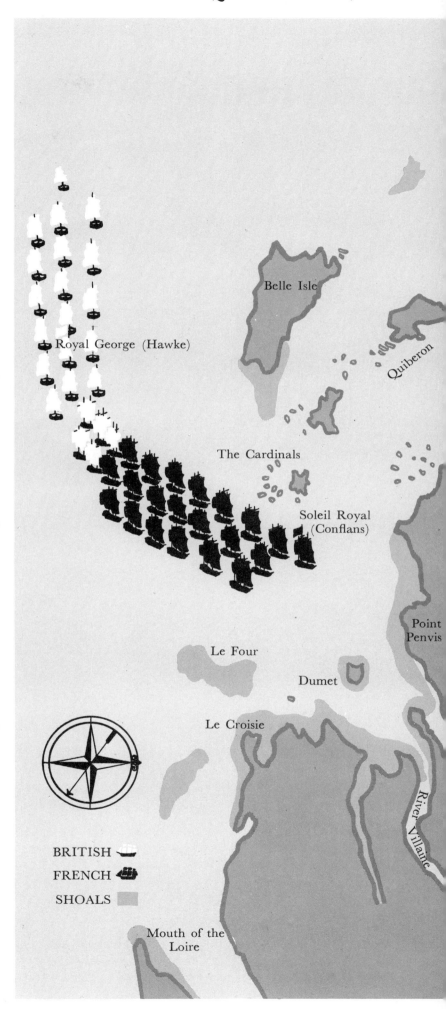

Royal George (Hawke)

Belle Isle

Quiberon

The Cardinals

Soleil Royal (Conflans)

Point Penvis

Le Four

Dumet

Le Croisie

River Villaine

BRITISH

FRENCH

SHOALS

Mouth of the Loire

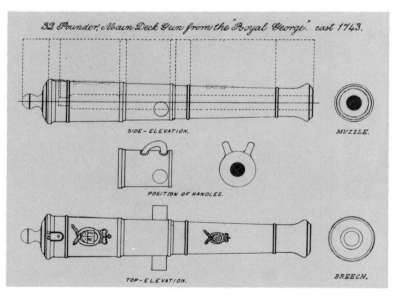

32 Pounder, Main Deck Gun from the "Royal George". cast 1743.

SIDE - ELEVATION.

MUZZLE.

POSITION OF HANDLES.

TOP - ELEVATION.

BREECH.

TOP: *A model showing the magnificent decoration of the* Dauphine Royale, *which fought at Quiberon Bay and was one of the French ships which succeeded in escaping to the Charente*

BOTTOM: *Details of the principal armament of the* Royal George. *She eventually sank at Spithead in 1782 with great loss of life*

RIGHT: *A contemporary painting by Richard Paton showing the sinking of the* Thésée *at Quiberon. The sea was so rough that water flooded in through her lower gun-ports. The* Torbay, *with whom she was engaged in action, narrowly escaped the same fate*

added to Hawke's toll when she foundered at the entrance to the Loire.

Hawke's victory, coming hard upon Boscawen's, not merely put an invasion of Britain beyond possibility, but it humbled the French navy under the eyes of her soldiers. 'Nothing could exceed the consternation of Court and Town,' wrote a naval officer from Paris, where he arrived a week later. 'This news has put everything else into the shade.' The results were indeed remarkable. A fleet of twenty-three ships of the line had chased another of twenty-one, and had defeated it under its own cliffs, with the direct loss of seven vessels and some two thousand five hundred men, and at the cost of two ships of its own, the crews of which were saved. It was a favourite maxim of Chatham's that 'the boldest measures are the safest'. Hawke had proved it.

The admiral had given his men such confidence that for the rest of the war they used the Quiberon anchorages almost as freely as their own. Parties were landed on French islets, several being used to grow vegetables for the benefit of the sailors.

Nothing sums up the victory more succinctly than a concluding passage in Hawke's despatch: 'When I consider the season of the year,' he said, 'the hard gales on the day of action, a flying enemy, the shortness of the day, and the coast they were on, I can boldly affirm that all that could possibly be done has been done. As to the loss we have sustained, let it be placed to the account of the necessity I was under of running all risks to break this strong force of the enemy. Had we had but two hours more daylight, the whole had been totally destroyed or taken; for we were almost up with their van when night overtook us.'

It was a ceaseless complaint on the part of critics of the conduct of earlier sea warfare that fleet encounters, as

LEFT: *The closing stages of the battle, painted by Richard Wright. In the right foreground is the* Resolution *wrecked on Four Shoal, with the* Soleil Royal *and* Héros *in flames behind it*

RIGHT TOP: *Admiral Sir Edward Hawke (1705–81), Commander of the squadron, whose daring pursuit of the French fleet into Quiberon Bay led to one of the most heroic victories in British naval history*

RIGHT CENTRE: *Captain Augustus Keppel, who commanded the* Torbay *at Quiberon Bay. This portrait is one of several by Sir Joshua Reynolds, a personal friend, to whom Keppel gave a passage to Italy in his ship-of-war in 1749, for which Reynolds was lastingly grateful*

RIGHT BOTTOM: *William Pitt, Earl of Chatham, whose vigorous policy as Secretary-of-State led to Britain's ultimate victory in the Seven Years' War*

opposed to single ship's actions, were so often indecisive. Fire was exchanged, honour was satisfied, little or nothing was achieved. By and large, lack of decision resulted from the official Fighting Instructions, which prescribed a formal line of battle, and ruin for the admiral or captain who did not follow the rules. A chase was another matter, and Hawke may be accounted fortunate that not once but twice in his life he was able to make use of tactics appropriate to a flying foe. But there are degrees of success even in chases, and Hawke's boldness at Quiberon is hard to equal. Yet it stopped short of rashness, since he was following the enemy into waters of whose every danger they must be presumed to have been familiar.

Hawke had absolute confidence in the quality of his ships and his captains, and it was not misplaced. He had watched them, year in and year out, on the work of blockade, which taxed every resource of seamanship. He also knew much of the psychology of his enemies. He had faced them before, and had studied them continuously. He knew their limitations, and the principle upon which

they used their fleet, which was as an adjunct to their armies, not as a service paramount in its own right, as was the way of his own country.

A man of coolness and reticence in his personal life, Hawke had a lasting effect upon the Navy he graced. He lived to see many of his Quiberon Bay captains rise to the highest ranks in their profession, though he also had the sadness to see his Service in adversity when, in his last retired years, Britain faced the rising strength of her own Colonies in America. Yet he had built well. The courage and decision which were his leading characteristics as an admiral were inherited by younger men, and in the final years of the eighteenth century, when British fleets were commanded by men of the calibre of Howe, St Vincent, Duncan and Nelson, the tradition of Hawke came into its full glory. The Navy looked back upon the triumphs of the Seven Years' War with natural pride, but with the assurance that its current achievements could rival even those of the man from whom so much had been learnt.

BELOW: *A quadrant of the Hadley type in use at the time of the Battle of Quiberon Bay*

RIGHT: *A detail of the sinking of the* Thésée *by Richard Paton*

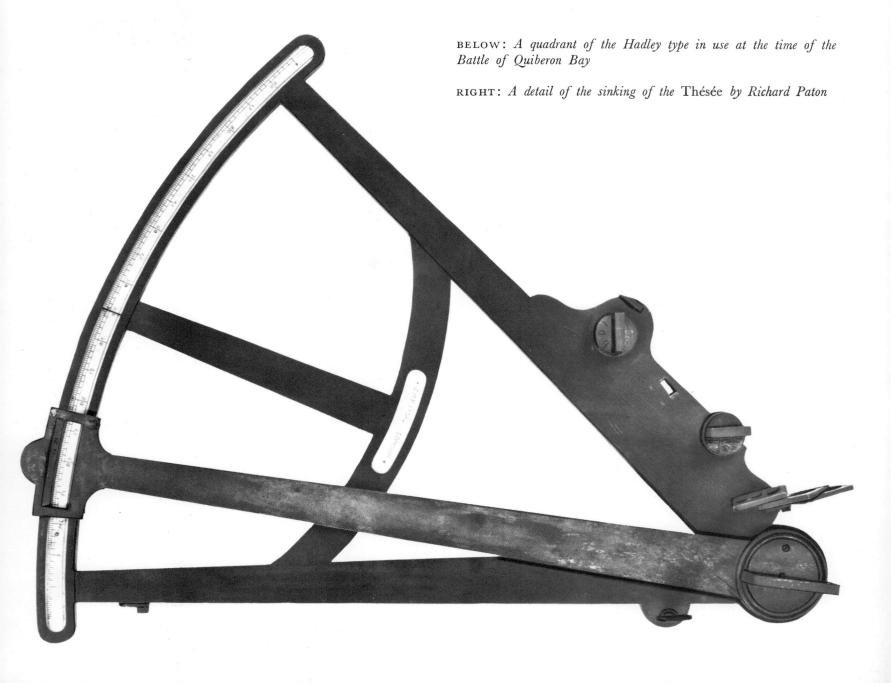

John Paul Jones

Flamborough Head
1779

The great naval hero of the American War of Independence triumphed in one of the most extraordinary sea-fights in history, against the British frigate 'Serapis'

BY THE AUTUMN OF THE YEAR 1779, when Paul Jones in the American ship *Bonhomme Richard* won an extraordinary action with a British frigate, Great Britain had been at war with her Colonies in North America for over four years. Things were going badly for King George III, and in particular for his navy. France and Spain were about to join his enemies: Gibraltar was threatened, and the islands of St Vincent and Grenada were ripe for capture. Britain was not to be spared humiliation nearer home, at the hands of a man born thirty-two years earlier at Kirkbean, Kirkcudbrightshire, a village which had been the birthplace of John Campbell, Hawke's flag-captain at Quiberon Bay.

John Paul Jones was the youngest surviving child of a gardener, John Paul. An elder brother had settled in Virginia, where he was doing well. John Paul Jones (he dropped his first Christian name, when he entered the American service, and assumed the surname by which he is remembered) learnt seamanship young, sailing as an apprentice in Whitehaven ships engaged in the North Atlantic trade. Then he joined a slaver, rising in due time to be master of a brigantine. Later he was employed in smuggling between the Solway Firth and the Isle of Man. In 1773, when he was trading in the West Indies, Paul Jones heard that his brother in Virginia had died. There-

upon, he took charge of the estate. Two years later, he joined the Revolutionary navy which was then forming. As his sea experience had been long and varied, he was given a commission and appointed first lieutenant of a 30-gun frigate. Soon afterwards he had independent command, first of a sloop, and then of a newly built frigate, the *Ranger*, in which he was ordered to France.

From Nantes, his first port of call, Paul Jones took his ship to Brest, where he re-fitted. On 10 April 1778 he sailed on a cruise, intending to harass shipping in the Irish Sea, and off his early haunts, the coasts of the Isle of Man, Cumberland, Wigtown and Kirkcudbright. He did some damage locally and caused much alarm, by far his most successful exploit being off Belfast Lough, where he fought and beat the *Drake*, a sloop of war, returning to Brest on 8 May with his prize, a justly proud man.

Paul Jones was lionized in France, but he was disliked by his crew, who gradually became mutinous. At length, Jones resigned command, and he was unemployed until the following spring, when he was able to commission an old French East Indiaman, the *Duc de Duras*, lying at L'Orient. He re-named her the *Bonhomme Richard*, out of compliment to his old friend Benjamin Franklin, whose publication *Poor Richard's Almanac* had recently been translated under the title *La Science du Bonhomme Richard*.

Jones's new ship carried forty guns, and she sailed on 14 August 1779 with a complement of 380 men, of whom some 150 were French volunteers. The rest were of many nationalities, mainly outcasts. With Jones sailed the

LEFT: *An engraving of Paul Jones as he appeared during the action with the* Serapis *off Flamborough Head*

A contemporary lithograph showing the Battle of Flamborough Head, with the British frigate Serapis *on the left and the American squadron on the right with Paul Jones's* Bonhomme Richard *at the extreme right*

Alliance, an American-built frigate commanded by Pierre Landais, a Frenchman who had taken service under the American Government, the *Pallas*, a French frigate, and the *Cerf* and the *Vengeance*, small French ships also sailing under the Stars and Stripes. Well handled, this could have been a formidable raiding squadron, but Jones, with all his gifts, did not possess the art of winning devotion, and from the first difficulties with his captains, with Landais in particular, were marked and serious.

As early as 23 May, off the coast of Ireland, one officer and twenty men deserted from Jones's own ship, the *Cerf* parted company, never to re-appear, and little more was heard of the *Vengeance*. Jones then took his squadron up the west coast of Ireland, rounded the north of Scotland, and sailed down the east coast, where it was likely he would be able to capture valuable prizes. He was not disappointed. Prizes came his way, but he found it increasingly difficult to keep his force together. Landais, with no tradition of discipline, regarded himself almost

as an independent privateer and frequently made cruises on his own, paying no regard to the rendezvous which Jones had been careful to arrange.

At one time, Jones made a show of force off Leith, spreading consternation in Edinburgh, but he was driven out of the Firth of Forth by a westerly gale. When it abated, he was far out to sea, and he decided that alarm and preparation would have destroyed his chances of success. Sensibly enough, he decided to attempt off the English coast what he had failed to do in the Forth. By a fortunate chance he fell in with the *Alliance*, which had once more become separated, on 23 September, shortly before a large convoy, believed to comprise the Baltic trade, was sighted coming southwards round Flamborough Head.

RIGHT: *A contemporary chart of the North Sea, including the scene of Paul Jones's famous cruise. It is taken from* A Complete Channel Pilot, *published in 1781*

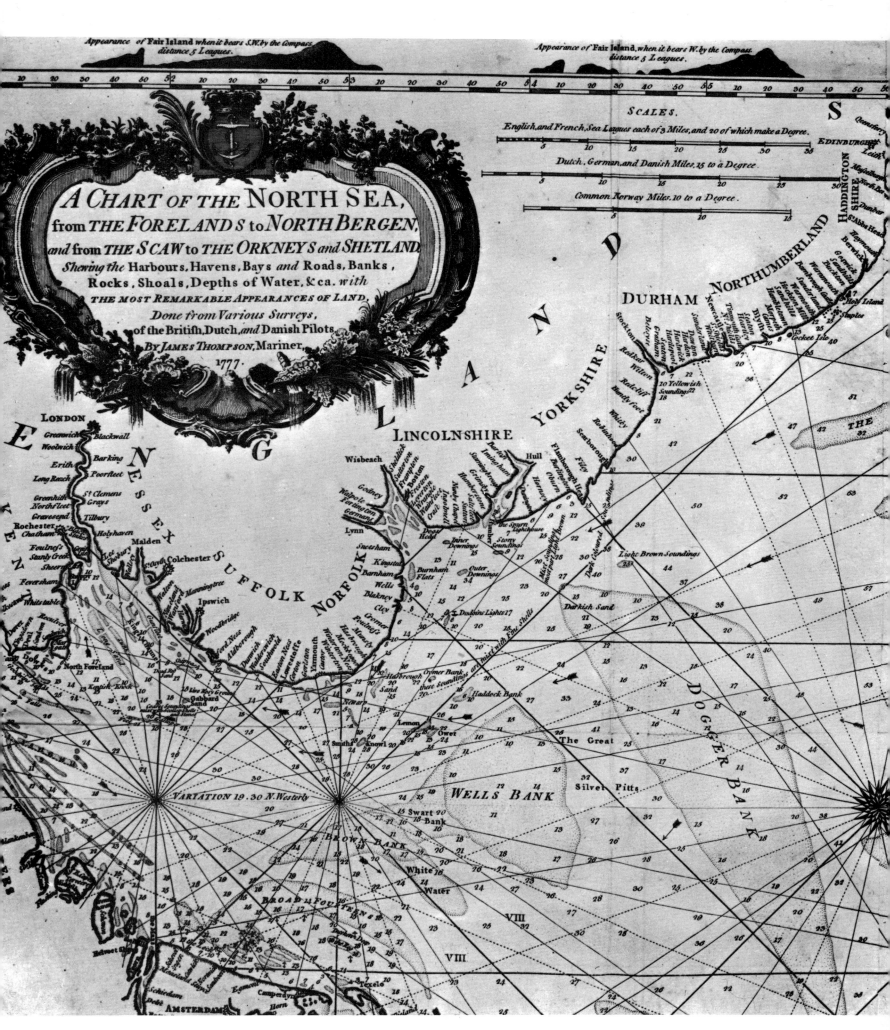

Extract from a letter of 1791, attributed to Paul Jones, and addressed to Vice-Admiral le Comte de Kersaint of the French Navy.

"You know, of course, my dear Kersaint, that my own opportunities in naval warfare have been but few. But I do not doubt your ready agreement with me if I say that the hostile ships and commanders that I have thus far enjoyed the opportunity of meeting, did not give any one much trouble thereafter. True, this has been on a small scale; but that was no fault of mine. I did my best with the weapons given to me. The rules of conduct, the maxims of action, and the tactical instincts that serve to gain small victories may always be expanded into the winning of great ones with suitable opportunity; because in human affairs the sources of success are ever to be found in the fountains of quick resolve and swift stroke; and it seems to be a law inflexible and inexorable that he who will not risk cannot win."

The merchantmen were under escort from the *Serapis* (Captain Pearson), a newly built frigate of 44 guns, and the *Countess of Scarborough* (Captain Piercy). The latter was a hired vessel mounting twenty 6-pounders – light guns, with few trained gunners.

The advantage of the wind was with the escorting ships. They at once stretched to the southward towards an enemy of whom they had probably had warning. Jones made the signal to form line of battle, but of this Landais took no notice. He stood towards the convoy, perhaps hoping to pass by the ships of war, and to make prizes while Jones fought for his life.

It was evening, and at about six o'clock the English tacked, crossing ahead of the Americans, keeping between them and the convoy. Flamborough Head itself was by now crowded with people that the rumours of the day had drawn to the neighbourhood. Even after the sun set, a harvest moon lit the scene for their benefit.

At half-past seven the first shots were exchanged between the *Serapis* and the *Bonhomme Richard*, while the *Pallas* was engaged with the *Countess of Scarborough*. The less important part of the battle was soon decided. The *Pallas*, more powerfully armed, found herself well able to deal with her opponent, which she took prize after the Englishman had made a creditable resistance. Unfortunately for Jones, she spent the rest of the night securing her capture, and her captain made no attempt to go to the help of his commodore. The *Alliance*, a powerful ship which could have rendered Jones's victory swift and overwhelming, gave up her pursuit of the convoy soon after dark, contenting herself with circling round the *Pallas* and the *Countess of Scarborough*, firing indiscriminately at both.

In the struggle between Jones and Pearson, the advantage should clearly have been with the Englishman. Not only was his ship new, his armament considerable, his crew well trained, but the *Serapis* was a good sailor. Moreover, within a few minutes of opening fire, two of Jones's guns burst, killing and wounding a number of men, and damaging the deck above them. After an hour's fighting, Jones knew that his only chance of success was to grapple his opponent. It should have been Pearson's particular care to prevent this, for his advantage was in mobility and ordnance, not in point of numbers.

It is a matter of debate how Jones caught the *Serapis*, but the details themselves are clear. The *Serapis*'s jibboom caught in the starboard mizzen rigging of the *Bonhomme Richard*. Jones lashed it to the mizzen-mast with his own hands. The *Serapis*'s starboard anchor then hooked her opponent's quarter, and the ships swung together bow and stern, their starboard sides touching.

In close fighting there was little to choose between the opponents, but their distribution of strength became

Captain Sir Richard Pearson, Commander of the Serapis, *who finally surrendered to Paul Jones*

A contemporary engraving showing the Serapis *and the* Bonhomme Richard *grappling together. The American frigate* Alliance, *commanded by Pierre Landais, can be seen intervening on the right*

important. The lower deck battery of the *Serapis* with its 18-pounders smashed the *Bonhomme Richard*'s hull into fragments and silenced her main deck ordnance, but the gun crews, driven above, reinforced the fighting tops, swept the quarter deck and forecastle of the Englishman with musketry and grenades, and forced her men below.

At this critical stage the *Alliance* which, had she been even tolerably handled, could have raked the *Serapis* and settled the issue within a few minutes, repeated her earlier manoeuvre of circling the combatants, firing at both, and doing more harm – or so Jones said later – to friend than foe. Even so, her mere presence had a dispiriting effect on Pearson and his men.

The English captain was even more discomforted by a display of individual daring worthy of Jones himself. One of the *Bonhomme Richard*'s crew crawled out on to a main-yard, carrying a bucket-full of hand-grenades. He succeeded in throwing one down the main hatchway of the *Serapis*, where a number of cartridges had been placed so as to be handy for the guns. The grenade fell among these. The explosions spread the length of the ship, disabled many of the guns, and killed, wounded or scorched

every man serving them. The effect was so severe that it seemed likely that the ship would have to surrender there and then.

Actually, matters were nearly as bad on board the American. The carpenter reported to Jones that there was so much damage below that the ship was in danger of sinking. Hearing this, the gunner ran aft, without orders, to haul down the flag, but finding that the staff had been shot away, he began to bellow, 'Quarter! For God's sake, quarter!', until Jones stove his skull in with the butt end of a pistol.

Shortly after this incident, both captains attempted to board. Although neither was successful, the next event might have given the day to the *Serapis*. In the hold of the *Bonhomme Richard* were about a hundred prisoners taken from prizes. Shortly after the carpenter cried for quarter, the American master-at-arms went below to release them. Over a hundred men rushed on deck, and had they been organized they should have been able, with the help of their friends in the *Serapis*, to overwhelm their captors. But they were confused, panic-stricken, half stunned with noise, in a condition to be ordered about, but not to take the initiative. Jones, with sublime presence of mind, instantly set them to work in parties at the pumps. There they stayed, like obedient sheep. Only one man kept enough self-possession to make his way over to the *Serapis*, and to tell Captain Pearson the true state of the *Bonhomme Richard*.

This act of initiative was too late to be of any use. Both ships were beaten, and it was almost a matter of chance which would give in first. The matter was decided by the near presence of the *Alliance*, and by the fact of the *Pallas*'s success becoming known to the English. At half-past ten the *Serapis* struck, Jones at once taking possession.

The *Bonhomme Richard* was with difficulty kept afloat during the night, and she sank about ten o'clock on the morning of the 26th. The state of the men was much the same as that of the ships: they were completely knocked up. The exact number of killed and wounded is uncertain but in proportion to those engaged it was the bloodiest combat of its time.

Flamborough Head was the greatest scene of Paul Jones's life. He managed to get his prizes to the Texel and later to France, where he received great honour. The King gave him a gold-hilted sword inscribed: VINDICATI MARIS LUDOVICUS XVI REMUNERATOR STRENUO VINDICI ('Louis XVI recognizes the services of the brave maintainer of the privileges of the sea'). His own authorities awarded him a gold medal, and he is honoured as one of the founders of the American navy, though he held no further active command.

The fate of the captains of the *Serapis* and the *Countess of Scarborough* is of some interest. They were tried by court martial at Sheerness on 10 March 1780, and were honourably acquitted. The Court held that 'Captains Pearson and Piercy, assisted by their officers and men, had not only acquitted themselves of their duty to the country, but had, in the execution of such duty, done infinite credit to themselves by a very obstinate defence against a very superior force'. The merchants of London, whose cargoes Pearson and Piercy had safeguarded, presented Pearson with a sword of honour. King George III, with what may appear to have been some excess of enthusiasm, actually knighted him. Pearson indeed had done his best, but in the circumstances it was far from good enough. He should have taken one of the various chances open to him to defeat his indifferently equipped though determined and skilful enemy, whose conduct of the engagement was in fact beyond praise. Above all, he should have kept his distance, and pounded the American to pieces. Paul Jones deserves the last word about the occasion. When he heard how his antagonist had been rewarded, he remarked: 'Should I have the good fortune to fall in with him again, I'll make him a lord!'

The oddest fact of all was the continuous assertion by Landais that it was *he* who had defeated the *Serapis*. He lived years after the battle, chiefly in America, and long before his death he had utterly convinced himself of the truth of his own story.

A French medal dated 1779 showing Paul Jones in a tie wig and on the reverse the Bonhomme Richard *in action*

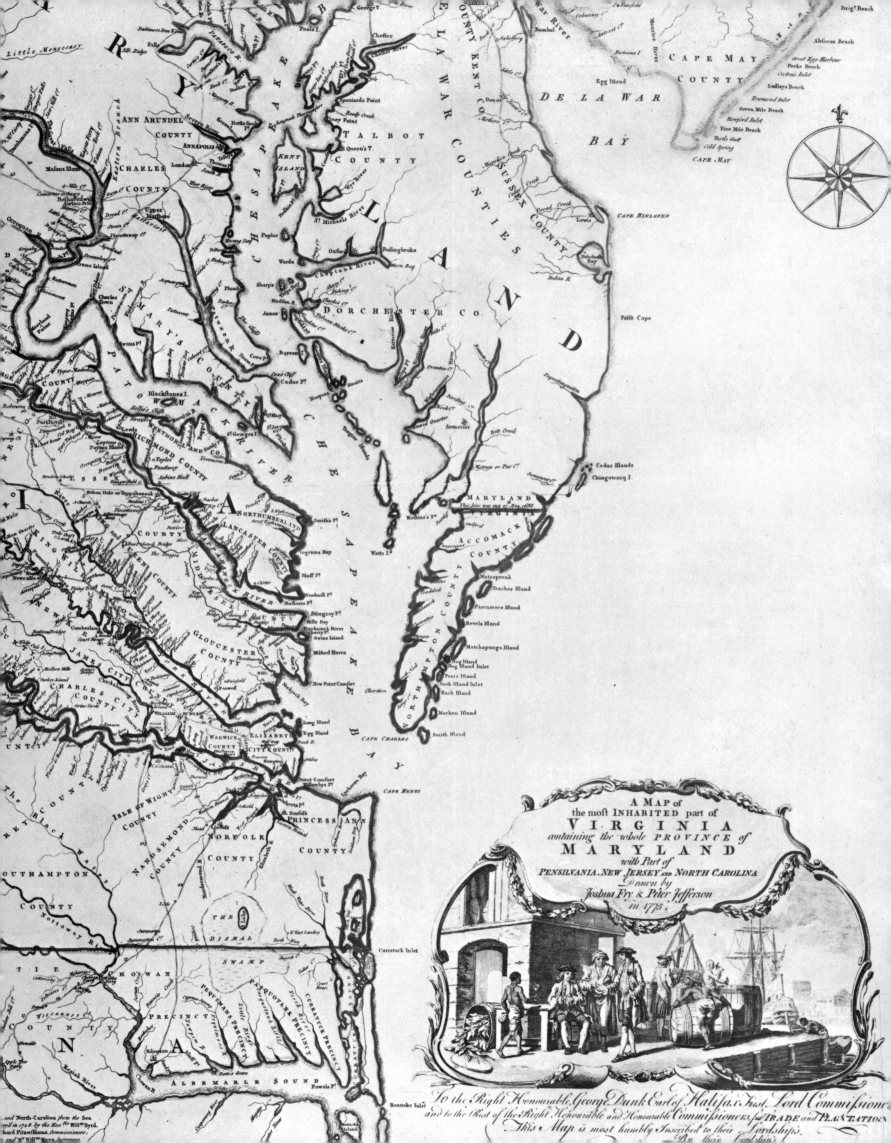

A MAP of
the most INHABITED part of
VIRGINIA
containing the whole PROVINCE of
MARYLAND
with Part of
PENSILVANIA, NEW JERSEY AND NORTH CAROLINA
Drawn by
Joshua Fry & Peter Jefferson
in 1775

To the Right Honourable, George Dunk Earl of Halifax, First, Lord Commissioner
and to the Rest of the Right Honourable and Honourable Commissioners, for TRADE and PLANTATION
This Map is most humbly Inscribed to their Lordships.

Chesapeake Bay
1781

During the last phase of the American War of Independence, the English lost local command of the sea, through their defeat by the Comte de Grasse's fleet

PAUL JONES'S VICTORY, exciting though it was, and demoralizing in its effect, decided nothing. American independence was achieved by the efforts of the Americans, by the genius of Washington, through the help of allies in France and Spain, and by sea power exercised not through raiding squadrons but by fleets. No event more strongly affected the issue of the war, or more powerfully helped to shape American destiny, than a battle, inconclusive in itself, which was fought in Chesapeake Bay between Admiral Graves and the Comte de Grasse. It took place on 5 September 1781, nearly two years after the *Serapis* had hauled down her colours off the Yorkshire coast.

In a military sense, the turning point of the war had come in 1777 after the battle of Saratoga, when a British army, attempting to march from Canada through the Hudson Valley to New York City, was compelled to surrender. When the news reached France it enabled Benjamin Franklin to conclude the treaty he had been working upon so long. Henceforward, Washington would be helped by French regulars. At sea, squadrons would threaten the navy of Britain both in its home waters, and far afield.

In 1781 the British made an attempt to conquer Virginia. Cornwallis, the general commanding, had done

LEFT: *Virginia and Maryland, enclosing Chesapeake Bay, the scene of Graves's action in 1781. Two sheets from an elaborate* American Atlas, *which was published in London in 1776*

much, and seemed to be through the more difficult part of his campaign. He had reached the great inlet of the Chesapeake, where he could expect to regain touch with the rest of British-held America through control of the sea. At the time of Graves's battle Cornwallis, although besieged to landward, was lying with his 7,000 men not too uncomfortably at York Town, on the York River which flows into Chesapeake Bay. He awaited with confident expectation the appearance of a British fleet.

Earlier in the year the naval situation had been favourable to the forces of George III. The main French and British fleets, respectively under the Comte de Grasse and Admiral Rodney, were in the West Indies. There was a smaller division based at New York and a French squadron under de Barras based north of it, at Rhode Island. The New York and Rhode Island forces had met earlier in the year in a desultory action off Cape Henry, after which the French had returned to Newport, leaving the British in control of local waters.

Washington and the French general, Rochambeau, with whom he was operating sent word to de Grasse that they hoped the next effort would be directed against either New York or the Chesapeake, but as the French Government had already declined to furnish means for a formal siege of New York, de Grasse told the generals that he would make for Chesapeake Bay. In fact, this would have been the choice preferred by the military commanders.

De Grasse gathered every available ship, and took pains to conceal his plans by passing through the Bahama

Two wash-drawings by an unidentified contemporary artist illustrating Graves's action against de Grasse. The upper drawing shows the French (left) coming out of harbour and the British (right) approaching in line ahead at 1 pm. The lower drawing shows the situation at 3.45 pm when Graves has the advantage of the wind and is attacking with his van. The rest of his fleet never came into action, and de Grasse escaped unscathed

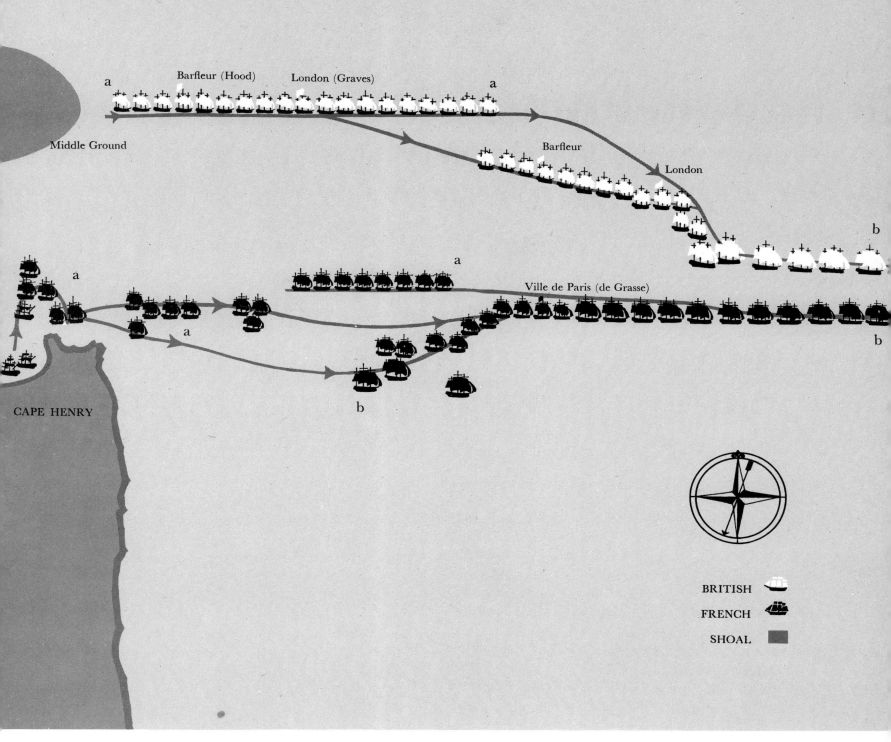

a

Barfleur (Hood)   London (Graves)   a

Middle Ground

Barfleur

London

b

a

Ville de Paris (de Grasse)

b

a

a

CAPE HENRY

b

BRITISH

FRENCH

SHOAL

Movement from 'aa' to 'bb' shows how the British centre and rear remained largely out of the battle. Despite the disarray of the French fleet at 'aa',
Graves's formal tactics allowed de Grasse time to compose his line

Channel, which was then little used. On 30 August he anchored in Lynnhaven Bay, just within the capes of the Chesapeake, with twenty-four ships of the line. Three days earlier the squadron from Newport, Rhode Island, eight of the line, four frigates and transports, all under command of de Barras, sailed for a rendezvous with de

Grasse, making a wide detour to avoid contact with the British. On 24 August troops under Washington and Rochambeau crossed the Hudson in a movement towards the head of Chesapeake Bay. Land and sea forces, all unseen, were converging upon Cornwallis.

The British were in every way unfortunate. Rodney,

A portrait of de la Touche-Tréville, one of de Grasse's captains in America, who afterwards played a leading part in Napoleon's fleet, successfully defending Boulogne against Nelson, by Georges Rouget

A mezzotint after a portrait by James Northcote (1746–1831) of Admiral Thomas Graves (c 1725–1802), painted in 1794 or 1795, showing his wounded arm and the medal he received for services under Howe on 1 June 1794

learning of de Grasse's departure, sent fourteen ships of the line under Admiral Hood to reinforce Graves in North America, while he himself returned to England on account of ill health. Hood reached the Chesapeake three days before de Grasse, looked into the bay and, finding it empty, proceeded to New York. There he was met by Graves, and although Hood's force was the larger, Graves, being the senior officer, took charge of the Fleet. On 31 August he sailed for the Chesapeake, hoping to intercept de Barras before he could join de Grasse. He had nineteen ships under command.

On reaching the Chesapeake, Graves was painfully surprised to find a fleet there which, from its size, could only be an enemy's. At worst, he had expected de Barras: at best, an empty anchorage. Although no tactical genius, Graves was a brave man, and his knowledge of affairs was such that he fully realized the immediate danger to Cornwallis if de Grasse were not defeated or at the very least forced to withdraw. He had the advantage both of the wind and of formation. The French fleet, when sighted, were in no order, and some of the ships were actually rounding Cape Henry. A Hawke or a Howe would probably have flown the signal for a general chase, and as Graves had for his second-in-command an

officer of the brilliance of Samuel Hood, it could have been a glorious day. A chase was, in fact, probably the only method by which de Grasse could have been driven from his position.

Graves, though in inferior strength, since de Grasse had twenty-four ships to his nineteen, did indeed attack, but, as Mahan remarked, 'his method betrayed his gallantry'. He was a formalist who believed in a regular line of battle, ship to ship from van to rear, and he signalled accordingly to his divisional commanders, Hood and Drake. As might have been expected, the result was indeterminate, Graves's tactics were those which de Grasse would have anticipated, and with which he was thoroughly familiar. The Frenchman was given precious time in which to order his squadrons, and the encounter resolved itself into a cannonade in the old style of warfare, with no close fighting, no unexpected moves.

Action began about four o'clock in the afternoon and continued for some two hours and a half, being broken off with the failing light. De Grasse's subordinates were as

RIGHT: *Louis-Antoine de Bougainville (1729–1811), a distinguished captain under de Grasse, who later became one of the foremost explorers of his age, rivalling Cook*

L . A . BOUGAINVILLE

COMTE DE L'EMPIRE

Sénateur, Grand-Officier de la Légion d'Honneu

Né à Paris, le 11 No.bre 1729.

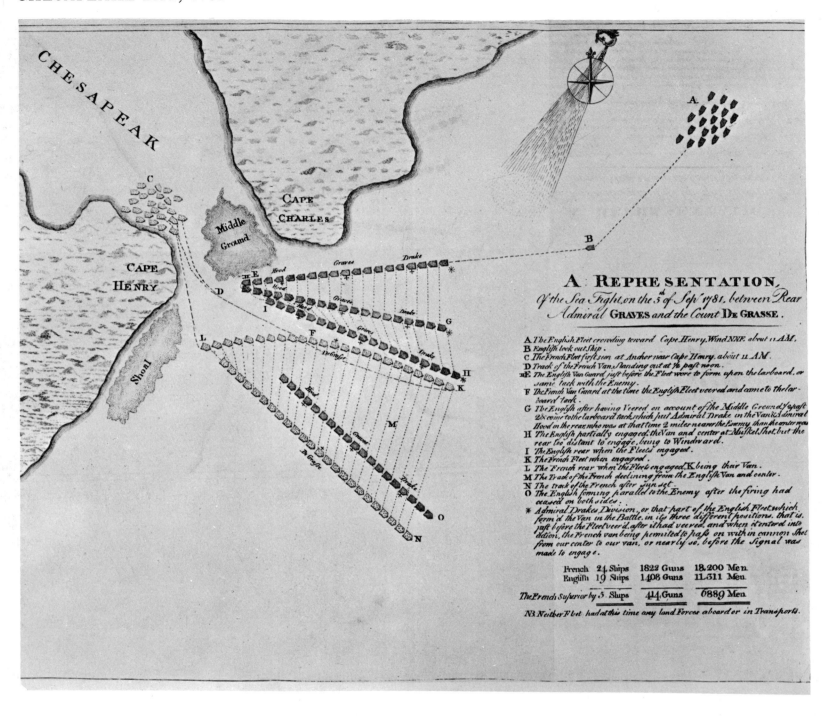

ABOVE: *One of the earliest and most elaborate diagrams of Graves's action of 5 September 1781, published in* Two Letters from W. Graves Esq Respecting the Conduct of Rear-Admiral Thomas Graves in North America

RIGHT: *Bow view of a model of a French frigate showing her in a later state flying the revolutionary Tricolour*

A coloured lithograph after a portrait by A. Maurin, of Francois-Joseph-Paul, Comte de Grasse (1722–88). Although he was later defeated by Rodney, he proved at Chesapeake that he was a considerable tactician. This battle ensured the surrender of Cornwallis's army ashore

distinguished as Graves's – Le Sieur de Bougainville, de La Touche-Tréville, and Le Sieur de Monteil. The French account of the battle states that:

> ... M. de Bougainville began the action with a very brisk fire, and successively the ships of the line of battle took part. Only the eight leading ships of the English line took any great part in the fight ... For the most part the centre of their fleet and their rear held themselves at half cannon shot ... the wind failed the nine last ships of our line entirely.

The sentences would have fitted a score of inconclusive actions, the only material success being severe damage to the British ship *Terrible*, which had to be sunk shortly after the encounter.

At a council of war held next day Graves decided that with a number of his ships more or less disabled, it would be too hazardous to attempt to re-engage: he also declined Hood's suggestion of trying to seize the former French anchorage by stratagem, an idea which Hood himself once put into effect with brilliant success against the same opponent in the West Indies.

Meanwhile, a north-east wind was carrying both fleets away from the scene of the land operations. By 9 September they were off Albemarle Sound, and the next day the British sighted Cape Hatteras. During the night of the 9th de Grasse lost touch with his opponent and returned to the Chesapeake, which he reached on the 11th. There he was joined by de Barras. Graves returned to New York, with a very discontented subordinate in Admiral Hood, whose fate it so often was to serve under men less brilliant than himself. Before the engagement of 5 September, American independence was probable. Afterwards, it was certain.

Graves was fully aware of the severity of his failure, and even of how it arose. The day after the battle, he issued a memorandum to his captains to the effect that the Line Ahead was intended as a means to an end, not as an end in itself, and that 'the signal for battle should not be rendered ineffective by strict adherence to the former'.

Example would have been better than either precept or post-mortem, and the flagships of both Graves and Hood were placed in positions in the line from which, though they could expect to exercise control, they could not initiate daring movements, and only a daring movement could have brought victory. Graves had an old established formal system, and an imperfect signal book, to blame for his disappointment, and he suffered no official displeasure, for both he and his captains had kept to the rules. No misconduct could be imputed to him.

Cornwallis and his army held out a little longer, but with de Grasse off-shore, only one issue was possible. Formal terms of surrender were signed on 19 October 1781, and although the conflict flickered through one more year, no sustained military operations were undertaken. When Cornwallis laid down his arms, a British band played *The World Turned Upside Down*, and soon a wave of rejoicing was felt throughout America. It is said that the aged doorkeeper of Congress died of joy when he heard the news.

No man was more aware than Washington of the importance of sea-power to the liberation of his country. 'In any operation', he wrote to Lafayette, 'and under all circumstances a decisive naval superiority is to be considered as a fundamental principle, and the basis upon which every hope of success must ultimately depend'. France had provided that basis.

RIGHT: *A view of the action off the Chesapeake showing a French detachment on the left and rear of the British line on the right, which illustrates very clearly the rigid disposition of Admiral Graves's fleet in accordance with official Fighting Instructions, painted by Theodore Gudin (1802–80)*

Suffren in
the East Indies
1782-3

*Admiral Suffren, twice captured by the English, fought five stern battles against them
in Eastern waters, and showed himself a great tactician*

ONCE FRANCE AND SPAIN HAD JOINED forces with the Americans, it became certain that the war would be world-wide, and that France, with a restored navy, would attempt to recover the losses she had endured at the hands of Great Britain earlier in the century. A particular scene of conflict was the Indian sub-continent, and it was in the waters of the Bay of Bengal that Suffren, by general consent the ablest naval tactician France ever produced, showed how much could be achieved by example.

Pierre-André de Suffren de Saint-Tropez was a younger son of a noble family of Provence. His parents destined him for service with the Knights of Malta, but before he joined the Order he experienced war at sea, at Toulon and in the West Indies, and in an action with Hawke during which his ship was captured. This began the first of two spells Suffren spent as a prisoner of the British, from whom he learnt much, and whose language he came to speak. The second occasion was when, after some six years at Malta, he was with de la Clue's fleet, and was taken prisoner by Boscawen in his action off Lagos.

After his exchange, Suffren rose slowly in rank, and by the time of the war of American Independence he was in command of a 64-gun ship, in which he served in North American and West Indian waters. His next appointment was to the *Zélé*, in which he took a leading part in the capture of a valuable convoy.

In 1781 Suffren was appointed to the newly built *Héros* of 74 guns, and was given command of a squadron of five ships which were about to sail to the East Indies. He left Brest at the same time as the Comte de Grasse, and he had orders, when past the Cape of Good Hope, to assume local rank as *chef d'escadre*, flying the broad pendant of a commodore. The opportunity had at last opened when, at the age of fifty-five, Suffren could use the knowledge accumulated, in good fortune and bad, during thirty-eight years at sea.

The Dutch had joined the alliance against Britain, and it became an immediate object for France to defend that country's possessions overseas, among which were the Cape of Good Hope and Trincomalee in Ceylon, both invaluable stages on the route to India. The Dutch navy was not then of the importance it had reached in the previous century, and the first duty enjoined on Suffren was to bring reinforcements to the Cape, and to prevent it falling into British hands.

A force with which to attack the Cape had been given to Commodore George Johnstone, and he was an unfortunate choice. Johnstone had made some stir in Parliament by attacking better officers than himself, including

Lord Howe. He now had the chance to prove himself in action, and his first false step was to allow himself to be caught provisioning at the Cape Verde Islands, with his men-of-war and transports in disorder.

Suffren was not a man to let such a chance go by. Disregarding Portuguese neutrality, he sailed into the harbour at Porto Praya, and, had he been better supported, might have destroyed most of Johnstone's transports. As it was, he did much damage and then, withdrawing under difficulty, made his way to the Cape as fast as possible. He arrived a month before Johnstone, and secured the colony. When the British arrived, Johnstone did not deem it prudent even to attempt to carry out his instructions. Suffren had scored his first success, and it was of first-rate importance.

The French squadron anchored at Mauritius, then called the Isle of France, on 25 October. Suffren's capital difficulties now began. The French position in India was uncertain. They had recently lost Pondicherry, and their best hope lay in support of Hyder Ali, ruler of Mysore, an inveterate enemy to Britain. Infusing new energy into M. d'Orves, whose squadron lay at Port Louis, Suffren and his colleague sailed for India on 17 December 1781, capturing on their way an English 50-gun ship, the *Hannibal*, which, with three others, had been sent by Johnstone to join Sir Edward Hughes at Madras.

Hughes, who was much the same age as Suffren, had had equally long experience. He was familiar with India, since he had held command there once before, in the previous decade. Both men were stout, genial, active, and enjoyed the pleasures of the table. William Hickey, a traveller who dined with them in turn, admired them

equally, though he noted that while Hughes's flagship, the *Superb*, was spick and span, the *Héros*, equally well armed, was indescribably dirty.

D'Orves, whose health had been failing, died on 9 February 1782, leaving the command to Suffren. Making his way straight to Madras with eleven of the line, three frigates and three corvettes, Suffren was disagreeably surprised to find Hughes with a respectable force, though inferior to his own, posted so strongly under the shore batteries that to attack there and then would have been foolish. After taking counsel with his captains, he stood out to sea. Hughes, with his nine ships, followed the example. He had two aims. The first was to damage the troop convoy which Suffren was protecting: the second was to guard against a descent upon Trincomalee. This place, with its splendid natural harbour, had been taken by the British, but it was lightly held.

By good seamanship, Hughes slipped past the French men-of-war during the hours of darkness, and he fell upon the convoy, which was to leeward of Suffren. At first the French captains were incredulous, but Hughes had seized six merchantmen, including a valuable transport, before he could be intercepted. When darkness fell, on 16 February, the squadrons were in line of battle, making ready for the inevitable clash.

Next day the wind, though irregular and squally, was in Suffren's favour. Hughes manoeuvred to try to weather him, but he was unsuccessful, and at about four in the afternoon, almost in a calm, the French were in a position to set about Hughes's five rear ships. During a partial but severe struggle the brunt of the fighting fell to the *Exeter* of 64 guns, wearing the broad pennant of Commodore King. King was heavily outgunned; his companions-in-arms could not move to his rescue owing to the light airs, and his captain was killed at his side. At the most critical stage, when it seemed the *Exeter* must be taken, the master approached King and asked what should be done. 'There is nothing to be done', said King calmly. 'Nothing to be done but fight her till she sinks'.

At about six o'clock, a squall enabled other ships to bear down, and the *Exeter*'s ordeal was over. The *Superb* had also been badly damaged, and the condition of both squadrons was such that, as if by mutual consent, both withdrew, the British to Trincomalee, and the French to Pondicherry, which had recently been re-occupied by France's Indian allies. The losses in men were about equal, but Hughes should in fact have been defeated had Suffren's captains given him better support. As it was, thanks to Hyder Ali's activity and to his own exertions, Suffren was able to land troops at Porto Novo,

RIGHT: *Suffren's second encounter with Hughes, 12 April 1782*

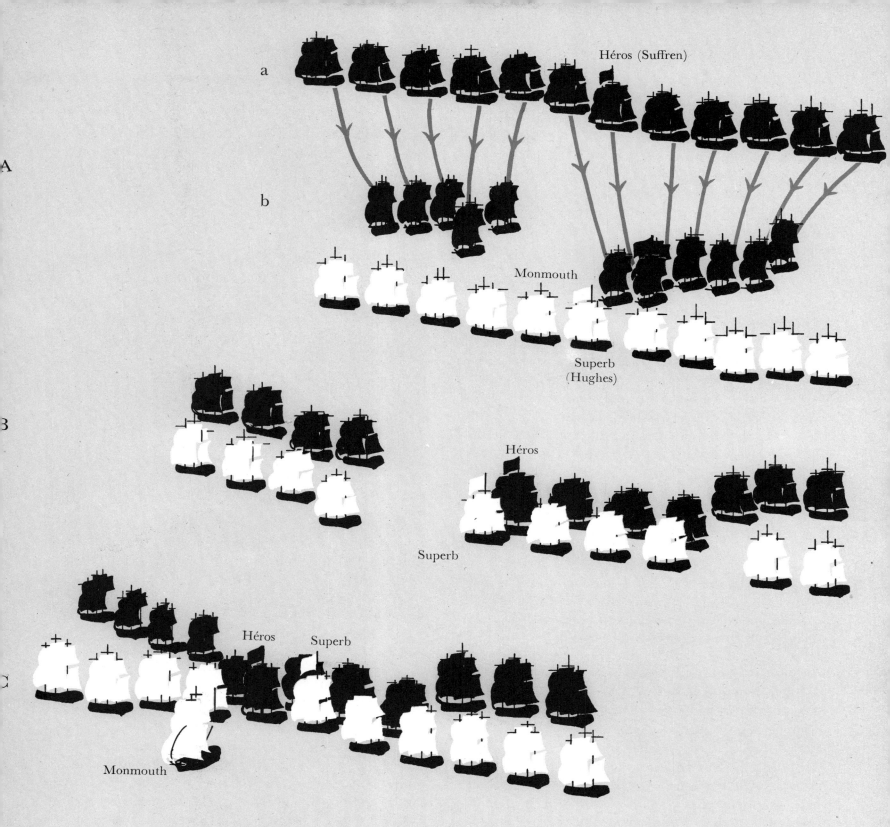

a

A

b

Héros (Suffren)

Monmouth

Superb
(Hughes)

B

Héros

Superb

C

Héros   Superb

Monmouth

FRENCH

BRITISH

a little south of Pondicherry, while Hughes, having re-fitted at Ceylon, returned to Madras to take soldiers aboard with which to reinforce the Trincomalee defences.

Hearing of Hughes's movements, Suffren followed him, and the squadrons met for their second encounter off Ceylon. When the French were sighted, on 12 April 1782, Hughes was at a disadvantage. He was close in-shore, with little room to manoeuvre, and he was to lee-ward: but he had eleven ships of the line with him, and he awaited Suffren's attack with the cheerful confidence which never left him.

It was Suffren's great chance to exploit his idea of overwhelming part of the enemy line by bringing superior force against it, meanwhile containing the rest. By an extraordinary chance, the feat was achieved the same day by an Englishman, Sir George Rodney, when opposed to de Grasse in the West Indies. Rodney's was a notable victory: Suffren had to be content with less.

The weight of the French fell upon Hughes's centre, and once more it was two ships only, this time the *Mon-mouth* and the *Superb*, which bore the brunt. The *Mon-mouth* was battered almost to a wreck, but she gave so good an account of herself that, with the help of the flag-ship, she so damaged the *Héros* that Suffren was obliged to transfer to the *Ajax*. Firing continued till about half-past five, when a violent squall, with heavy rain, caused confusion to both sides. The ships then anchored for the night. By that time the *Héros* was aground, and the squadrons had become so mixed up that Suffren's flag-lieutenant, sent away with a message, went by accident on board the *Superb*, and was taken prisoner.

The loss in men was once more about equal, but while it was fairly evenly distributed with the French, most of the British casualties occurred in the two ships severely engaged. For no less than seven days the squadrons lay refitting within sight of one another. Then the French withdrew, and Hughes landed his troops and stores.

By this time, both squadrons were suffering badly from sickness, including scurvy, and Suffren was fortunate, when he anchored on 5 June at Tranquebar, to find store-ships sent him from Batavia by the Dutch. From Tranquebar he moved north to Cuddalore, which had recently been occupied by French troops. He took aboard a force for the recapture of Negapatam, a Dutch settlement which had fallen to the British earlier in the war. He sailed on 3 July, with the knowledge that Hughes, who had left Trincomalee, was anchored off his own destination. Suffren intended to bring Hughes to battle a third time, then to land his troops and carry on the siege. Hughes's immediate object was to keep his squadron between Suffren and the shore.

The battle duly took place on 6 July, on Hughes's terms. He began it, about ten o'clock, by engaging ship-

ABOVE: *Commodore George Johnstone, who had been ordered to attack the Cape of Good Hope, then a Dutch possession. He proved no match for Suffren, who arrived at the Cape a month before him and was able to prevent a British landing*

to-ship, in accordance with time-honoured 'Fighting Instructions'. The result, as so often under the system, was bloody and indecisive. When action was broken off, Hughes returned to Negapatam, and Suffren to Cudda-lore. Far from having his opponent's measure, Suffren had failed in his mission, and Hughes had scored. There had been, moreover, an unfortunate incident. During a sudden shift of wind the *Sévère*, a French 64-gun ship commanded by M. de Cillart, actually struck to the *Sultan*. De Cillart's officers were incredulous and refused obedience, firing on and causing loss to the British ship when she hove-to and sent a boat to take possession. The captain was sent home and cashiered, and although Suffren, who for all his personal valour found too little support from his captains, and at one time or another sent others back to France, M. de Cillart was the only one who was punished. As if by deserved contrast, Suffren himself learnt, while on the Coromandel Coast, that the

The scene at the encounter off the Cape Verde Islands when Suffren surprised Johnstone while he was provisioning. Suffren's flagship, the Héros *is slightly left of centre with British ships on either side*

Grand Master of the Knights of Malta had honoured him with the insignia of Bailiff, and it is by this title that he is often distinguished. As Hughes's blue coat was already adorned by the star of the Order of the Bath, the commanders were appropriately recognized.

Hughes refitted at Madras, and it was there that he was surprised by the news that Suffren had left Cuddalore, for he had refused to credit information to that effect which had been given him by the Governor. He hurried forward with his preparations, fearing for the safety both of Negapatam and Trincomalee. He was too late. Baffling winds made his passage unusually long, and when, on 2 September, he arrived off the familiar harbour, he found that Trincomalee had been surrendered to the French two days before. Suffren, having achieved his greatest success, resolved to crown it by beating Hughes at sea. He had fifteen ships to oppose to Hughes's twelve, and his intention this time, with the advantage

of the wind, was to throw his weight upon the British rear.

By now, some of the French captains were almost mutinous, and few obeyed Suffren's signals. Battle continued in an irregular way for about three hours, when the wind shifted. Three French ships, and the *Héros* and *Illustre* in particular, did most of the fighting. Hughes was in no position to press any advantage he could gain, while Suffren, as darkness fell, was forced to withdraw to his anchorage. Although but a short distance away, he was to leeward of it, and in bearing up, the *Orient*, which was badly handled, grounded heavily on a reef, and could not be got off. Even her main-mast, ear-marked for the *Héros*, was lost by the carelessness of a lieutenant. It was broken off at the level of the upper deck.

It was Suffren's bitterest hour. He had been robbed of his victory by what he conceived to be the treachery, as well as the apparent cowardice, of some of his officers.

Naval Cannon in the 18th Century

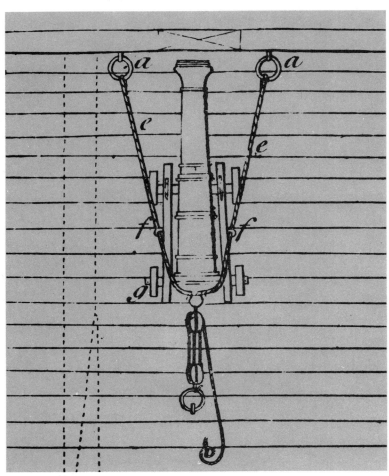

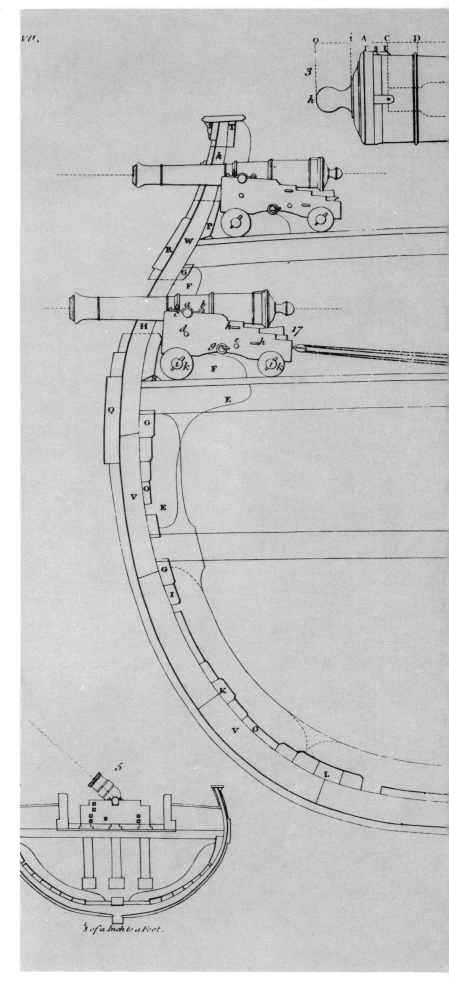

CANNON

from *An Universal Dictionary of the Marine* by
William Falconer (London, 1769)

'*Cannon are charged by putting down into the bottom first a quantity
of powder, one-third or one-half the weight of the ball. This is done with
an instrument termed a* ladle *(figure 7), which is a kind of cylindrical
spoon, generally made of copper... Upon the powder is put in a wad of
rope-yarn, formed like a ball, which is pressed down upon the powder
with the* rammer *(figure 10). Upon this wad is put the ball or shot;
and to secure it in its place another wad is firmly pressed down upon
it... The touch-hole of the piece is then filled with powder.*'

*Apart from figure 5, which shows the section of a bomb-vessel, the re-
maining figures on these pages illustrate the parts of the cannon (figure 3)
– the breach (A–C), the trunnions (T), the muzzle (H–B); the cross-
section of a 32 pounder (figure 15); the plan and elevation of a sea-
carriage (figures 16 and 17); gun-tackles – the train-tackle, which
prevents the cannon from rolling into place until it is charged (figure 17),
and the tackles used to draw the loaded piece into place (figure 18);
cannon housed – showing the breech lowered so that the muzzle bears
against the upper-edge of the port – (figure 19); breeching, the rope used
to restrain recoil (inset); loading and cleaning equipment – worms, for
drawing (extracting) the charge (figures 6 and 9); ladle, for measuring
powder (figure 7); hog-bristle sponge, for cleaning the barrel (figure 8);
rammer/sponge (sheepskin) (figure 10) – the loader could shorten this
rammer by bending its flexible handle and thus remain sheltered from
enemy musket fire; and the different types of shot – bar-shot, the middle
of which the French sometimes filled with 'combustibles', set alight when
the shot was fired to set fire to the sails (figure 11); chain-shot, designed
to destroy the masts and rigging (figure 12); grape-shot (balls in a
canvas bag) (figure 13); and case-shot (musket bullets in a tin box),
'principally used by the French to scour the decks of the enemy' (figure 14).*

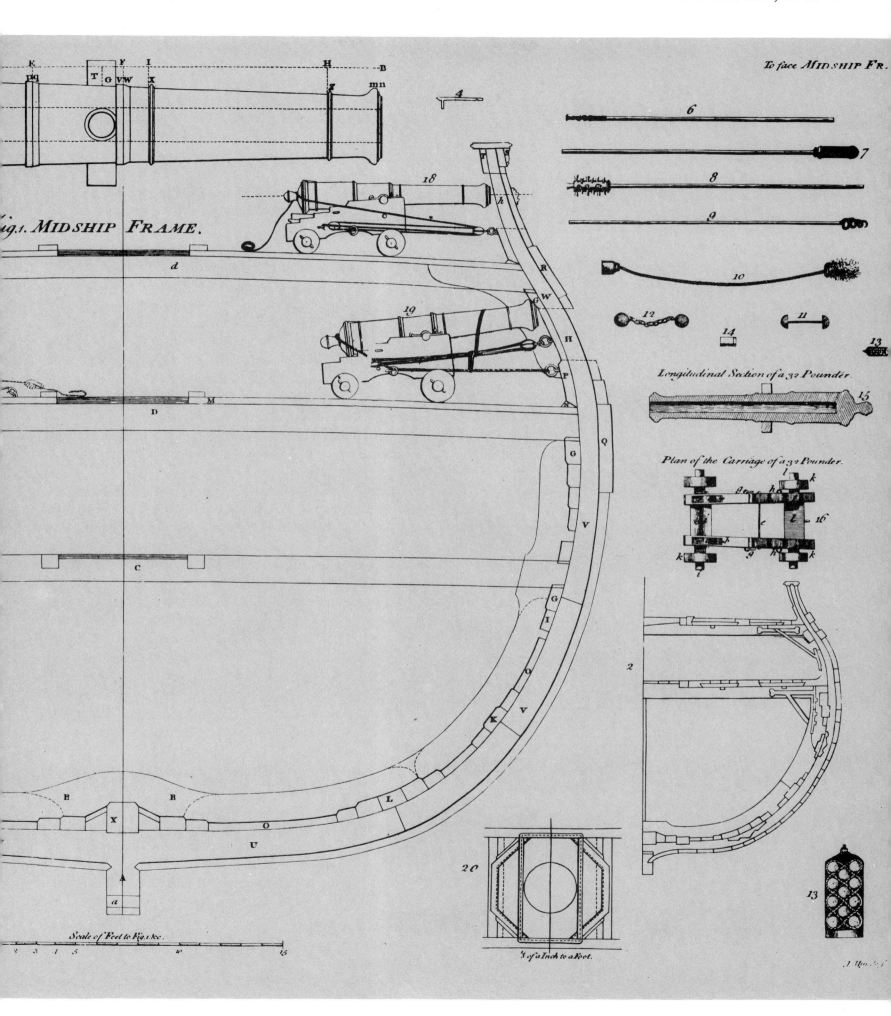

To face MIDSHIP FR.

Fig.1. MIDSHIP FRAME.

Longitudinal Section of a 32 Pounder.

Plan of the Carriage of a 32 Pounder.

Scale of Feet to Fig.1 &c.

⅛ of a Inch to a Foot.

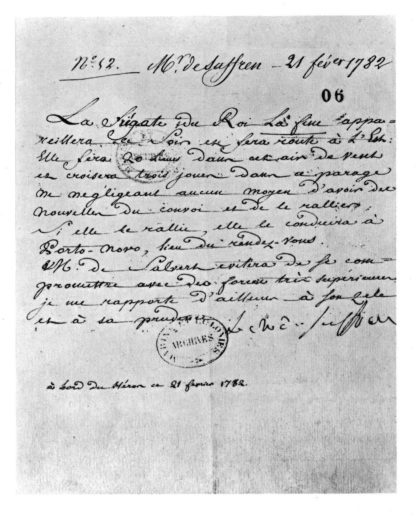

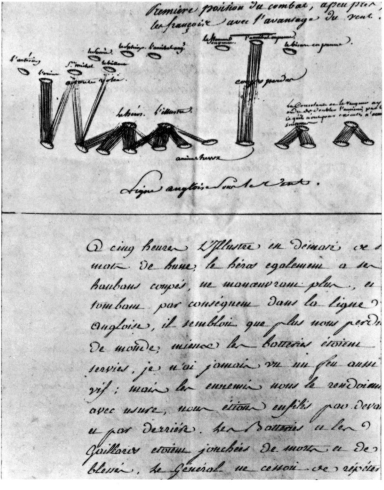

Four of them, including M. de Tromelin of the *Annibal*, the senior captain, were sent to the Isle of France, vacancies being filled by commanders of the smaller ships, including Villaret de Joyeuse, who was later to make a name for himself in the Revolutionary Navy.

After refitting at Trincomalee, Suffren resolved to go into winter quarters at Sumatra, visiting stations on the Coromandel coast on his way. At Cuddalore the *Bizarre*, a 64-gun ship, was run ashore by the carelessness of her captain, one of the new promotions: again valuable masts and spars were lost, this time by the capture of a transport which was bringing them to Suffren. Hughes wintered at Bombay, where he was reinforced by five of the line under Sir Richard Bickerton. The ships included the *Gibraltar*, a fine 80-gun ship taken from the Spaniards.

Suffren was recalled to the Coromandel coast by rumours of the death of Hyder Ali. When he arrived off Cuddalore in February 1783, he found the news confirmed, but he was reassured to hear that Hyder's son, Tippoo Sahib, had inherited his father's policy and warlike spirit. Suffren thereupon sailed for Trincomalee, where he was strengthened by three ships of the line, a frigate and much needed stores. There were also troops for Porto Novo, and these were taken to India towards the end of March.

Having disembarked the regiments, Suffren was anxious to return to Trincomalee, for he knew that Hughes, reinforced, might attempt the recapture of that place. Indeed, as the French entered the bay, the British were sighted to seaward. Hughes was actually making for the Coromandel coast, where he established a blockade, though a high rate of sickness was beginning to cause him serious difficulties.

It was off Cuddalore that the fleets met once again. Suffren's object was to establish communication with the town, which was under siege. He succeeded. He passed his fleet inside the British position, and anchored close inshore. He borrowed troops from the garrison and then, taking advantage of the wind, weighed and stood out to sea, eager to engage.

After nearly three days spent in manoeuvering, Hughes hove to, in line of battle, to await Suffren's attack. Battle opened at five o'clock and continued until dark. It was not conducted with the energy which had marked the earlier clashes. Hughes's ships were short-handed: as for Suffren, he had received an order from France, resulting from the capture of the Comte de Grasse, that he was not to expose himself in action, and on this occasion he flew

LEFT TOP: *Detailed instructions in Suffren's own handwriting to one of his frigate commanders in February 1782*

LEFT BOTTOM: *Admiral Suffren showing his interest in gunnery tactics and concentration of fire*

Trincomalee, the finest natural harbour in Ceylon, taken by the French during Sir Edward Hughes's second command in the East Indies

his pendant in the *Cléopatre*. Both sides suffered, but no immediate decision was reached, and no ships were lost. Afterwards, Hughes withdrew to Madras, thus raising the blockade of Cuddalore.

It was the last encounter. On 29 June 1783 news arrived of the ending of hostilities.

The protracted episode of Suffren and Hughes had a happy ending, for on his way back to France, the Frenchman was everywhere received as a hero, most warmly of all by his late enemies. When he was at the Cape, a division of nine of Hughes's ships anchored in the harbour. Commodore King, the hero of the *Exeter*, waited upon Suffren with a party of captains. 'The good Dutchmen received me as their saviour,' wrote the Frenchman, 'but among the tributes that have most flattered me, none has given me more pleasure than the esteem and consideration testified by the English.'

In Europe, Suffren was royally received, and the honorific post of Vice-Admiral of France was given him. He died in 1788. Sir Edward Hughes outlived him by six years, and as the result of two spells as a Commander-in-Chief in India, he was able to leave his step-son £40,000 a year.

A medal struck by the French in 1784 to commemorate Suffren's campaign in the East Indies

The Glorious First of June
1794

The name given to the naval victory of Lord Howe over the French, which was fought four hundred miles out in the Atlantic in the latitude of Ushant

THE FIRST MAJOR CLASH AT SEA in the war between France and Great Britain, which with one interval lasted from 1793 to 1815 and involved to a greater or lesser degree all the principal nations in Europe, took place over four hundred miles into the Atlantic. Known as 'The Glorious First of June', since the principal action took place on that day, it was in fact a series of tactical engagements in which success went to Lord Howe, who defeated the fleet of Admiral Villaret de Joyeuse. Nevertheless, it was a strategic failure for Great Britain, since her opponent succeeded in the object for which he fought.

An immense grain convoy, assembled in the Chesapeake for the relief of a starving country, reached France safely, and Villaret de Joyeuse, far from feeling himself disgraced, considered, with some justice, that in spite of the loss of seven ships of the line, France had come off best. Equally important – to the admiral at any rate – he had kept his head, for he had been told that if the grain were captured, he would answer for it at the guillotine.

The task set the Brest fleet was to prevent the British from approaching the track of the convoy, which had a close escort of only four ships of the line. Villaret de Joyeuse, who had been promoted to flag rank at record speed owing to the disruption of the old French navy at the time of the Revolution, had with him in his flagship an official, Jean-Bon Saint-André, whom later generations would know as a Political Commissar. Saint-André's job was to see that the sailors did their duty.

Howe had made a westerly cruise from his base at Torbay in April 1794, but he had met nothing. He sailed again, early in May, with a strong force, thirty-four ships of the line and a galaxy of admirals, Graves, Alexander Hood, Pasley, Gardner, Bowyer, Caldwell and Montagu – reminiscent of the large fleets of the old wars with the Dutch. As he had orders to cover an outward-bound convoy, he was forced to detach eight warships, under Montagu, ordering them to rejoin him after seeing the merchantmen safely to the latitude of Cape Finisterre.

By 5 May Howe was off Ushant. There he learnt that his opponent was still in harbour. Not wishing to prevent him from leaving Brest (for Howe was as eager to fight the French fleet as to intercept their convoy), he made no attempt to watch Brest but advanced westerly, putting himself, as he believed, between the grain ships and the probable course which would be taken by Villaret de Joyeuse. He was thus in a fair way to capture the convoy first and deal with the fleet later.

A week passed, and Howe met nothing. He returned to Ushant, off which he arrived on 19 May. There he learnt that Brest was empty. The French had sailed three days earlier with twenty-five of the line. Villaret de Joyeuse had been joined at sea by one additional ship,

RIGHT: *An oil-painting by Nicholas Pocock (1741–1821), who was himself present at the Battle of the Glorious First of June, showing the French* L'Achille, *the British* Brunswick *and the French* Le Vengeur *in action; the last ship struck and sank after a tremendous duel*

A lieutenant with a party of seamen at Tower Hill, London, are impressing men for service in the Royal Navy; a late eighteenth-century print

and had actually passed close to the British, unseen in the misty weather.

The moment Howe had firm news of the French course, he went off in pursuit, without waiting for Montagu. On the 25th, two French corvettes were seen steering after the British fleet, which they mistook for their own. Both were captured and burnt, since Howe could not spare enough men to make up prize crews. The French officers and men had perfect confidence that when the two main fleets met, they would be released.

Early on 28 May, with a rough sea running, Lieutenant Edward Codrington, at the mast-head of the *Queen Charlotte*, Howe's flagship, reported the enemy to windward, about ten miles away. The British were then slightly further from Brest than the French, a fact which speaks well for the pursuit. At first Villaret de Joyeuse, who had the windward position, seemed inclined to run down to attack his opponent, but when the size of Howe's fleet had been reported by his frigates, he held his wind, intending not only to keep his advantageous position but to prevent Howe from approaching the convoy. This was far out of sight on a southerly course.

Howe had formed his leading ships into a flying squadron, led by Admiral Pasley in the *Bellerophon*, and he signalled him to engage as soon as wind, distance and the enemy permitted. Pasley was an active officer, and four of his ships managed to get into action with a detachment of the French, among them the three-decker *Révolution-*

naire. After some stiff fighting the Frenchman was rendered unfit for further action, at the expense of one disabled British vessel, the *Audacious*. Some reports said that the *Révolutionnaire* struck her colours, but with darkness approaching, she could not be secured, and she managed to escape next day, though it was a near thing. She was sent home with a 74-gun ship to protect her.

On 29 May, Howe was still to leeward of the French, but he was determined to gain the wind before sunset. If the French stood, as he beat towards them, he meant to break through their line and bring on a mêlée. His van failed him, thanks to the wretched handling of the *Caesar*, the leading ship, but he himself set an example in the *Queen Charlotte*, and with Pasley's *Bellerophon* and the *Leviathan*, commanded by Lord Hugh Seymour, Howe broke through towards the rear of the French line, and cut off three two-decked ships.

Villaret had no intention of losing the services of these ships but, in order to save them, he was forced to run to leeward and so yield the advantage of the wind to his opponent. Howe had got his way, as he usually did. Moreover, although Villaret had saved his ships, he was forced to send them home, so battered was their state. So far, he had lost the services of four ships to Howe's one: but the convoy was undiscovered and that was what mattered most.

Next day, 30 May, was misty, and Howe was content merely to keep contact. Villaret de Joyeuse, edging away

Admiral of the Fleet Earl Howe, KG, (1726–99) is wearing Admiral's undress uniform in this portrait by John Singleton Copley (1737–95)

A lithograph portrait by Antoine Maurin (1793–1860) of Louis Villaret de Joyeuse (1750–1812), showing the French admiral in his last years in Napoleon's service

to leeward, was lucky enough to meet with and be reinforced by four ships of a detached squadron, so that his fleet was once more brought up to its original strength. On 31 May, about noon, the mist began to disperse, and Howe, with that moral strength which is the characteristic of a great commander, decided to postpone his attack until next day, meanwhile keeping touch. He meant to have all day in which to gain his victory: his captains should be under his eye, obeying his signals as he intended, and he believed he could afford the time. He was seen to smile, and the news spread like lightning through the *Queen Charlotte*. 'Black Dick', as Howe was called from his dark complexion, smiled rarely. When he did so, it meant business.

Howe's plan, which he intended to carry out at dawn on 1 June, was designed to overcome the usual withdrawing tactics employed by a fleet when fighting to leeward. The conventional attack would have been to engage the French, from the windward position in a line parallel with theirs, from a comparatively long range. The French would have aimed high, as they generally did, intending to cripple the windward fleet by damage to masts and spars, and then to withdraw in an orderly fashion. Howe's idea was to run down almost bows on, break through at all points, so preventing Villaret's escape, and then to destroy the French in detail. He prophesied that for every ship which did as he intended, he would take a prize. In the event, he was exactly right.

The attack was made in the early morning. Six ships, the *Queen Charlotte*, *Defence*, *Marlborough*, *Royal George*, *Queen* and *Brunswick*, acted as Howe wished, and brought on a mêlée in the manner of Monck and Rupert. Many of the other ships either misunderstood the signals, or considered the method of attack permissive, though with the exception of the *Caesar* there was no lack of eagerness to engage closely, and when the smoke of battle cleared, after a morning's encounter, Howe had taken six prizes, while a seventh French ship, *Le Vengeur du Peuple* had been sunk after a tremendous duel with the *Brunswick*.

The French fleet was in much confusion during and after the battle, and Howe has been criticized for not following up his victory, and for not detaching some proportion of his force to seek out the convoy. There is reason behind the charge, but at least three circumstances have to be recalled when weighing the matter. The first was Howe's age and state. He was sixty-nine, one of the oldest admirals to have won a victory on such a scale, and he had been exhausted by four days of close manoeuvring, during the course of which he had had no chance to recover. Sir Roger Curtis, his First Captain or Chief-of-Staff, although a far younger man, was cautious in the extreme: no initiative could be looked for in that quarter.

The second circumstance was that most of the ships which would have been likely to do best in pursuit of the French were those very units which, having done best in action, were the most damaged.

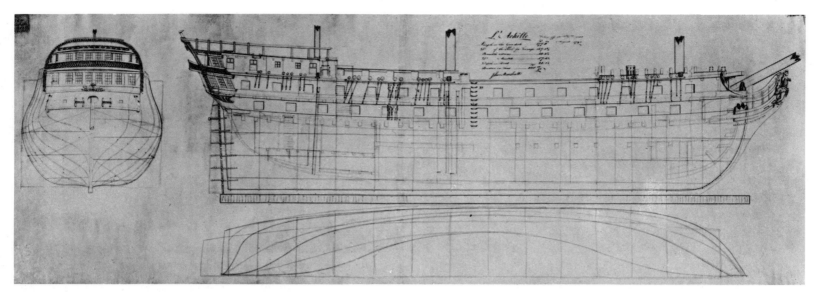

The lines of L'Achille, *a French 74-gun ship of the line, which surrendered to Lord Howe's fleet, drawn in an English dockyard after capture*

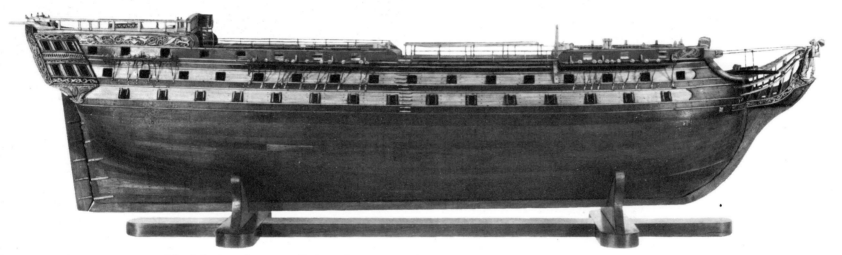

A good contemporary model of the French 74-gun Eole, *whose commander, Captain Bertrand Keranguen, was killed at the First of June*

As for the convoy, it was Howe's hope that the *Audacious*, when she returned home, would report the French to be at sea, and that a force would be sent from Plymouth in a 'cleaning up' operation. In fact, this was what happened. Montagu, having seen his outward bound ships safe, returned home, and when news of Howe's encounter of 29 May reached him, he sailed at once for Brest. If Howe had been in pursuit of the French, Villaret de Joyeuse would have been in a dreadful predicament with a victorious fleet on his tail, and Montagu, with fresh ships, barring the way to his base.

Years later, the French admiral told an English officer that when he saw Montagu's sails in the neighbourhood of Brest he was petrified. 'My ships were in a shocking state,' he said, 'the lower decks crowded with invalids and wounded. A fight was the very last thing we would have chosen.' Villaret de Joyeuse was spared this final

horror. Montagu allowed himself to be driven away, and, forgetting the possibility of being able to capture the convoy, or being unaware that it had not already reached France, he returned to Plymouth. The night after Villaret's appearance off his home port, the lights of the merchantmen were seen in the Raz de Sein, the southern passage by which Brest is approached, and grain ships and fleet made harbour together. Jean Bon Saint-André (who had prudently gone below during the battle) loudly proclaimed a success to his political colleagues in Paris, and made an heroic legend of the last fight of *Le Vengeur du Peuple*.

Of the many episodes which arose from the fighting on 1 June 1794, two stand out, and they both concern flagships. One of them is related by Codrington, who first sighted the French fleet. He was a favourite with Howe, and he had, in his turn, unbounded admiration for his admiral. Codrington was a man whose devotion was worth winning. He was later to serve under Nelson at Trafalgar and when, in due course, he himself achieved flag rank, it was to command, at Navarino, in the last full-scale battle to be fought wholly under sail.

On 1 June, when it was clear that Villaret de Joyeuse would stand and fight, Lord Howe's face, said Codrington, showed 'an animation which, at his age, and after such fatigue of body and mind, I had not thought it capable. He seemed to contemplate the result as one of unbounded satisfaction.' In fact, the dashing captain of the *Magnanime*, foremost at Quiberon Bay, had matured into the most experienced admiral of his day, without losing a particle of his resolution. 'Now, Sir,' said Howe to Sir Roger Curtis as the opposing fleets drew near: 'prepare the signal for close action.' Curtis pointed out that there was no such signal. Howe knew this well enough, and said: 'No, Sir, but there is a signal for *closer* action . . .', and he made sure that it was made, so that every captain would know that a mêlée was intended. 'Then,' continued Codrington, 'turning to us by whom he was surrounded, and shutting the little signal book he always carried about him, he said: "And now, gentlemen, no more book, no more signals. I look to you to do the duty of the *Queen Charlotte* in engaging the French admiral. I do not wish the ships to be bilge to bilge, but if you can lock the yard-arms so much the better, the battle will be the sooner decided."'

The other case, that of the *Queen*, was equally striking. The *Queen* was the flagship of Admiral Gardner, who in more peaceful times was of a nervous disposition, often fearful of damage from his next astern if she drew too

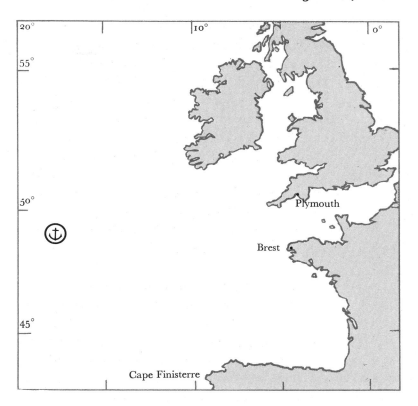

close. In action, he was transformed. The *Queen* fought nobly on 29 May, and in the course of that day her captain, Hutt, received so severe a wound that he died soon after the battle, while her sailing master, Mitchell, was killed outright. For the remainder of the sortie the ship was handled by the admiral in person, aided by a number of able lieutenants, one of whom, Mr Ballard, kept a log covering the operations.

On 1 June the *Queen* was again in the very thick of it, and she received so much damage that, had the French shown more enterprise, Howe might have had a task to

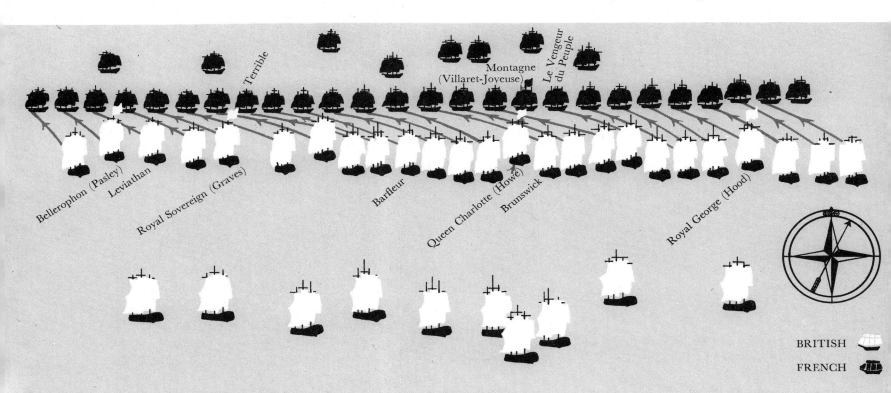

rescue her. At the most critical stage she was forced some distance to leeward, dismasted, and almost helpless. 'Observed eleven sail of the enemy's line and their frigates starting for us,' noted Ballard at this time. 'Our fleet so much disabled to windward, no hopes of relief from them. *Beat to arms*. Swayed a fore studding-sail up . . . At half-past one, they began a heavy fire on us, which was so faithfully returned, occasioned them to pass on, not wishing to have any more fire from a disabled British ship.' This was one of the finest instances of self-help in the annals of any navy. Howe was soon able to send help to the *Queen*, but she needed none, and she returned to Spithead under jury-masts, the admiration of every seaman.

The sortie which ended with the fighting of the Glorious First of June has an interest apart from its strategy and tactics. It was the first occasion on which awards to the principal officers engaged were made on a regular system. This has since been extended, to a greater or less degree, to the armed services of almost every country. Honours for prowess in action had been bestowed from early times in the form of grants of rank, of stars of the orders of chivalry, and of monetary rewards to principal commanders. What was newly ordained by George III in the year 1794 was the giving of a gold medal, struck to a

A midship section of a 74-gun ship typical of those which fought under Howe at the First of June

RIGHT: *The sinking of* Le Vengeur *after her duel with the* Brunswick, *by Robert Dodd (1748–1815)*

Numb. 13669.

[541]

The London Gazette
EXTRAORDINARY.

Published by Authority.

WEDNESDAY, JUNE 11, 1794.

Admiralty-Office, June 10.

SIR Roger Curtis, First Captain to the Admiral Earl Howe, arrived this Evening with a Dispatch from his Lordship to Mr. Stephens, of which the following is a Copy.

Queen Charlotte at Sea, June 2, 1794,
Ushant E. Half N. 140 Leagues.

SIR,

THINKING it may not be necessary to make a more particular Report of my Proceedings with the Fleet, for the present Information of the Lords Commissioners of the Admiralty, I confine my Communications chiefly, in this Dispatch, to the Occurrences when in Presence of the Enemy Yesterday.

Finding, on my Return off of Brest on the 19th past, that the French Fleet had, a few Days before, put to Sea; and receiving, on the same Evening, Advices from Rear-Admiral Montagu, I deemed it requisite to endeavour to form a Junction with the Rear-Admiral as soon as possible, and proceeded immediately for the Station on which he meant to wait for the Return of the Venus.

But, having gained very credible Intelligence, on the 21st of the same Month, whereby I had Reason to suppose the French Fleet was then but a few Leagues farther to the Westward, the Course before steered was altered accordingly.

On the Morning of the 28th the Enemy were discovered far to Windward, and partial Actions were engaged with them that Evening and the next Day.

The Weather Gage having been obtained, in the Progress of the last mentioned Day, and the Fleet being in a Situation for bringing the Enemy to close Action the 1st Instant, the Ships bore up together for that Purpose, between Seven and Eight o'Clock in the Morning.

The French, their Force consisting of Twenty-six Ships of the Line, opposed to His Majesty's Fleet of Twenty-five (the Audacious having parted Company with the sternmost Ship of the Enemy's Line, captured in the Night of the 28th) waited for the Action, and sustained the Attack with their customary Resolution.

In less than an Hour after the close Action commenced in the Centre, the French Admiral, engaged by the Queen Charlotte, crowded off, and was followed by most of the Ships of his Van in Condition to carry Sail after him, leaving with us about Ten or Twelve of his crippled or totally dismasted Ships, exclusive of One sunk in the Engagement. The Queen Charlotte had then lost her Fore Topmast, and the Main Topmast fell over the Side very soon after.

The

standard pattern, from a design by the Italian artist Thomas Pingo, to all admirals and captains who had particularly distinguished themselves. The medal itself has on the obverse a figure of Victory, standing on the prow of an antique galley, placing a laurel wreath on the head of Britannia. At Britannia's side there is an oval shield, charged with the crosses of the Union flag. Britannia's right foot rests on a helmet, and she holds a spear in her left hand. The reverse carries a wreath of oak and laurel, within which are engraved the name and rank of the recipient, and the date of the action for which it is conferred. The inscription on Lord Howe's own medal runs:

RICHARD EARL HOWE, ADMIRAL AND COMMANDER-IN-CHIEF ON THE I OF JUNE MDCCXCIV. THE FRENCH FLEET DEFEATED

The King's idea was in itself excellent, and had the medal been granted in the case of every admiral and captain engaged, it would have given much satisfaction. Every ship's company would have taken the medal as a compliment to their unit. Most unfortunately, the Admiralty called for individual recommendations, and although Howe protested that any distinction between one officer and another must necessarily cause offence, nevertheless a choice was insisted upon. Howe judged rightly. The admirals and captains who gained his special notice received their medals; others did not, and as a result the awards gave as much offence in cases where officers were omitted as they caused pleasure among those who were included.

LEFT TOP: *First news of the earliest naval victory against Revolutionary France was brought to England by Sir Roger Curtis, who sailed ahead of the fleet with despatches for the Admiralty.* LEFT: *A contemporary cartoon showing Sir Roger Curtis, the Admiral's first captain, licking Lord Howe's boots: a reference to the unsatisfactory honours list published after the battle, for which Curtis was known to have been responsible*

RIGHT: *Brest in 1794, by J. F. Hue: a general view of the base from which Villaret de Joyeuse sailed with his fleet to protect the grain convoy from America*

OVERLEAF: *Lord Howe stands with drawn sword on the quarter-deck of his flagship, the* Queen Charlotte; *Captain Neville of the Queen's Regiment, mortally wounded, is supported by his friends; the Captain of the ship, Sir Andrew Snape Douglas, wilting slightly from a head wound, stands on the right.*

A lieutenant of the Revolutionary Navy, a watercolour by Goichon, dating from the late nineteenth-century

An idealized portrait of a French sailor in the early days of the Revolutionary Navy, also by Goichon

The choice of recipients was, in fact, eccentric. Captain Collingwood for instance, who commanded the *Barfleur*, was omitted from the distinction, while Rear-Admiral Bowyer, whose flag-captain he then was, and who lost a leg early in the battle, was included. Collingwood never quite forgave Howe, but three years later, when he played a notable part at the battle of St Vincent, the Admiralty made amends by sending him *two* medals. Later he gained yet another for Trafalgar.

Perhaps it was inevitable that the matter of awards should adjust itself in the course of time through trial and error. Certainly there was no discontent after later victories at sea, when all captains except the rare creatures who disgraced themselves (or had the ill fortune to be killed) received their coveted medals.

It was over half a century before the system of giving medals was extended to others than commanding officers, but it came in time. Long after most of the survivors of Howe's battle were dead, a Naval General Service medal was instituted, with a clasp commemorating the principal actions of the war with France. Since that time, not only have rewards been made on a more generous scale, but they have been given more promptly. This is as it should be, and it is an odd but verifiable fact that there has been a greater prolification of decorations and medals in ultra-democratic countries than in monarchical Britain. A man who has fought well values visible recognition of the fact. His is a natural and legitimate aspiration.

This example of the gold medal and chain, designed by Thomas Pingo, which was presented to the British flag officers after the victory of the First of June, belonged to Vice-Admiral Sir Alexander Hood, later Lord Bridport

The Nile

1798

The British fleet under Nelson sailed into Aboukir Bay and, in a night encounter, destroyed Bonaparte's ships of the line under Admiral Brueys

ONE OF HOWE'S WARMEST ADMIRERS was John Jervis, Earl St Vincent, and St Vincent's most illustrious pupil was Horatio Nelson. Howe had served under Hawke, Hawke under Anson, and Anson remembered officers who had fought in the last of the old wars with the Dutch. The chain of naval tradition was unbroken.

From the age of twelve, when he first went to sea, Nelson was dedicated to a single end, to make his country great by means of her fleet. Born in 1758, he had served as a youth in the East Indies under Hughes against Hyder Ali. He had fought by land and sea: by land against the Spaniards in Nicaragua and against the French in Corsica, where he had lost the sight of his right eye: by sea in the West Indies, in North America, against the Spanish and French in the Atlantic and the Mediterranean, losing his right arm in an attempt on Teneriffe.

His first great chance had come as a commodore, when he had been present at the battle of Cape St Vincent. The year was 1797, and it had brought Jervis an earldom. Nelson had turned out of the line, without orders, and, by his own initiative, ensured the surrender of two ships. It was not an incident which his Commander-in-chief was likely to forget, and when, in the spring of 1798 Nelson rejoined the fleet as a rear-admiral, recovered from his wounds, Jervis gave him an opportunity for distinction such as seldom falls to any man, and armed him with means to accomplish it.

To Great Britain, the times seemed as hard as they had been during the War of American Independence. On land, the French were all-conquering, for in Napoleon Bonaparte they had discovered a prodigy whose skill matched fantastic ambition. Jervis's fleet had had to withdraw from the Mediterranean, and although his successful battle had been a tonic, its effects did not last. They were forgotten in the horror which filled every breast when it was known first that Channel and then Spithead ships were in mutiny.

To crown everything, it was clear by the early months of 1798 that the French were planning something very big and secret. Bonaparte had visited the coast of Northern France and Flanders, and had reported to Paris, 'We shall not for some years gain the naval supremacy. To invade England without that supremacy is the most daring and difficult task ever undertaken'. Alternatives must be found, to 'shake England to her marrow-bones', in the phrase of the time. Possibilities were considered and discarded: finally Bonaparte flung out the idea that 'an Eastern expedition would menace Britain's trade with the Indies'. France had not forgotten her hopes of a great destiny in India. Bonaparte would not only revive them, he would translate them into fact.

An Eastern expedition was not merely possible but inviting, and, unless the British returned in strength to the Mediterranean, there was nothing to prevent it. Within weeks of the decision, every major port on the

RIGHT: *Napoleon: an engraving after Sir Charles Eastlake (1793–1865), who made sketches of Bonaparte when he was a prisoner aboard the* Bellerophon *in Plymouth Sound in 1815*

French and Italian riviera was at work preparing for a project whose aim was known only to a handful.

Both sides hastened, for different reasons. Nelson was only two days in company with St Vincent before he was off on a mission to discover what was happening in the Mediterranean, and to shadow and if possible destroy the French armada before it had achieved its purpose. Nelson passed through the Straits of Gibraltar on 8 May with three ships of the line, two frigates and a sloop. It was the day before Bonaparte reached Toulon. Less than a fortnight later, the *Vanguard* was dismasted and nearly wrecked in a Gulf of Lions gale, Nelson's frigates had been scattered, and the French had got clean away – their direction uncertain.

'You are hereby authorized and directed to proceed with your squadron to ascertain, by every means in your power, the destination of the considerable armaments . . . at Toulon, Marseilles and Genoa,' ran Nelson's orders. Conjecture suggested Sicily, Malta, Corfu on the one hand, Portugal or Ireland on the other. St Vincent, by dividing and so weakening his fleet, had in fact staked everything on Bonaparte's being an eastern, not a western destination. The unforgivable sin would have been for Nelson to let the French pass westwards through the Straits of Gibraltar without warning: and now he had been driven from his station, and for all he knew the enemy might be doing that very thing.

Bad as they seemed, things were not quite so serious as that, and when Nelson, with the help of the other ships of the line, had re-fitted the flagship at sea and been joined by the ten further vessels which were to make up his full force, he knew, at least, that the worst had not happened – but where *was* Bonaparte?

Bonaparte was at Malta. His huge armada had descended upon the island on 9 June. The Knights of St John were decadent, and the French members had refused service against their compatriots. The Grand Master surrendered with scarcely a show of resistance. Within a few days Bonaparte had plundered the island's treasure, reorganized its affairs from top to bottom, left a garrison at Valetta, and sailed on.

Nelson's captains were all experienced, and when the admiral found he could get no news of the French, even from Naples, which was usually a mine of information, he took counsel with the senior officers, Sir James Saumarez of the *Orion*, Troubridge of the *Culloden* and Darby of the *Bellerophon*. All agreed that Egypt was the likeliest point of French attack, and to Egypt Nelson hurried. Having no frigates, he could not spread his search, and

LEFT: *One of several extant versions of the portrait of Nelson by Leonardo Guzzardi, made in Sicily after the Battle of the Nile*

his ships overtook those of Bonaparte during hours of darkness (French officers actually heard British signal guns during one night). Nelson looked into Alexandria, found the harbour empty, and beat wearily back to Sicily. He could scarcely believe himself wrong, and indeed, as his top-gallants disappeared over the horizon, the French, their course close inshore, began preparation to disembark. As Nelson put it, 'the devil's children have the devil's luck'.

On his second cast, Nelson found his quarry. Bonaparte's transports were snug in Alexandria, but his fleet, under Brueys, thirteen of the line including the giant *L'Orient*, were at anchor in Aboukir Bay, near the Rosetta mouth of the Nile.

It was in the afternoon of 1 August that Nelson's lookouts sighted the French. From the moment that the signal for an enemy fluttered from the halliards, every officer and man in the squadron knew what Nelson would do. He would attack that day. The frustration of the last few weeks had had one compensation: it had enabled the most brilliant young flag-officer of his day – Nelson was not yet forty – to turn his captains into the best trained team of officers ever assembled. There was not one weak link.

Edward Berry, the flag-captain, described his chief's methods:

> It had been his practice during the whole of the cruise, whenever the weather and circumstances would permit, to have his captains on board the *Vanguard*, where he would fully develop to them his own ideas of the different and best modes of attack, and such plans as he proposed to execute upon falling in with the Enemy, whatever their position might be, by day or by night. There was no possible position in which they could be found, that he did not take into his calculation, and for the most advantageous attack of which he had not digested and arranged the best possible disposition of the force which he commanded.

Berry went on to describe the confidence and understanding which made signals almost unnecessary. Nelson had given his trust to his subordinates. They knew his inmost thoughts: they also knew that in calling them, as he did, a 'Band of Brothers' he was using a phrase from his favourite play, Shakespeare's *Henry V*, and that in the day of battle he would look to them to behave like the

LEFT: *A French engraving of Admiral Brueys, whose fleet was destroyed by Nelson in Aboukir Bay on 1 August 1798, and who was himself killed in the action*

OVERLEAF: *The Battle of the Nile at about 6.30 pm, a painting by Nicholas Pocock (1741–1821). The* Goliath *and* Zealous *are rounding the bows of the French* Guerrier

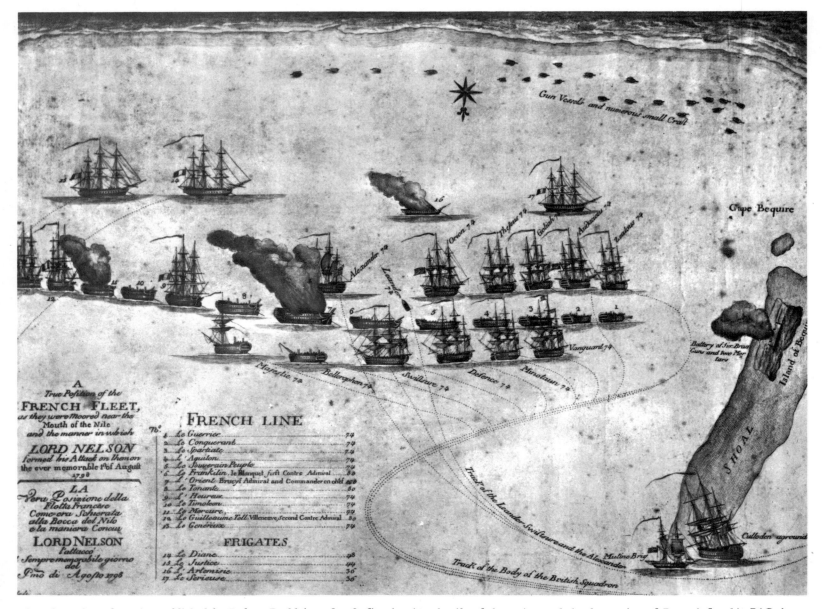

Within the image:

A
True Position of the
FRENCH FLEET,
as they were Moored near the
Mouth of the Nile
and the manner in which

LORD NELSON
formed his Attack on them on
the ever memorable 1st of August
1798

LA
Vera Posizione della
Flotta Francese
Come era Schierata
alla Bocca del Nilo
e la maniera Concui

LORD NELSON
l'attacco
Sempre memorabile giorno
del
1mo di Agosto 1798

FRENCH LINE

1. Le Guerrier _____ 74
2. Le Conquerant _____ 74
3. Le Spartiate _____ 74
4. L'Aquilon _____ 74
5. Le Souverain Peuple _____ 74
6. Le Franklin, le Blanquet first Contre Admiral _____ 80
7. L'Orient, Brueys Admiral and Commander en chief _____ 120
8. Le Tonante _____ 80
9. L'Heureux _____ 74
10. Le Timoleon _____ 74
11. Le Mercure _____ 74
12. Le Guillaume Tell, Villeneuve Second Contre Admiral _____ 80
13. Le Généreux _____ 74

FRIGATES

14. Le Diane _____ 48
15. La Justice _____ 44
16. L'Artemise _____ 36
17. La Serieuse _____ 36

An adaptation of a print published by Robert Dodd (1748–1816), showing details of the action and the destruction of Brueys' flagship L'Orient

heroes of Agincourt. He gave much, but he expected much, and he was never disappointed.

Nelson might be eager to attack, but what of Brueys? He had had time to make his position impregnable. He was anchored in a sandy bay, protected by shoals. One flank rested on the mainland, the other on a small island, Bequier, on which the French had placed a battery. The frigates and lighter craft were inshore of the ships of the line. Had he been a confident kind of man, Brueys might have smiled at the thought of the reception Nelson would get if he were fool enough to rush in. Had they been in his shoes, Nelson, and a dozen other British admirals, would have wished for nothing better than for an enemy to bash his head against such an obstacle as an anchored fleet awaiting battle on its own terms.

Brueys had parties ashore watering. Although it was an hour or two before he was convinced that Nelson would attack, that afternoon at any rate, he recalled them and made ready for action. Nelson had the wind in his favour and just the necessary time, before darkness, to complete a tactical masterpiece. The core of his plan was so simple that he was able to explain it to Lord Howe in under thirty words: 'By attacking the Enemy's van and centre, the wind blowing directly along their Line, I was enabled to throw what fire I pleased on a few ships.' In the event, Nelson achieved what had been the hope of every admiral since the beginning of time. He was helped by two mistakes of his enemy.

Nelson had to sail into the bay under the concentrated fire of most of Brueys's fleet, which lay in a slight curve, the van to the west. Owing to the relation of the enemy to Bequier Island, the attack had to be made from north-east to south-west, and had Brueys placed artillery ashore to guard his flank in any strength, instead of only a few light pieces, the British must have suffered cruelly. As it was, their advance was at no time checked, and as de-

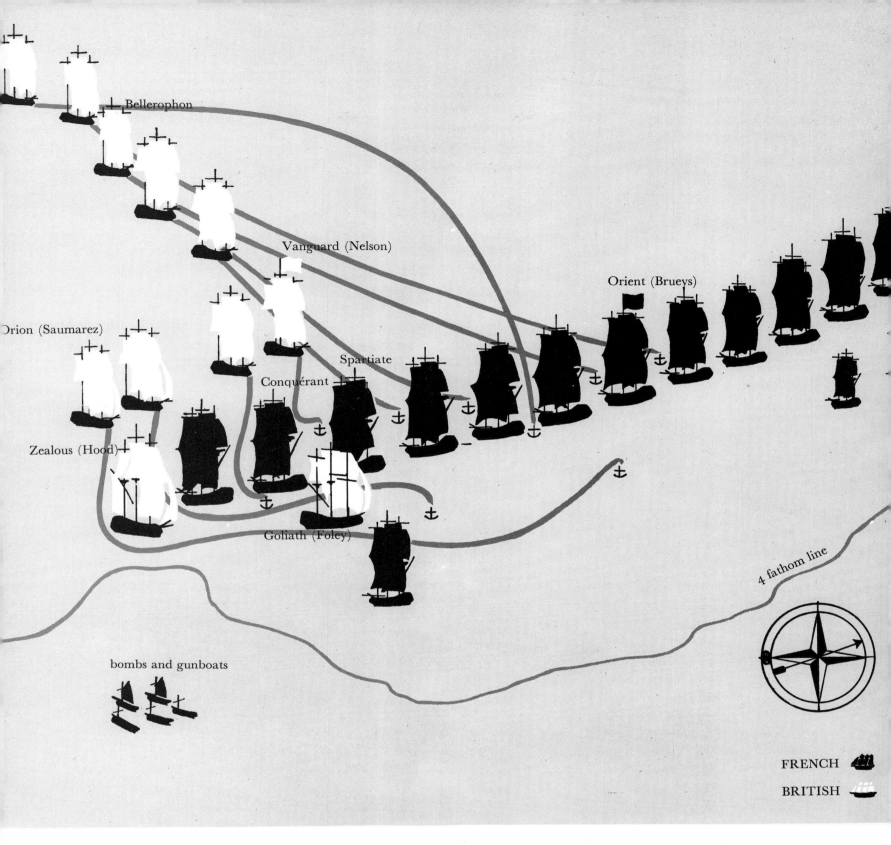

Bellerophon

Vanguard (Nelson)

Orient (Brueys)

Orion (Saumarez)

Spartiate

Conquérant

Zealous (Hood)

Goliath (Foley)

4 fathom line

bombs and gunboats

FRENCH

BRITISH

tails of the French position became clear, Foley, the captain of the leading ship, saw to his surprise and glee that Brueys had been careless enough to leave room for him to round the head of the French line, and to attack from inshore, where the enemy's guns were likely to be unready. Other captains later noticed that the French were not anchored close enough to one another, and that there were places where a skilful man could break through the line, raking an enemy as he did so.

Where Foley led, Samuel Hood, a kinsman of the famous admiral, followed in the *Zealous*. The *Audacious*

anchored – like all Nelson's ships, by the stern, with a spring on the cable to allow manoeuvring – where she could rake the *Conquérant*. The *Theseus* followed, then Sir James Saumarez in the *Orion*. By the time Nelson himself came up in the *Vanguard*, daylight was beginning to fade. The flagship and all succeeding vessels attacked the French on the seaward side, slowly advancing down the line, blasting everything in their path. The only unlucky captain was Nelson's life-long friend Troubridge. He ran the *Culloden* on to a shoal off Bequier Island, but he was able to guide the last two ships safely into the Bay. Once

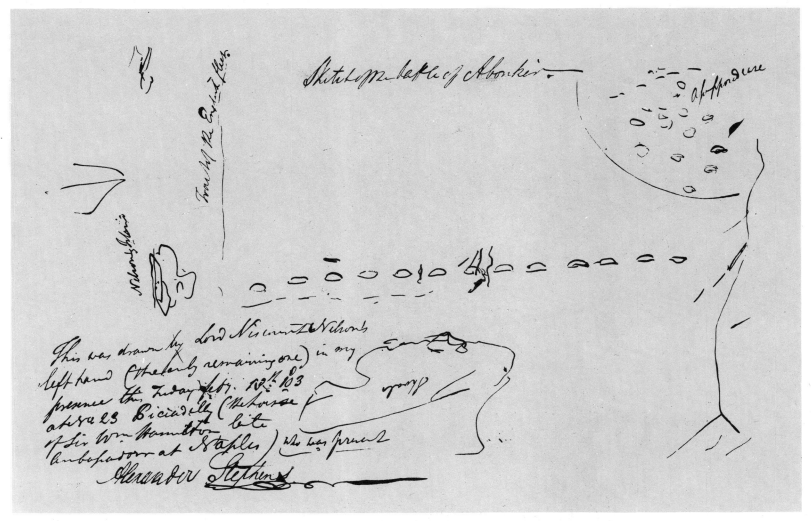

A rough sketch of the battle made by Nelson on his return to England, showing his approach, and Bequier Island in Aboukir Bay

there, gun-flashes and blazing ships lit up the soft Egyptian night, and they took up their position. 'Each knew his duty,' said Nelson. 'I was sure each would feel for a French ship.'

Brueys's *L'Orient*, her hold stuffed with treasure, was in the centre of his line, and it fell to the *Bellerophon* to attack her. The *Bellerophon* was a 74-gun ship, twelve years old, and much knocked about already. The *L'Orient* had the pick of the French fleet, carried 120 guns, and her strength was enormous. Her early broadsides nearly blew the British out of the water. Within the first hour and a half, Captain Darby and every officer had been either killed or wounded, and the *Bellerophon* was forced from the line, almost dismasted and a wreck. She was saved mainly by the initiative of a volunteer, Mr Hindmarsh, who managed somehow to hoist a scrap of sail and make off into the darkness. Shaken as the *Bellerophon* was, she had done her work. The *L'Orient* was on fire, and her

LEFT: *A dramatic reconstruction of the most awe-inspiring incident in the battle, the explosion of* L'Orient, *the French flagship, by Mather Brown* (c *1763–1831*)

teeth were so drawn that she became an easy prey for the *Alexander* and *Swiftsure* who, one on each side, made her survival unlikely.

After the *Vanguard* had been engaged for some time with the *Spartiate*, Nelson was wounded. A piece of iron shot hit his forehead, above his sightless eye. He streamed with blood, and he was forced to go below, believing himself to have but a brief time to live. He refused to claim attention before the 'brave fellows' who were already in the sick berth, which was the sort of consideration which is never forgotten, but the surgeon soon reassured him that, although messy and painful, his injury was not serious. Nelson returned on deck, to view the most terrible incident of a tremendous night.

At about ten o'clock it was seen that fires on the French flagship were spreading beyond control, and that men had begun to throw themselves into the water. Suddenly, with a roar so shattering that every ship in the harbour believed she had herself been struck, the ship blew up. This marked the one great, unnatural, awe-inspired pause in the battle. After a shower of flaming debris had descended, some of it setting fire to sails in the

Nelson, his head bandaged, attends prayers on board his ship, the Vanguard, *after the battle. A coloured aquatint after J. A. Atkinson, published in 1816*

Alexander, men sank down by their guns, exhausted. There they slept 'side by side, as it were, of their sleeping enemy', as a captain described it. When battle was resumed, only two French ships of the line and two frigates were left unsunk, ungrounded or untaken. They were beating out of the Bay in charge of Rear-Admiral Pierre Villeneuve, whom Bonaparte was later to call a lucky man!

The state of Aboukir Bay as dawn broke on 2 August 1798 was one of the most extraordinary in history. 'Victory is not a name strong enough for such a scene,' said Nelson, and as usual he was right. He had achieved his masterpiece, and in his letter to Lord Howe he said: 'Had it pleased God that I had not been wounded and stone-blind, there cannot be a doubt but that every ship would have been in our possession.' Then, thinking that perhaps this implied a reflection on his 'Band of Brothers', he added: 'But here let it not be supposed that any Officer is to blame. No; on my honour, I am satisfied each did his very best.' The 'bests' may have differed, but even the least of them was creditable by any standard. Nelson's captains had set an example for all time, and the admiral himself, in Conrad's words, had 'brought heroism into the line of duty'.

Nelson always preached completion. It was not enough to beat your foe, as Howe had done on the Glorious First of June: the matter must be pursued relentlessly, the harvest gathered in. After giving thanks to the God in whom he believed so trustingly, Nelson set about the business of exploiting his triumph. Ships were repaired, prizes made sea-worthy, despatches written (in duplicate, a wise precaution, as the originals were captured in the *Leander*), a blockade of the coast was organized, and an officer was sent to India to notify the East India Company of the result of the battle. The effects of Nelson's success would undoubtedly be felt in India, and the gratitude of the Directors was such that they sent Nelson a present of £10,000.

Not only was the victory one in which consummate skill and judgment had been shown; its effect upon Europe was electric. It was the first major reverse Bonaparte had suffered. The French army was cut off in Egypt, and although, given luck, the Commander-in-Chief, by deserting his army, might escape, it would be secretly. His idea of an advance towards India was for ever shattered.

A few months after the battle Captain Collingwood, then commanding HMS *Excellent*, wrote to a relative from Portsmouth: 'I know, my dear Sir, what joy you would feel at the unparalleled victory of Nelson. It was indeed a charming thing. It was the promptitude as much as the vigour of the attack which gave him the superiority so very soon; the Frenchman found himself assailed before he had determined how best he should repel the assault, and when victory had decided on our side the fruits of it were carefully gathered in.'

This was the professional judgment of a brother officer. Other tributes were more sensational: for instance when Lord Spencer, then at the head of the Admiralty, heard the news of Nelson's exploit, he fell to the floor in a faint, so severe had been his anxiety. Nelson won a peerage, and honours from many sovereigns. Much more: he established a place in the hearts of his countrymen, even of mankind, which he has never lost.

LEFT: *HMS* Foudroyant, *which long survived Nelson's own era, served as his flagship in the Mediterranean after the Battle of the Nile*

Elephant off Copenhagen
3rd April 1801.

Sir,

Elephant
Defiance
Monarch
Bellona
Edgar
Russel
Ganges
Glatton
Isis
Agamemnon
Polyphemus
Ardent

Amazon
Desiree
Blanche
Alcmene
———
Sloops.
Dart
Arrow
Cruizer
Harpy
Fire Ships
Zephyr
Otter.
Bombs
Discovery

    In obedience to your
directions to report the proceedings
of the Squadron (named in the Margin)
which you did me the honor to place
under my Command.

    I beg leave to inform
you, that having by the Assistance
of that Able Officer Captain Riou and the
unremitting exertions of Captain ~
Brisbane, and the Masters of the Amazon
and Cruizer (in particular) buoyed
the Channel of the outer deep, and
the ~~~~~~~~ of the middle Ground, the
~~~ Squadron
passed in safety, and anchored off
Draco the Evening of the 1st and that
Yesterday Morning I made the Signal
for the Squadron to Weigh and to
engage the Danish line, consisting
of seven Sail of the line, ten floating
batteries mounting from 26, 24 pounders
to 18, 18 pounders, and one Bomb Ship,
besides Schooner Gun Vessels ~~~ were
supported by the Crown Islands mounting 88 Cannon, and four Sail of the line
moored in the harbours mouth, and
some batteries on the Island of ~
Amack,
    The Bomb Ship and Schooner
              Gun

Sir Hyde Parker Bart.

Copenhagen

1801

Nelson, in a celebrated incident in naval history, affected not to see Sir Hyde Parker's signal for recall and continued action until he compelled the Danes to agree to terms

IN A PROTRACTED STRUGGLE AT SEA, neutrals usually profit, but they expose themselves to war risks which sometimes lead to ugly incidents, and even to spreading the conflict.

In 1800, while Nelson was settling the affairs of Naples and Sicily before returning to England, a crisis occurred between Britain and Denmark. The Danish *Freja*, of 40 guns, was met off Ostend, while escorting six merchant-men, by an English squadron, whose commander insisted on a search for contraband of war. Krabbe, the Danish captain, refused, and fired on an English boat. An action began, and after half an hour the *Freja* struck her colours. She was taken, with her convoy, to the Downs, but was left under her own flag. Lord Whitworth was sent to Copenhagen, and on 29 August an agreement was arrived at whereby the *Freja* should be repaired, at British charge, and should be released together with her convoy. The whole vexed question of belligerents' right of search would be discussed later, in plenary session.

Peace between Denmark and Britain had been pre-served for the time, but it was not to last. Paul I, Emperor of Russia, had conceived an intense admiration for Bonaparte's military genius, and an almost equal dis-like for the British. Paul, who had become titular Grand Master of the Knights of Malta, had been angered at French seizure of the island, but Bonaparte, realizing

LEFT: *A secretary's copy of Nelson's despatch to Sir Hyde Parker, describing the action of 2 April 1801*

that the fall of Valetta was inevitable, offered to transfer the island to the Tsar. The idea worked upon his vanity to such an extent that when, on 5 September 1800, the island fell to the blockaders, and when the British showed no sign of withdrawing, Paul retaliated by seizing all British ships in Russian ports. He did more. In December of the same year, in concert with the Danes, Swedes and Prussians, he revived the idea of an Armed Neutrality of the North, specifically to resist Britain's claims. This was equivalent to a threat of war, and Britain's circum-stances were such that she had no choice but to act.

Nelson had landed at Great Yarmouth on 6 November, and was re-employed almost at once with the Channel Fleet. On 17 February 1801 he was ordered to place him-self under the command of Admiral Sir Hyde Parker, in a force destined for the Baltic. On 2 March he left Spithead to join his new chief.

Nelson was not pleased. He felt the cold acutely after years of the Mediterranean sun; his eyes were inflamed; his marriage had broken up; and the prospect of a campaign in the Baltic, an area he had not visited since he had been a junior captain, was uninviting. Nor did Parker's character reassure him. Parker was very senior – he was nearly twenty years older than Nelson – very rich, and he had recently married a young wife irreverently known in the fleet as 'batter pudding'. Nelson had served with him before, and had not been impressed by his capacity. Finally, he felt slighted. Was this a fit assignment for a Vice-Admiral of the Blue who had

Sir Hyde Parker (1739–1807), a mezzotint after George Romney, painted in 1779 when Parker was a Captain. He was relieved of his command when the news of Copenhagen reached London

Horatio Nelson in the year of Copenhagen, a portrait by G. Shepperton after John Hoppner. He had lost the sight of his right eye in 1794, but the damage was not easily apparent to artists and public

proved himself a masterly tactician, and a man, more-over, able to handle greater affairs, as he had shown by his vision and skill immediately after the Nile? He suspected, with reason, that certain members of the Board of Admiralty wished to remove him from the influence of Lady Hamilton, with whom he had returned home, old Sir William Hamilton in tow.

Parker, as Nelson had expected, was reluctant to sail, but his armament was formidable: twenty-six of the line, seven frigates and twenty-three smaller vessels. It needed to be so, for in theory Russia had 48 battleships in the Baltic, Denmark had 28, and Sweden 12. Actualities were different. If Parker could intimidate one Power before the three could combine, he would have done his work, and Denmark was the obvious place to start.

Vansittart, a foreign service envoy, had been sent ahead in a frigate in an attempt to detach Denmark from her allies, but no great hope was built on his success. Parker anchored just outside the Sound on 21 March. Two days later, Vansittart reported failure. The Danes were getting ready to defend their capital.

Now, at once, was the time to act. So Nelson urged; but he found it as difficult to gain Parker's confidence as to stir him into movement, and it was not until 30 March that the Fleet was away. Parker had been told by the Governor of Kronborg, on the Danish shore of the Sound, that he would resist the British passage, and at seven o'clock shore-guns opened fire. A few British ships replied, but Parker moved over to the Swedish side,

RIGHT: *An engraving of the principal Danish officers who served in the Battle of Copenhagen, together with a sketch of the battle and a memorial to those killed in the action*

made his run safely, and about noon came to an anchor near Hven.

As soon as it became clear that the British would reach the Baltic before the northern countries could coalesce, the Danes gave their energies to preparation. Eighteen ships of varying strength were moored in a line stretching southwards from the Trekroner battery along the shore of Amager Island. In Copenhagen harbour itself were blockships, also the nucleus of an active fleet, ready to serve where occasion required.

During the afternoon of 30 March, Parker, Nelson and Rear-Admiral Thomas Graves (the latter a cousin of the man who had fought at Chesapeake Bay), reconnoitred the Danish position. As a result of his observation, Nelson offered to lead an attack with ten of the smaller ships of the line and the lighter vessels. Parker accepted the proposal, adding two more ships. He himself would take station off the mouth of the harbour, ready to deal with any Danes who might put to sea. His heavy ships would be likely to ground in shallow water, and his dispositions were sensible. Graves would go with Nelson.

Amager, a natural protection to Copenhagen, has a sister island to the east. The channel between them is divided by a shoal, known as the Middle Ground. The Danish line ran along the edge of the western channel, and Nelson intended to attack from the south.

On the morning of 1 April the whole fleet left the anchorage at Hven, re-anchoring near the northern end of the Middle Ground. At about 1 pm, with the wind at north-west, Nelson's ships got under way again, and at night-fall anchored just east of the southernmost point of the shoal. Captain Thomas Masterman Hardy, whom Nelson had brought with him from the *St George*, his regular flagship, to the smaller *Elephant*, from which he would direct the assault, went by boat, during the hours of darkness, to investigate the channel. At eleven o'clock he returned with the opinion that the intended attack was feasible. All that was needed was a change of wind, and Nelson spent the rest of the night, with a number of his captains and some diligent clerks, dictating orders.

The battleships were to proceed in line ahead. As at the Nile, they were to anchor by the stern on reaching their appointed stations. The Trekroner battery was to be engaged by the *Russell* and the *Polyphemus*. The frigates, under Captain Riou of the *Amazon*, were to help in the attacks on the northernmost ships. Bomb vessels were to take station to starboard of the battleships in the centre of the line, and gun-brigs were to be employed against

RIGHT: *The Battle of Copenhagen by Nicholas Pocock, painted in 1806. It shows the two fleets engaged, with the city in the background*

A Danish line-engraving, viewing the action from the island of Amager, with the dockyard in the foreground. The normal work of the dockyard continued even during the height of the action

Captain Edward Riou (1758–1801), a portrait by John Jackson. Riou was killed after engaging the great Trekroner battery with his small frigates

the southernmost Danes. Nelson's twelve 74's had the duty of reducing eighteen moored ships of varying size, plus the Trekroner battery, which mounted 66 guns. He would need the help of every single vessel which could be brought into action, for the advantage of situation lay with the Danes: they had supplies and their city behind them, and they had been given essential time.

Nelson got his favourable wind next day, and soon after nine o'clock on 2 April his ships were under way. An hour and a half later the *Provesteen* opened fire on the *Edgar*, and action began. The first four British ships took up their positions exactly, but then things began to go wrong.

First the *Agamemnon*, a 64-gun ship in which, years before, Nelson had made his name, failed to weather the tip of the Middle Ground. Then the *Bellona*, 74 guns, kept too far to starboard, and ran aground. So did the *Russell*, 74 guns, which was following her closely. The *Bellona* was in charge of a Nile captain, Sir Thomas Thompson formerly of the *Leander*, and both his ship and the *Russell* could use their guns, though not to much effect. Perhaps it was as well, for Thompson's were so old that some of them burst, killing their crews.

On seeing these misfortunes, Nelson re-formed the remaining ships, and it was for this reason that Riou, with the lightly armed frigates, found himself trying to subdue the fire of the great fixed battery, the Trekroner. It would have been a stiff task for ships of the line; it was a hopeless one for Riou, though he would never have admitted it. The bomb-vessels were able to take some part in the action, but the gun-brigs failed to round the shoal.

Parker's heavy ships, at the northern end of the Middle Ground, were by now beating up towards the head of the Danish line. Their progress was slow, and it soon seemed clear to Parker that Nelson was meeting much more resistance than had been expected. The *Agamemnon* could be seen, distantly, aground, and the *Bellona* and *Russell* were flying signals of distress. At about 1.15 pm Parker signalled to Nelson, 'Discontinue action'.

The result, which was described by Colonel Stuart, senior officer of the soldiers serving with Nelson's detachment, is one of the more celebrated incidents in naval history, and is fully in keeping with Nelson's whole outlook. When the signal was hoist, the admiral, said Stuart, 'continued his walk, and did not appear to take notice of it. The (signal) lieutenant meeting his Lordship at the next turn asked whether he should repeat it? Lord Nelson answered, "No, acknowledge it." On the officer returning to the Poop, his Lordship called after him: "Is No. 16 (for close action) still hoisted?" The lieutenant answering in the affirmative, Lord Nelson said, "Mind you keep it so." He now walked the deck considerably agitated, which was always known by his moving the stump of his right arm. After a turn or two he said to me, in a quick manner: "Do you know what's shown on board the commander-in-chief – No. 39." On asking him what that meant he said: "Why to leave off action." "Leave off action!" he repeated, and then added with a shrug, "Now, damn me if I do!" He also observed, I believe to Captain Foley, "You know, Foley, I have only one eye – I have a right to be blind sometimes": and then with an archness peculiar to his character, putting the glass to his blind eye, he exclaimed: "I really do not see the signal".'

Unfortunately Riou did, and with the remark, 'What will Nelson think of us?', he prepared to obey it. As the stern of his frigate wore round, she was raked by the Trekroner, and Riou himself was cut in two.

If ever disobedience was justified, it was Nelson's at Copenhagen. The *Dannebrog*, the enemy flagship, was on fire, and at 12.30, with nearly a third of her men killed or wounded, and all but three of her guns disabled, her flag was hauled down. Commodore Fischer moved to the

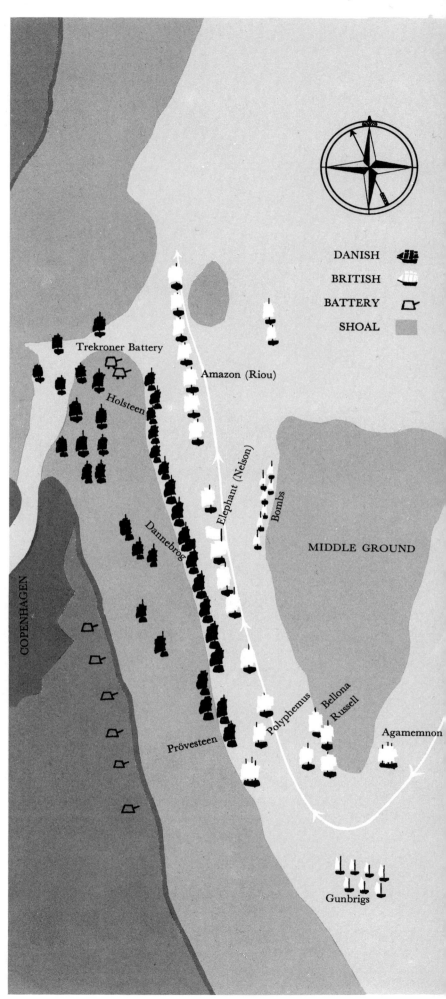

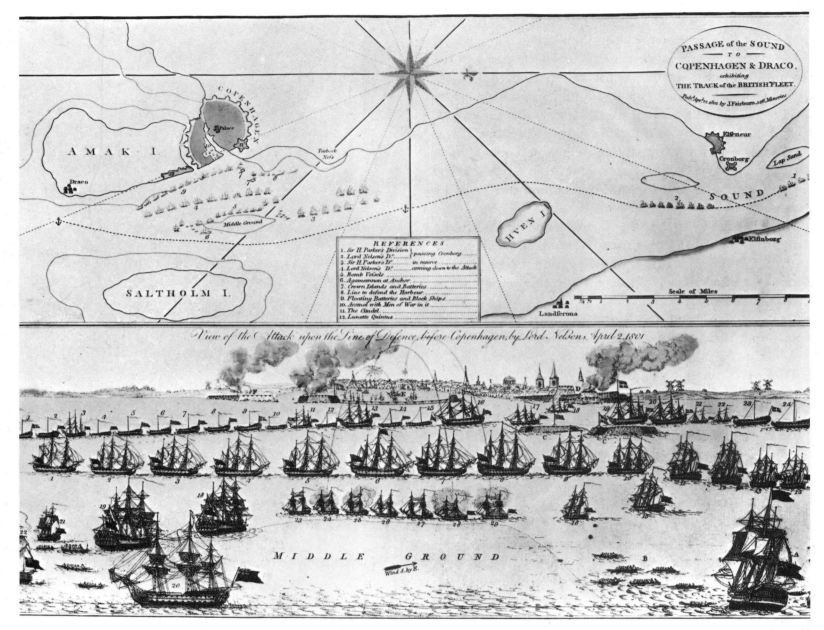

A plate published by J. Fairburn three weeks after the battle, showing the line of approach of Parker's fleet from the Sound to Copenhagen, and details of Nelson's tactical dispositions

Holstein of 60 guns, and when she in her turn was disabled, to the Trekroner. Everywhere, fire was slackening, and at about two o'clock Nelson sent ashore a flag of truce with a note addressed to the Danish Crown Prince. This he was careful to seal, so that no sign of haste should appear. He demanded to be allowed to take possession of his prizes, saying that if he were not permitted to do so unmolested he would be compelled to burn them without being able to remove their crews.

The Crown Prince sent his Adjutant General across to the *Elephant*, upon which Nelson hoisted a white flag, and sent a message ashore saying that he *consented* to an armistice until he could remove or burn his prizes, and that, on conditions, he would land the wounded Danes. Nelson sent the officer on to Parker, who was then some four miles away, in order to draw up a more definite

agreement. Seeing the flag of truce hoisted, the Crown Prince ordered a cease-fire. The action was over by a little after three o'clock, but the burning *Dannebrog* later blew up, like *L'Orient* at the Nile.

Nelson thought of Copenhagen as his severest action, and the casualties on both sides were heavy indeed. The British lost 253 killed in action, (rather more than at the Nile), and had 688 wounded. The Danes had 790 killed, not all of them regular men-of-warsmen. They had nine hundred wounded, and two thousand were made prisoners of war. Twelve Danish ships were captured.

As soon as battle ended, Nelson set to work to get his ships out of range of the Danish batteries, but in the course of joining up with Parker both the *Elephant* and Graves's *Defiance* went aground near the Trekroner. The *Désirée*, going to the help of the *Bellona* and *Russell*, got

The British fleet off Elsinore in their passage of the Sound, a vital moment in their approach to Copenhagen. A coloured aquatint after Nicholas Pocock

into difficulties herself, and the general situation of the British fleet was such that it was fortunate that the armistice was extended.

With Denmark immobilized, Parker had Sweden and Russia to deal with. He anchored in Kjoge Bay on 18 April, having sent frigates ahead into the Baltic to discover the whereabouts of the Swedish fleet. Palmquist, the Swedish admiral, was encountered off Bornholm, but he had by then received orders to return to Carlskrona. He did this, mooring his ships in a line across the harbour. Parker arrived off the port on 20 April, and was assured that Sweden, while not prepared to abandon her allies, was ready to come to terms if a satisfactory agreement could be reached.

Parker then started for Revel, intending to face the most formidable Baltic power, but three days after leaving Carlskrona he had word from the Russian Minister at Copenhagen to say that Paul I had been murdered, and that his successor, Alexander I, had ordered his fleet to abstain from hostilities. By a 'home stroke', Britain had made her point, and she could continue her great struggle with France with one less distraction.

The Baltic expedition of 1801 had a sequel six years later, when the danger recurred of a Danish fleet being added to the forces arrayed by Napoleon against Britain. On this occasion the naval Commander-in-Chief was Admiral Gambier, a man who had fought with great distinction at Howe's victory of 1794. Gambier brought 17,000 troops with him from England, and he arrived off Gothenburg on 1 August 1807, anchoring off Helsingor two days later.

The Danes had as yet no clue to Gambier's intentions, but as a precaution they began to put Copenhagen into a state of defence. A message was conveyed to the Danish Crown Prince, who was then at Kiel, stating that, since it was evident that his country would be forced to go over to the side of France, it was requested that the fleet be handed over to Britain until the conclusion of peace. If the conditions were accepted, Britain would protect Denmark from a French attack, but in the event of refusal the fleet would be taken by force and would be retained. Not unnaturally, such terms were rejected out of hand, and the Danish Crown Prince left at once for Copenhagen to organize the City's forces. By 13 August, Gambier received orders to proceed to active measures.

There was fighting by land and sea, and this time, since they had with them a substantial army, the British were able to mount a regular siege. Early in September they were in a position to bombard the Danish capital. Resistance was stubborn, but by 5 September great fires had devastated part of the city, and the Danish General Peymann sent to ask for a truce as a preliminary to capitulation. Gambier insisted on the surrender of the Danish fleet as essential to any arrangement, but the bombardment ceased, and on the morning of 7 September a convention was signed, by the terms of which the fleet and its stores were ceded, and all hostilities ceased.

Late in October, the last of the British troops re-embarked, and the Danish ships were sailed for England. Both expeditions to Denmark are remembered with some bitterness in that country, but Britain was fighting for her life against a continent armed against her, and with power in the hands of the most ruthless and brilliant leader France ever produced. Necessity knows no law, but of all types of war, that which has become known as 'preventative' is one of the least satisfactory. The weaker side can feel little but humiliation, while the stronger has none of the elation which follows victory against a well matched or superior enemy.

A Queen Anne crown, the reverse engraved immediately after the Battle of Copenhagen, with a memento of the occasion

A sketch by Rowlandson of a midshipman of Nelson's day. A sextant, lightly pencilled in, is carried in his left hand

RIGHT: *The dramatic destruction of the* Dannebrog, *the Danish flagship. A coloured aquatint after J. T. Serres (1759–1825)*

Trafalgar
1805

*The last and greatest of Nelson's victories, which destroyed the main Franco-Spanish fleet,
ensured British command of the sea for the rest of the war*

THERE HAD BEEN NO RESPITE FOR Nelson after the ardours of Denmark. The Admiralty had superseded Parker as soon as news of the battle reached them, putting Nelson in his place. It was an unwelcome step to him, for he bore no resentment against his chief, and his health was such that, now that there was no need for further active measures in the Baltic, he would have wished to return home. For once their Lordships met his wishes without demur, perhaps more for the reason that they had a new use for his services than because they wished to gratify him. Hardly had he arrived home than he was put in charge of the seaward defences of his country. His orders were to organize the flotillas and 'sea fencibles' which would be a principal means of defeating any attempt at invasion on the part of the Grand Army which Bonaparte had encamped about Boulogne.

The appointment brought Nelson little but frustration, and the one attack which he mounted on Boulogne itself – another of those 'home-strokes' in which he so much believed, like Drake and other notable leaders before him – failed disastrously on the night of 15 August 1801. The French were thoroughly prepared, and the assault was beaten off with loss. It was Nelson's last service before the Treaty of Amiens, signed in May 1802, brought a brief respite in the titanic struggle. The Treaty in fact held good for one year only, and settled nothing. It gave

the main protagonists, the principal land and sea Powers, a breathing space in an exhausting war, but when the conflict re-opened, Bonaparte's huge army was still encamped on the shore of the Channel, ready for the day when French sailors would secure at least temporary command of the sea, and so enable it to cross.

The bed-rock of British defence was, as ever, her home fleet. It was commanded by William Cornwallis, whose station was off the western end of the Channel. Cornwallis, who like Nelson was a disciple of Hawke, believed in a close watch upon Brest in all weathers, and while he had charge of affairs, matters at sea in the northern area were in the safest hands.

The French Mediterranean Fleet, with its base at Toulon, was soon to become Nelson's own settled object. The day after war was renewed, he was given the command he would have chosen, and on 18 May he hoisted his flag in the great three-decker *Victory*, which had been laid down during the Seven Years' War, when he had been a child, and which had carried the flags of most of the leading admirals of her era. He rarely left her during the remaining years of his life. She became his stately home, fit to carry the flag of a man as steadfast on watch as in battle.

It was an axiom of Monck, hero of the Four-Days' Battle, and one which applied equally to the admiral's as the general's art, that

LEFT: *Nelson embarks for his last campaign; a popular reconstruction of the scene at Portsmouth, by Andrew Gow*

if a man faint under the burden of such tediousness as usually attendeth upon warlike designments, he is in no way

171

fit for enterprise: because the two chief parts of a soldier are Valour and Sufferance; and there is as much honour gained by suffering wants patiently in war, as by fighting valiantly, and as great achievements effected by the one, as by the other . . . and yet it is an easier matter to find men that will offer themselves willingly to death, than such as will endure Labour with patience.

Labour and patience were now Nelson's lot. The campaign which ended at Trafalgar had a resounding climax, but it began with a long spell in the Gulf of Lions, and so it continued through the years 1803, 1804, and much of 1805. Admiral Mahan, Nelson's generous American biographer, stated the case in words which have become renowned: 'They were dull, weary, eventless months,' he wrote of the ceaseless, silent pressure of Nelson's navy, 'those months of watching and waiting of the big ships before the French arsenals. Purposeless they surely seemed to many, but they saved England. The world has never seen a more impressive demonstration of the influence of sea-power upon its history. Those far distant, storm-beaten ships, upon which the Grand Army never looked, stood between it and the domination of the world.'

Nelson seldom had enough ships for the work in hand, but it was his way to make full use of what he had, and at last his transcendent services had brought him the post he deserved. The Mediterranean, observed St Vincent, required 'an officer of splendour'. She now received one.

As time passed, and Spain once more joined the war on his side, Bonaparte conceived what he believed to be a masterly scheme. His blockaded squadrons should escape, from Toulon, from the Biscay ports, from Brest, they should be joined by Spaniards from Cartagena and Cadiz, and the forces should combine in the West Indies in a huge armada, far surpassing anything dreamed of by Philip of Spain. The Admirals should sail back to Europe, sweeping everything before them by sheer numbers, and gain command of the Straits of Dover. Then, at Bonaparte's signal, the soldiers should cross. Under his commanding genius, the issue could not be in doubt. Britain, the seemingly unconquerable, would become his vassal.

Bonaparte, despite the rude experience of his fleet at Aboukir Bay, continued to treat his sailors like generals. He made no allowance for the element in which they worked, and paid scant regard to possible reactions by the enemy. This was natural in the world's greatest soldier, but it was misguided. Even so there were times when it looked as if some at least of his plans might succeed, for not once but twice, early in 1805, his 'lucky' Admiral Villeneuve escaped from Toulon.

The first venture came to nothing: the French returned, battered by weather which Nelson had had to face since 1803. Nelson, when he knew that Villeneuve had eluded him, fearing that Egypt might once more be Bonaparte's ambition, made a false cast, and sailed all the way to Alexandria. He found the port deserted, as he had done once before, in 1798, and he returned dejected. So old a hand at war should not, he felt, have made that particular mistake.

The lesson was well learnt. When Villeneuve got away a second time, Nelson waited off Sardinia, and it was there, in a favourite anchorage, that he had the news he most dreaded. Villeneuve had been seen to pass through the Straits of Gibraltar on 8 April – ten days earlier – and it appeared possible that he might have picked up the Spaniards from Cartagena on his way. It was one of the darkest hours in Nelson's life. He had had his fill of 'Sufferance'. Was he to be denied his hour of Valour?

It was not until 4 May that Nelson was able to provision off Tetuan, for the winds were foul. Two days later he anchored off Gibraltar, and he sailed the same evening. His problem was complex, for not only had he to guess the enemy's direction, but he had to give cover to an expeditionary force under General Craig, destined for the Mediterranean. Having seen Craig safe, and knowing that Cornwallis was in strength to the north, Nelson made for the West Indies.

Again his luck was out. He made a good passage to Barbados, and would have pushed on to Martinique had not faulty intelligence sent him south to Trinidad. He found nothing. This was all the more mortifying since Nelson himself never believed Trinidad to have been an object of Villeneuve's, but he could not disregard what seemed to be unimpeachable evidence from an army officer with whom he had served before, and in whom he had confidence.

Villeneuve, after summoning such Spaniards as were ready at Cadiz, had made his crossing, though his ships were not in the best order. Then, hearing that Nelson was on his heels, instead of waiting for the French Atlantic squadrons which Bonaparte had told him to expect, he sped back to Europe. Nelson, when he learnt the Frenchman's movements, sent a fast brig direct to England, her captain having orders to warn the Admiralty. The brig actually sighted the Allied fleet on passage, and was thus able to give the latest news to Whitehall.

Nelson returned to Gibraltar, a bitterly disappointed man. He had leave to return home, and made use of the

RIGHT: *A print after a painting by T. Davidson, showing the quarter-deck of the* Victory *at the time when Nelson's signal 'England Expects that Every Man will do his Duty' was about to be hoisted*

A popular print, published by Edward Orme in 1806, showing Nelson with his Trafalgar captains explaining his tactics for winning the forthcoming battle

chance, taking with him the *Superb*, which needed docking. Meanwhile Lord Barham, then head of the Admiralty, ordered a strong squadron under Sir Robert Calders to intercept the Combined Fleet when, as was expected, it made a landfall off Cape Finisterre.

By the time Nelson anchored at Spithead, Calder had fought his action, but Villeneuve, undefeated, was safe in Ferrol. Calder was amazed at the outcry which resulted from what he considered a success. Had he not, with an inferior force, taken two Spanish ships? What had escaped him was the fact that the days of the creditable but indecisive fleet action were over: that at the Nile Nelson had preached the gospel of total war, and that – at least while Nelson lived – his fellow admirals would be judged by his standards. It was hard on them no doubt, but war is a hard business, and it is better to learn ruthlessness from friends and colleagues than from the hands of the enemy.

Nelson spent twenty-five days in England, at his home at Merton and in London: then, on 14 September 1805, he re-hoisted his flag on board the *Victory*. Barham had pressed him to resume his command, and he could not refuse. Villeneuve and his fleet had by now moved south to Cadiz, watched by a squadron under Collingwood. 'Depend upon it, Blackwood,' said Nelson to his best frigate captain, who brought him news of the enemy, 'I shall yet give Monsieur Villeneuve a beating.'

Nelson made no secret of his tactical plan. He wrote about it officially and unofficially, and discussed it with politicians as well as with fellow-officers over the dinner-table. It became so familiar that it was even suspected by

RIGHT: *Monumental in scale and conception,* Trafalgar *by J. M. W. Turner (1775–1851), which was commissioned by George IV for the Painted Hall at Greenwich in 1824, ultimately derives from sketches made by the artist when the* Victory *returned to England after the battle*

The Redoutable *about to surrender in the closing stage of the battle. It was from this ship that Nelson was shot by a marksman in her fighting tops*

the enemy who, ever since the Nile, had studied Nelson's character and methods with the fascinated attention which was their due.

'One day,' said Captain Keats of the *Superb*, 'walking with Lord Nelson in the grounds at Merton, talking of naval affairs, he said to me:

"No day can be long enough to arrange a couple of Fleets and fight a decisive battle, according to the old system. When *we* meet them (I was to have been with him), for meet them we shall, I'll tell you how I shall fight them.

"I shall form the Fleet into three Divisions in three lines. One Division shall be composed of twelve or fourteen of the fastest two-decked ships, while I shall always keep to windward, or in a situation of advantage; and I shall put them under an officer who, I am sure, will employ them in the manner I wish, if possible. I consider it will always be in my power to throw them into Battle in any part I may choose;

but if circumstances prevent their being carried against the Enemy where I desire, I shall feel certain he will employ them effectively, and perhaps in a more advantageous manner than if he could have followed my orders.

"With the remaining part of the Fleet formed in two lines, I shall go at them at once, if I can, about one third of their line from the leading Ship." He then said: "What do you think of it?" Such a question I felt required consideration. I paused. Seeing it, he said: "But I'll tell you what *I* think of it. I think it will surprise and confound the enemy. They won't know what I am about. It will bring forward a pell-mell battle, and that is what I want." '

That, indeed, was not only the core of the matter – but Keats had caught something of Nelson's infectious enthusiasm. The *Superb* could not be ready in time, Keats missed the battle, and Nelson would not have enough

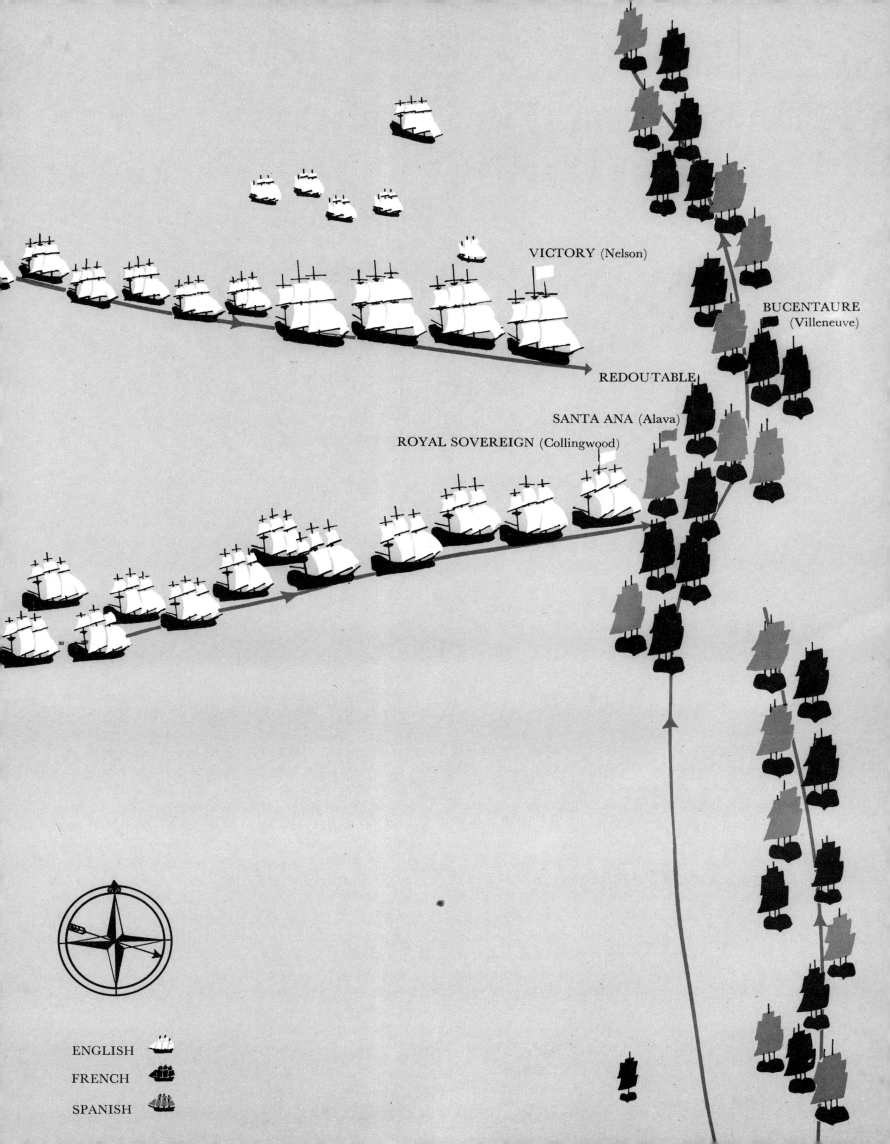

VICTORY (Nelson)

BUCENTAURE
(Villeneuve)

REDOUTABLE

SANTA ANA (Alava)

ROYAL SOVEREIGN (Collingwood)

ENGLISH

FRENCH

SPANISH

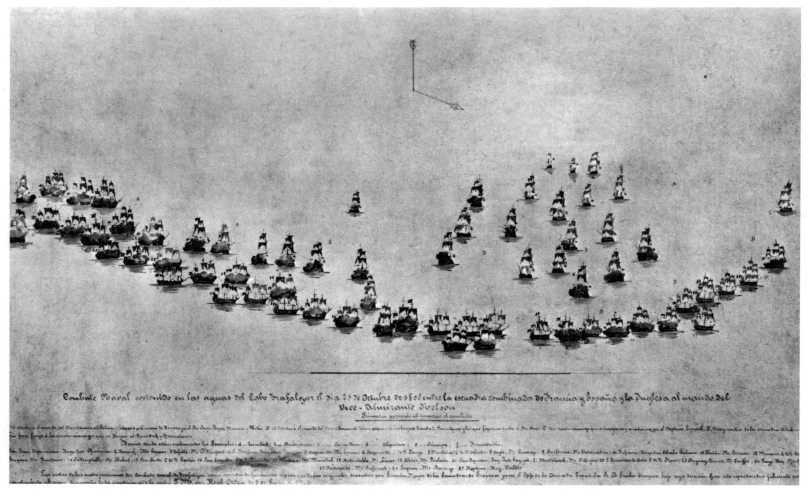

A version of the formation of the rival fleets as battle was joined by the officer who served as Chief-of-Staff to the Spanish Admiral Gravina

ships to form his flying division, but the mode of attack held good, even to the element of surprise. Villeneuve, though he knew, and wrote, that Nelson 'will not trouble to form line parallel to our own and fight it out with the Gun . . . he will try to double our rear, cut through the line, and bring against the ships thus isolated, groups of his own to surround and capture them', did not know all the details of Nelson's idea, which was so daring, tactically, so unlike anything which had gone before, and which would be so inappropriate as a model for lesser leaders that it could be regarded as a plan to succeed only once, under particular circumstances, and with a fleet incontestibly superior not in numbers but in fortitude, gunnery, seamanship and training.

The *Victory* joined the fleet off Cadiz on 28 September, and Nelson infused it with a new zeal. 'The reception I met with,' he said, 'caused the sweetest sensation of my life.' He added: 'I believe my arrival was most welcome to every individual . . . and when I came to explain the "Nelson touch" (his plan) it was like an electric shock. Some shed tears, all approved. "It was new – it was singular – it was simple!", and from admirals downwards,

it was repeated: "It must succeed, if ever they will allow us to get at them!"'

Some of the more experienced captains did not believe that the Combined Fleet would leave port. The season was late, and Villeneuve might stay snug the whole winter. Nelson thought it would prove otherwise, and Bonaparte played into his hands, first by ordering Villeneuve to make his way into the Mediterranean at the first opportunity, and then by sending another Admiral to supersede him. Bonaparte considered that Villeneuve's luck had deserted him: certainly his grandiose schemes for invasion were at an end. He would use his army another way. He would march it to the heart of the Continent, and add new victories to the many he had won before.

On 19 October, when Nelson had been granted a few necessary weeks in which to shape his fleet, Blackwood signalled from the frigate *Euryalus* that the enemy were on the move. What had happened was that Villeneuve, preparing for his sortie, had ordered part of his force to drive Blackwood and the inshore squadron away – Nelson kept his main force well out of sight. The French

A painting of the battle by George Chambers (1803–40) after Clarkson Stanfield, whose original was supervised by officers who had served in the action. In the right centre is the Victory, *with the* Redoutable *and the* Temeraire *alongside her to starboard*

move had not succeeded, but as the ships concerned in the operation could not get back, Villeneuve had no choice but to sail his entire force. He did not know Nelson's exact numbers – which were in fact twenty-seven available ships of the line, but he himself had thirty-three, fifteen of them Spanish, and he believed that, with such strength, he should be able to carry out his master's instructions.

When Nelson had news that the enemy were stirring, he was well out to sea. He signalled his ships to steer for the Straits of Gibraltar, intending to bar Villeneuve's passage to the Mediterranean. He was now sure of his destination. It was no time of the year for a French admiral to head north.

The night of 19 October and the day and night following it were spent in manoeuvre, Villeneuve struggling, not with marked success, to get his ships into proper order, Nelson still keeping his main strength out of sight, so that his adversary should commit himself irrevocably to an attempt to reach the mouth of the Straits.

At first light on 21 October, the Fleets were in sight of each other, Villeneuve still heading south. Nelson sig-

nalled his ships to dispose themselves as previously arranged, the windward column under his own direction, the leeward under that of Collingwood. There were light airs only, with a swell from the west presaging a storm, but the wind was rather north of west, which was what Nelson would have hoped.

As early as eight o'clock, Villeneuve reversed course. This was an action which Nelson would have expected, for as it was now impossible for the Combined Fleet to make good its passage past Gibraltar without a fight, Villeneuve's best plan was to return to Cadiz where – if a full scale clash could not be avoided – at least he could make good his damage afterwards.

The frigate captains were summoned to the *Victory*, to be given their final orders. These amounted to no more than that they were to tell the rear ships to get into action as well as they could, and as quickly, without regard to the formal 'Order of Sailing' which Nelson had drawn up. One of the captains said later, 'we scrambled into battle as best we could', a sentence which would have horrified that meticulous tactician Lord Howe and most earlier commanders-in-chief.

Nelson's famous prayer before battle was entered in his personal journal on 21 October 1805

The admiral then went the rounds of the *Victory*, praising all Hardy's arrangements and encouraging the crew. A considerable proportion were volunteers, their numbers including seventy-one foreigners of nearly every nationaality, among them twenty-two Americans, and three emigrant Frenchmen! When he had seen everything for himself, Nelson retired to his cabin, where Pasco, the signal lieutenant, found him on his knees. He was committing a prayer to his private diary which has since become part of the treasury of the English language:

'. . . May the Great God I worship,' Nelson wrote, 'grant to my Country, and for the benefit of Europe in general, a great and glorious Victory; and may no misconduct in any one tarnish it; and may humanity after Victory be the predominant feature in the British Fleet. For myself individually, I commit my life to Him who made me, and may His blessing light on my endeavours for serving my country faithfully. To Him I resign myself and the just cause which is entrusted me to defend. Amen. Amen. Amen.'

When Nelson returned to the upper deck, he said to Blackwood, 'I'll now amuse the Fleet with a signal,' asking if there was not one yet wanting. Blackwood said he thought everyone knew exactly what they were about, but Nelson held to his opinion. Pasco related that 'his Lordship came to me on the poop, and about a quarter to noon said: "I wish to say to the Fleet, ENGLAND CONFIDES THAT EVERY MAN WILL DO HIS DUTY", and he added, "You must be quick, for I have one more to make, which is for close action". I replied: "If your lordship will permit me to substitute *expects* for *confides*, the signal will soon be completed, because the word 'expect' is in the vocabulary, and 'confides' must be spelt". Nelson replied in haste, and with seeming satisfaction: "That will do, Pasco, make it directly".' It was thus that the Fleet went into action, Collingwood complaining (and he was not alone) that he wished his old friend would stop signalling, since they all knew their business well enough.

Trafalgar was unlike other great sea battles in many respects, one of them being that Nelson in the *Victory* and Collingwood in the *Royal Sovereign* led their respective lines. Collingwood was in action first, at about twelve o'clock, and for some moments, which seemed like eternity, he fought alone. 'See how that noble fellow Collingwood carries his ship into action', exclaimed Nelson – and indeed, the great three-decker, splendidly handled, was awe-inspiring to friend and foe alike. Soon,

RIGHT: *A. W. Devis (1763–1822) went on board the* Victory *on her return to Portsmouth to interview witnesses and make sketches for his famous painting,* The Death of Nelson. *Captain Hardy stands over the dying Admiral, Dr Beatty feels his pulse, and Scott, the Chaplain, rubs his chest*

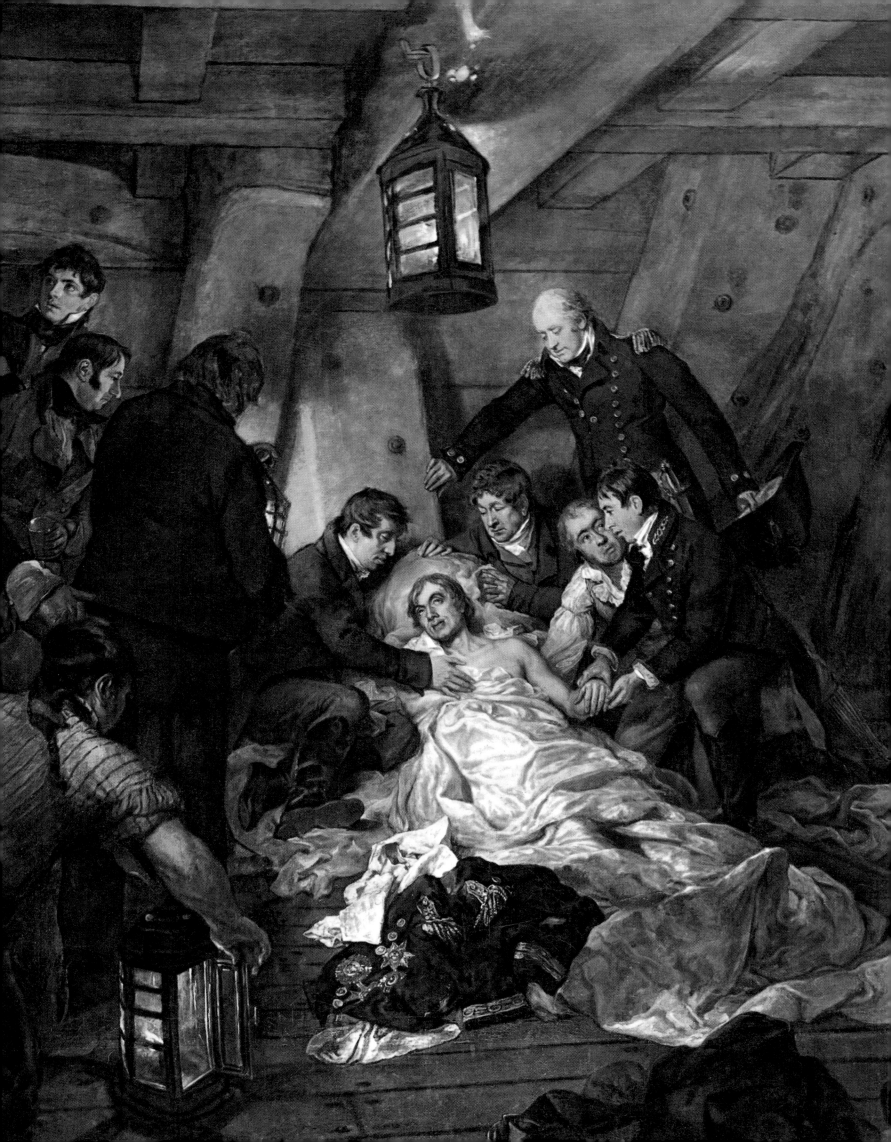

other ships in Collingwood's division were attacking the rear of the Combined Fleet, and before one o'clock the *Victory* herself was hotly engaged.

Everything went according to plan. The enemy line was pierced as Nelson had intended; their van ships could not turn to help those behind until decision had been reached in the centre and rear, and the most unorthodox battle of the sailing era burnt all through the autumn afternoon, until the Combined Fleet of France and Spain was reduced to utter disorganization.

At about 1.15, as he was pacing the quarter deck with Hardy, Nelson was hit through the shoulder by a bullet fired from the *Redoutable*, a French 74-gun ship which was superbly fought by Captain Lucas. 'They have done for me at last', said Nelson. 'My backbone is shot through!' He was carried below to the cockpit by Sergeant Secker of the Marines and a party of seamen, his face covered with a handkerchief, so that the ship's company should not be discouraged by seeing their admiral wounded.

Nelson lingered for some three hours, in great pain, but he lived to know from Hardy's lips the news he longed for – at least eighteen of the enemy had struck their colours. His own line had achieved its purpose of preventing interference with Collingwood, and Collingwood had smashed the allied rear. Villeneuve himself, and all his staff, were prisoners of war.

Having done his duty, as he said so often and so thankfully in his last moments, Nelson could die happy, and in the hour of his great fulfilment. He had achieved the end for which he had lived, and in the years of war with France which were still to come there was never again the need or indeed the chance for another full-scale encounter at sea. In effect if not quite in appearance, the enemy were annihilated, and the dominating position achieved by the British fleet endured for more than a century.

Of the many records of Nelson's death, none is more simple, complete and formal than the sentence in which it is described in the log of the *Victory*. 'Partial firing continued until 4.30,' so runs the record, 'when a victory having been reported to the Right Honourable Lord Viscount Nelson KB and Commander-in-Chief, he then died of his wound.'

RIGHT TOP: *Admiral Villeneuve, Commander-in-Chief of the allied fleet at Trafalgar, had already survived Nelson's victory at the Nile, but died soon after his return to France in 1806*

RIGHT BOTTOM: *This portrait of Nelson's close friend and second-in-command at Trafalgar, Admiral Lord Collingwood, by Henry Howard, was commissioned posthumously to hang in the Painted Hall at Greenwich*

We'll teach you, you *mira see Frog
eaters what it is to board an English
Man of War, have you forgot the Battle of
the Nile already*

*D-mme Jack, why here we have
got both Parleevous & Dons at
the same time, upon us*

*what! you'll never do so again
eh I'll just take off a Wing or
two by way of Security*

det &c AN ENGLISH. SET-TOO, or *British Jars clearing the Deck of the* Temeraire *of French and Spaniards* .
*a Circumstance which occur'd during the Battle of Trafalgar 21 Oct 1805 which strongly marks the invincible spirit of British Seamen when engageing the Enimies of their
Country, the* Temeraire *was boarded by accident or design by a French Ship on one side and a Spaniard on the other, the Contest was Vigorous but in the End the
combin'd Ensigns where torn from the hoop and the British hoisted in their Stead*

A popular cartoon showing an imaginary scene on HMS Temeraire, *which was erroneously supposed to have been boarded by the enemy during
the battle*

Despite the magnitude of the success, only four prizes were brought into Gibraltar after the battle. A storm blew up such as Nelson had feared, and it was with difficulty that the battle-weary victors could save even their own ships. In the long run, it signified little. Collingwood would continue the work he had shared with his friend, and Nelson's genius and example would be remembered and revered by all future students of war. As Collingwood wrote, in words which arose from knowledge extending over most of Nelson's sea career: 'Lord Nelson is an incomparable man, a blessing to any country that is engaged in such a war . . . An enemy that commits a false step in his view is ruined, and it comes on him with an impetuosity that allows him no time to recover.' Collingwood wrote with thoughts in his mind of the Nile and Copenhagen. His words were prophetic of Nelson's last battle, in which he himself took so splendid a part.

*Nelson's flag-captain, Thomas Masterman Hardy, was the only senior
officer who served in all Nelson's principal battles, St Vincent, the Nile,
Copenhagen and Trafalgar. A portrait by an unknown artist*

Cross-section of HMS Victory

*Built to the design of Sir Thomas Slade, her keel was laid down at the
Old Single Dock, Chatham, on 23 July 1759, and she was launched on
7 May 1765. Preserved now at Portsmouth Dockyard, she flies the flag
of the Commander-in-Chief. This cross-section is drawn by Colin Mudie*

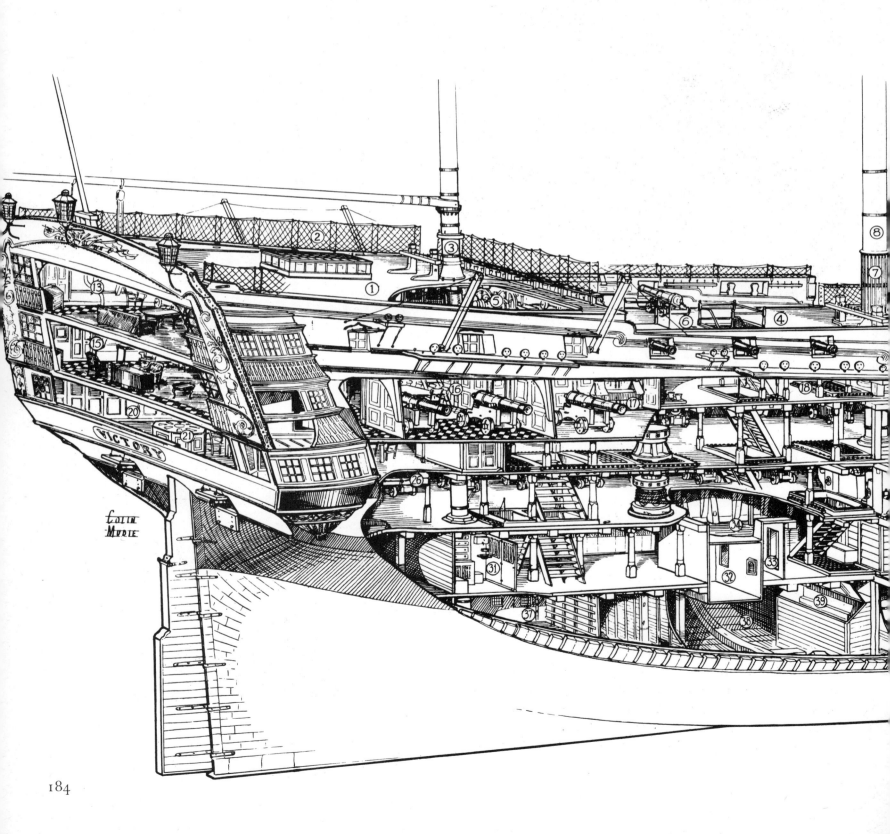

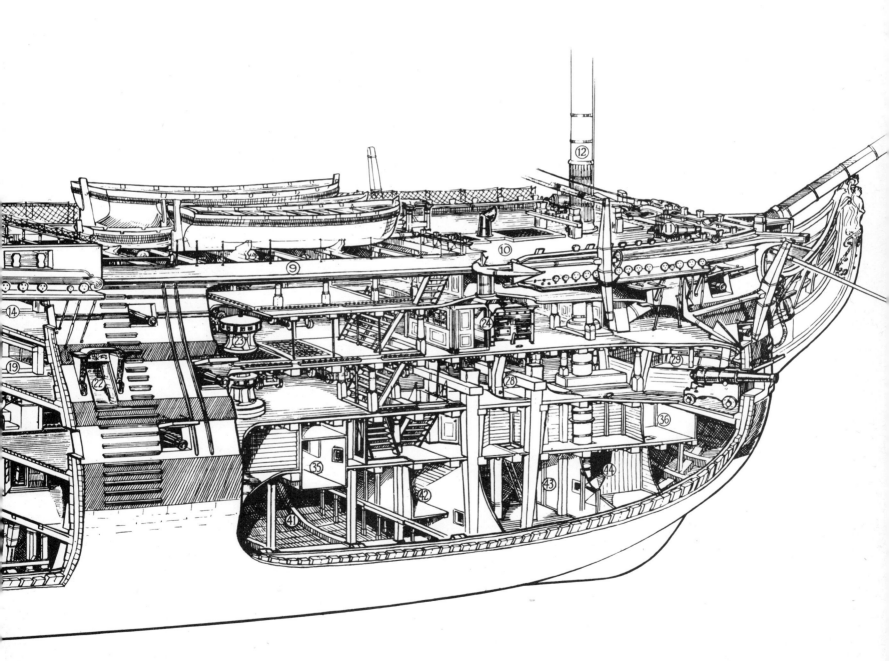

Lissa

1811

An action of the Napoleonic wars fought off the Dalmatian coast, notable for the French commander's imitation of Nelson's tactics at Trafalgar

WHEN NELSON COMMISSIONED the *Agamemnon* on the outbreak of war with France in 1793, he took with him to sea a number of youngsters from his own County of Norfolk. Among them was William Hoste, then twelve years old, who became one of his best officers. Hoste was slight but strong, quick and ardent; dark, with tousled hair. Everybody liked him.

The eager disciple served under Nelson in many battles, including St Vincent and the Nile, and he was a post-captain by the age of twenty-two. He never looked back, though he had the disappointment of being on detached duty at the time of Trafalgar. Hoste made his name in smaller ships of war, brigs and frigates, and it fits his character that his reputation derives from services, largely in independent command, in the comparatively isolated area of the Adriatic.

Hoste's greatest achievement was a victory on a miniature scale in which his largest ship carried only 38 guns. Its claim on remembrance is that it was won by an inferior force with an artistic completeness which would have satisfied Nelson. And by an odd chance, it showed how inappropriate were the tactics of Trafalgar when

LEFT: *The opening of the battle at Lissa, 1811. The closely formed line of the four British ships can be seen on the right, with the first Franco-Venetian ships coming in to attack*

OVERLEAF: *A general view of the action at Lissa, showing the starboard division of the Franco-Venetian forces bearing down under the stern of the* Amphion, *Commodore Hoste's flagship*

applied against an enemy compact, well prepared, and resolute.

Such control of the Adriatic as was possible to British forces, after the main decision in the war at sea had been reached, was exercised mainly by frigates. Since the littoral was in the hands of France or her dependants, and the nature of the coast-line, particularly on the eastern side, in what is now called Yugoslavia but which was then known as the Illyrian Provinces, favoured irregular warfare, the Adriatic provided scope for such a man as Hoste. He could exercise his initiative to the full.

It was during March 1811 that Hoste, with a commodore's pendant flying in the *Amphion*, a frigate given him by Nelson and long overdue for repairs, had his most famous encounter. He was making use of Lissa as a base and anchorage, and it was close upon the shores of that island that his little force, the *Amphion*, 32 guns, the *Active*, 38 guns, the *Volage*, 22 guns, and the *Cerberus*, 32 guns, sighted a squadron of French and Venetian ships – Venice having since 1797 been under French control – consisting of five frigates, a corvette, a brig, two schooners, a gunboat and a xebec.

Although saddled with such miscellaneous resources, the commodore, Dubordieu, who had crossed from his base at Ancona in the territory of the old Papal States, was able to put six of his ships into the line. His strength was imposing, for the *Favorite*, *Flore*, *Danae* and *Carona* all carried 44 guns; the *Bellona* had 32 and the *Carolina* 28. Dubordieu's object was first to beat Hoste, and then to

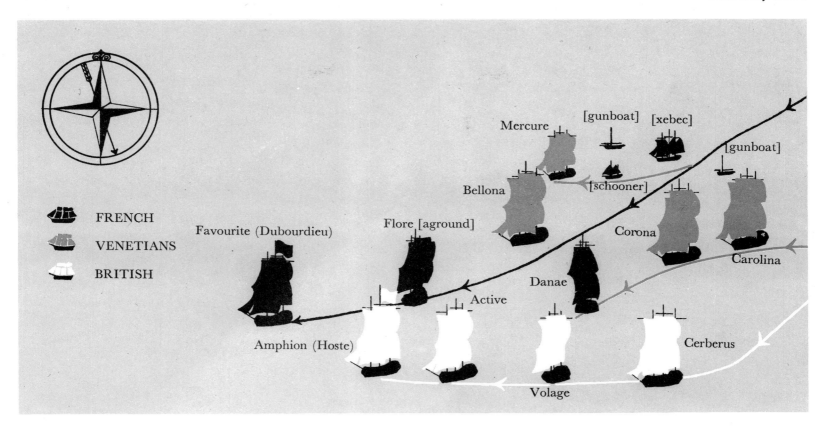

FRENCH

VENETIANS

BRITISH

Mercure [gunboat] [xebec] [gunboat]

Bellona [schooner]

Favourite (Dubourdieu) Flore [aground] Corona

Carolina

Danae

Active

Amphion (Hoste) Cerberus

Volage

occupy Lissa. Being on the opposite side of the Adriatic to his own base, occupation of the island would have given him the chance to control the northern part of the Sea, including Venice and its approaches.

At first light on 13 March 1811, the *Active* signalled she had seen a strange fleet to windward. As morning drew on, the enemy were observed lying-to off the north point of the island, the wind being from the north west. Dubordieu wasted no time. He formed in two divisions, and in Hoste's own words, 'instantly bore down to attack us under all possible sail'. Hoste had not been Nelson's pupil for nothing, and knew the right counter. 'The British line,' he said, 'led by the *Amphion*, was formed by signal in the closest order on the starboard tack to receive them.'

'In the closest order' – those were the vital words: no gaps, as with the French at the Nile and Trafalgar, by which the line could be pierced, turned or doubled. The captain of the *Volage*, Hornby, records that before fire opened, Hoste flew one special signal: 'Remember Nelson'. The effect was like a shock. 'It was worth a thousand cheers,' said Hornby. 'Never again so long as I live shall I see so interesting or so glorious a moment.'

It was Hoste who began firing, at about nine o'clock. In bearing down, the enemy were exposed, without being able to use their broadsides. It was the time to inflict damage without receiving it, and Hoste made the most of it. There were three ships in each enemy division, the

LEFT: *The later stages of the battle with Dubordieu's* Favorite *exploding on the left*

lighter vessels bringing up the rear, and they faced Hoste's compact four. 'The intention of the enemy appeared to be to break our line in two places,' Hoste related, 'the starboard Division, led by the French commodore, bearing upon the *Amphion* and *Active*, and the leeward Division on the *Cerberus* and *Volage*. In this attempt he was foiled (though almost aboard of us) by the well-directed fire and compact order of our line.'

Dubordieu, checked at the first shock, then attempted

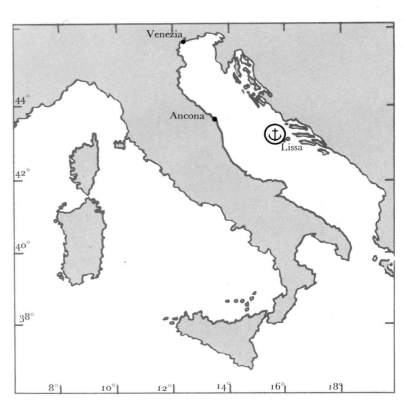

Wednesday 13th March 1811

H.	K.	F.	Courses.	Winds.	Nº. of Signals.	Remarks and Occurrences.
						AM
						Light Breezes
1	2		NNE	NW	Amphin General	2.30 K Ship & set the Main sail at 3 saw
					3	the Fleet & heard the report of two Guns (gun?
2	3				44 Active	to Windward with a Blue light And each
					108	with a blue light at the Cerberus & Volage
3	1	2			Gun Isle graph	in 6ª Columns of Lissa from WBW to NbE
	1	6	WbS		1714	Dist off shore one mile to 20 and 2 Reefs
					694	and made all sail on the Larbd Tack at
4	4		West	NNW	to Volage	Obsd the Active to the Nº & Wd & 5 Frigates 1
					95	Corvette 1 Brig 2 Schooners 1 Zebeck & 1 Gun
5	4	2	NE		R	Boat all drawing sails set in chace of Do cleared
						Ship for Action — Tackd Ship and as I working tow—
6	4		NbE	Vble	Ship for Action	the Enemies Squadron at 6 saw the Enemies
						Squadron form in two Divisions and bear down to us with
7			) Working to			all sail set — made the Active's signal to close & General
8			) Windward			signal to form the line of Battle a head in close order
						and prepare for Action — At 9 commenced firing on
9						the Enemies Van Ship the Enemies leading ships steering
						so as to break the line between the Amphion & the Active
10			) OffJ			9.15 came to close action with the Enemies leading ships —
						Within half a cables length of the shore

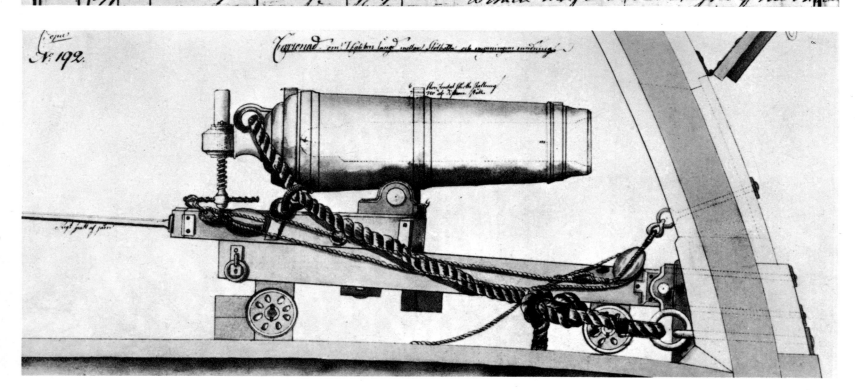

No. 192.

TOP: *Commodore Hoste's log recording the opening moves of the battle.* BOTTOM: *A typical short range cannon of the period, known as a carronnade, which often proved decisive in close action*

A portrait of Sir William Hoste, Bart, painted in 1817

to round the *Amphion*, his idea being to place Hoste between two fires. 'But,' said Hoste, 'he was so warmly received in the attempt, and rendered so totally unmanage-
able, that in the act of wearing he went on shore on the
rocks of Lissa in the greatest possible confusion.'

First blood was to Hoste. Then came the inevitable
mêlée. Some of Dubordieu's ships got to leeward of the
Amphion, though perilously near the shore, but the greater
part stayed to windward, engaging the other ships.
Action was general until after 11 o'clock, when first the
Flore and then the *Bellona* struck. The remaining Franco-
Venetians tried to make off, but were chased as fast as
the disabled state of the British allowed. The *Corona* was
next to surrender, her captors hearing in the distance the
sound of Dubordieu's *Favorite* blowing up – she had been
ablaze for some time. The smaller ships scattered in
every direction, but Hoste had nothing with which to
pursue them.

While he was taking possession of the *Bellona*, the larger
Flore, although she had struck, took the chance to get
away, and neither threats nor diplomacy after the battle
could make her officers give her up; they claimed that
their colours had been shot away.

Dubordieu, a member of the Legion of Honour, was
killed in the action. 'In justice to a brave man,' said
Hoste, 'I must say he set a noble example of intrepidity
to those under him. They sailed from Ancona with 500
troops aboard, and everything necessary for fortifying
and garrisoning the Island of Lissa. Thanks to Providence, we have this day prevented them.'

Four frigates had defeated six, captured two, or if the
Flore is counted, three, and driven the enemy leader
ashore. Hoste's loss was high, 45 killed and 145 wounded,
just over a fifth of the seamen and marines engaged, for
he was short-handed. He himself was wounded in the
right arm and had severe contusions in the body, but he
would not quit the deck until the action was finished.

RIGHT: *The victorious* Amphion *at the close of the action at Lissa*

Lake Erie

1813

The naval actions of the Anglo-American war of 1812 were confined to smaller ships-of-war. This battle resulted in American control of Lake Erie

AT THE WESTERN END OF LAKE ERIE, close to an island on the American side, stands a tall monument to Commodore Oliver Hazard Perry. It commemorates the services of an outstanding personality in one of the most unfortunate wars in history.

Through lack of patience and understanding on both sides, a conflict between the United States of America and Great Britain imposed itself in 1812 on the larger, life-and-death struggle upon which Europe had for so long been engaged. The cause was two-fold: disruption of American trade through Britain's stranglehold on the Continent by sea blockade, and a continuous series of annoyances, sometimes amounting to actual bloodshed, due to the boarding of American ships by British naval parties in their search for deserters. Britain was ravenous for seamen for her extended fleet: there were never enough, and officers were not always scrupulous in those they seized.

During the course of the war, in which the United States saw an opportunity to invade Canada, much of the

fighting took place on the Great Lakes, and in particular on Lake Erie. Their waters, though fresh and inland, were the scene of operations involving regular naval officers and sizeable vessels, which have a claim to consideration as producing at least one considerable battle. They called for the exercise of as much skill, resolution and initiative as anything which then took place on the ocean.

The opposed forces on the Great Lakes were rarely in a state of equilibrium. First one side wrested superiority, then the other. There were raids, sorties, captures of outposts, marches, skirmishes on land and water, and always three problems pressed both sides: shortage of manpower, difficult supplies, and the need not merely to fight but to launch ships. Most of the vessels could not long have survived the open sea. They were built of unseasoned timber – this year's tree was next year's ship – they were of shallow draft, and were held together by wooden pegs even where nails would ordinarily have been considered essential. Their armament was whatever could be raked together, and it ranged from cannonades to muskets.

In the summer of 1813, Perry won command of Lake Erie. He was twenty-eight, a man of strong emotions, fiery and energetic, new to the area. He had a vein of sentiment not uncommon with such characters. In Captain R. H. Barclay RN, he had a worthy opponent, a seasoned officer who had served at Trafalgar, where he had lost an arm.

LEFT: *Commodore Perry, commander of the American squadron at Lake Erie, leaving the battered* Lawrence *and transferring his flag to the* Niagara. *This spectacular piece of bravery transformed apparent defeat into a decisive victory for the Americans, as the undamaged* Niagara *was able to round up the disabled British ships*

OVERLEAF: *The end of the action at Lake Erie. The* Niagara *is forcing her way through the British line, her cannon firing on both sides*

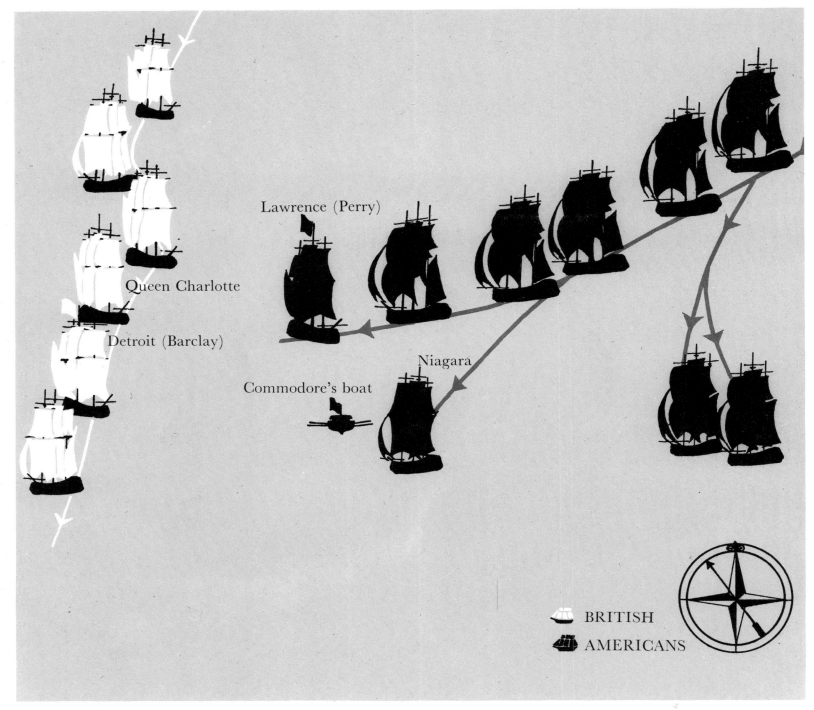

Lawrence (Perry)

Queen Charlotte

Detroit (Barclay)

Niagara

Commodore's boat

BRITISH

AMERICANS

Perry was about to launch a new ship when he heard news of the capture of the American frigate *Chesapeake* by Sir Philip Broke, off Boston, and the death of her gallant captain. He made the chastening incident serve as an inspiration, christened the new ship the *Lawrence* after the dead commander, and had a blue flag made, on which Lawrence's words were embroidered: 'Don't give up the ship'. A modern expert in propaganda would have condemned the sentiment as pessimistic or at best negative, but his own men knew quite well what he meant. Perry's second ship was the *Niagara*, and his third the *Caledonia*, a vessel which had been taken from the British by Elliott, his second in command, the previous autumn.

A shipwright would have found it hard to classify the

larger ships on either side, so unorthodox was their build. Although there were a number of schooner-rigged gunboats, the large *Lawrence* and *Niagara* between them represented about two-thirds of Perry's strength. As Perry had had no earlier operational experience, it was fortunate for him that the British allowed him five weeks in which to train before the day of battle. Barclay's biggest ship was the new *Detroit*, named after a British success early in the war. She was comparable in size, though not in strength, to the *Lawrence* or *Niagara*. The only other major British unit was the *Queen Charlotte*, and the smaller vessels were inferior in weight of metal to

RIGHT: *The later stages of the action at Lake Erie. The abandoned* Lawrence *can be seen on the right*

A popular representation of Perry shifting to the Niagara *carrying his broad pendant*

Perry's. Arithmetically, Barclay's whole force may have been two-thirds as strong as his opponent's – scarcely more.

Perry's main base was at Presqu'Isle, about mid-way along the American side of the lake. Barclay's was at Malden, away to the west, and when Perry had strength enough to blockade, he used an anchorage off Bass Island, in what is now known as the Put-in-Bay cluster, close enough to the British to threaten them. The British had command of the Straits of Detroit and Lake Huron, but they were running short of supplies, food included, nothing was to be had from the west, and their position was so precarious that it could only be restored by regaining command of Lake Erie.

On 10 September, Barclay attacked, at first with the advantage of the wind. This shifted, and Perry, equally willing to engage, then bore down upon the British line. Barclay had a schooner ahead, then the *Detroit*, then

another schooner, then the *Queen Charlotte*, with a schooner bringing up the rear. Perry's order of sailing had allotted the *Lawrence* to the *Detroit* and the *Niagara* to the *Queen Charlotte*, since it was between these four ships that the issue would be decided.

At first, Perry's flagship bore the brunt of the action: probably the wind dropped, certainly it was the *Lawrence* and *Detroit* which took the shock, and Perry looked in vain for support. Barclay's men – the Canadians, soldiers and a handful of seamen who made up his crew – stood to their guns with a bravery that was only equalled by Perry and his Kentuckians. The *Detroit*'s guns were primitive. They were fired by snapping pistols over loose powder piled in the touch-holes. In the smaller craft, American superiority soon told, though in

RIGHT: *A contemporary broadsheet celebrating Perry's victory in 1813 at Lake Erie*

BRILLIANT NAVAL VICTORY.

YANKEE PERRY, BETTER THAN OLD ENGLISH CIDER.

"TUNE---THREE YANKEE PIGEONS."

HUZZA ! for the brave Yankee boys,
  Who touch'd up John Bull on lake Erie,
Who gave 'em a taste of our toys,
  From the fleet of brave Commodore *Perry*.

They were not made of 'lasses but lead,
  And good solid lumps of cold iron,
When they hit JOHNNY BULL in the head,
  They gave him a pain that he'll die on.

Now the *Niagara* bore down,
  To give 'em a bit of a whacking,
The *Lawrence* came up and wore round,
  And set her nine pounders a cracking.

They soon felt the *Scorpion's* sting,
  And likewise the *Æriel's* thunder,
The *Porcupine* give 'em a quill,
  And made the Queen Charlotte knock under.

The *Somers* now gave 'em a touch,
  And the *Tygress* she gave him a shock sir,
Which did not divert Johnny much,
  For it put him in mind of the BOXER.

The *Trip* she was hammering away,
  The *Oris* soon made 'em smell powder,
The brave *Caledonia* that day
  Made her thunder grow louder and louder.

We gave 'em such tough yankee blows,
  That soon they thought fit to surrender ;
That day made 'em feel that their foes,
  Were made in the masculine gender.

Poor Johnny was sick of the gripes,
  From the pills that we gave them at E
And for fear of the stars and the stripes,
  He struck to brave Commodore PERRY.

Now as for poor old Johnny Bull,
  If we meet him on land or on Sea sir,
We'll give him a good belly full,
  Of excellent gun powder tea sir.

Old England is fam'd for her perry and bee
  Which quickly bewilders the brain,
But such PERRY as she's taken here,
  She never will wish for again.

Huzza ! for our brave Yankee Tars,
  Who pepper'd the British so merry,
Who fought for the stripes and the stars,
  Under brave Commodore PERRY.

☞ Printed by N. COVERLY, Milk-Stre

A general view of the engagement on Lake Erie at the height of the action. The Queen Charlotte *is second from the left, while on the right Perry can be seen crossing from the* Lawrence *to the* Niagara

one case a gun leapt from its carriage and fell down the hatchway, while another burst.

In the heat of battle the *Queen Charlotte*, which had been attacked neither by the *Niagara* nor the *Caledonia*, moved up the line and brought her guns to bear on the *Lawrence*, which was already grappling with the *Detroit*. Perry's flagship was soon shot to pieces. Casualties mounted on both sides. In the British ships the captains and lieutenants were all killed or wounded, Barclay himself being hit in five places. Perry survived, kept his head, and saved the day for the Americans. More than two hours after action began, he still had one uninjured boat. In this he had himself rowed to the *Niagara*, in the manner of an admiral in the old Dutch wars, taking his precious blue flag with him.

The *Lawrence* was by now silent, and it was thought by the weary British that the battle was over and that they had won. Perry had different ideas. As soon as he reached the *Niagara* the wind freshened, and he took command. He saw the chance to bear down with a fresh ship on a disorganized line. By this time the British, their leaders casualties, were in trouble. Their smaller ships had dispersed to leeward, mostly disabled, and the *Detroit* and *Queen Charlotte* fell foul of one another. Elliott was sent off to rally the smaller Americans, and the next thing the British knew was that the *Niagara* was upon them, Perry burning for revenge. The *Detroit* and *Queen Charlotte* had little fight left in them, and after they had been taken the smaller vessels were gradually rounded up. Total defeat, which had looked so unlikely, stared the

LEFT: *An engraving showing Commodore Perry about to board the* Niagara, *in which he won the action*

British in the face. Before daylight faded the flag was hauled down, and Perry returned triumphantly to the battered *Lawrence*.

With Lake Erie secured as a result of the action, the British army ashore, near to starvation as it was, could only retreat. The town of Detroit, Britain's proudest capture, fell to the Americans and the whole United States was, for the time, clear of invaders. 'We have met the enemy and they are ours.' That was Perry's summary of his exploit. It was in a special sense his own. Resourceful, refusing to admit defeat, he had thrilled his countrymen, and he deserved his monument.

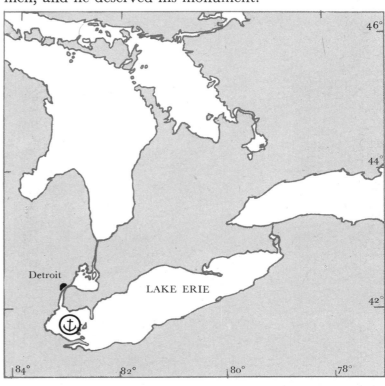

TRANSPORTS

Middle Island

BRITISH

RUSSIANS

FRENCH

TURKO-
EGYPTIAN

(Tahir Pasha)

Asia
(Codrington)

Sirène
(de Rigny)

(Moharem Bey)

Azov (Geiden)

Citadel

ISLE OF NAVARINO

Navarino Bay

1827

French, English and Russian squadrons, united for the cause of Greek freedom,
defeated the Turks in the last battle fought wholly under sail

THE LAST SEA BATTLE FOUGHT wholly under sail was not the least extraordinary in a long sequence. It took place in that classical area of great actions, the Morea, scarcely a hundred miles from the scene of Lepanto, in circumstances of complexity. It involved six nations, and in itself it was a landmark in the struggle for the liberation of Greece.

The War of Greek Independence lasted for some eight years, from 1821 onwards. Starting as a series of revolts against Turkish rule by Greek partisans who found fighting more natural than uniting, even among themselves, it soon became a matter of concern to all the greater European powers. Byron's writings, crowned by his service in Cephalonia and his death at Missolonghi in 1824, added fire to a movement for freedom which stirred everyone among the liberally minded and the classically educated.

Matters were made difficult in at least three ways. First was the fact that Greek seamen, caring nothing for the niceties of international law, tended to treat any ships trading with Turkey as enemies. Second was the attitude of Austria, a reactionary Empire hostile to Russia, with a Turkish trade so ramified that she maintained a large fleet in the Levant. Third was the suspicion with which the powers friendly to Greek aspirations, Britain, France and Russia, treated one another. Russia, for territorial and other reasons, was anti-Turkish. British sentiment inclined strongly to the Greeks, but her Government was unwilling to weaken Turkey to Russia's advantage. France, anti-

Russian to the extent that some of her naval officers took service in the navies of Turkey and her vassalage, Egypt, yet shared to the full Britain's sympathy with Greece.

Early in 1826 the Duke of Wellington was sent to St Petersburg. The result of his visit was the signing of a Protocol by which it was agreed that Britain should urge Turkey to recognize Greece as a self-governing, though still a tributary part of her dominions. Turkey, though willing to withdraw from the Danubian Principalities of Moldavia and Walachia, remained adamant about Greece.

Early in 1827 there was a conference of the Powers. Austria and Prussia declined to take any steps against the Porte, but by the Treaty of London, signed in July 1827, Britain, France and Russia openly agreed to secure autonomy for Greece, and secretly undertook to obtain this by a 'pacific' blockade of Ibrahim Pasha, the Turkish Commander-in-Chief on the spot. British officers, including Sir Richard Church, Lord Cochrane and Captain F. A. Hastings, were already engaged on the Greek side. A Russian officer of a family settled in Corfu was elected President of the Greek Republic, while the French were represented by Colonel Fabvier, who had been fighting with the insurgents four years.

At the time of the London Treaty, the British fleet in the Mediterranean was commanded by Admiral Sir Edward Codrington, with his flag in the *Asia*. He was a man of striking presence who had served as a lieutenant in Howe's *Queen Charlotte* at the Glorious First of June,

and who as a captain had commanded the *Orion* at Trafalgar. The French fleet was led by the Comte de Rigny, the relationship between the two admirals being cordial. They met at Smyrna on 1 August 1827 to discuss their future policy. Both knew of the signature of the Treaty, but neither had yet received instructions from their Governments. Codrington had his a week later, when both admirals learnt they were to be sent reinforcements: two ships of the line for Codrington and four for de Rigny. They were further told that a Russian squadron would soon be on its way to join them. Meanwhile, a Turkish and Egyptian fleet had sailed from Alexandria for Navarino, in the south west corner of the Morea. The force anchored without incident on 8 September.

The British and French fleets left the Gulf of Smyrna on 15 August for Nauplia, on the opposite side of the Morea to the Turks. There they informed the provisional Greek Government that proposals for an armistice were about to be presented to the Porte. On the 21st they separated, Codrington returning to Smyrna and de Rigny sailing to Milo, his usual base.

On 7 September Codrington learnt that terms had been rejected by the Sultan. He also received authority 'to *enforce* the maintenance of an armistice by sea', in view of the Greek acceptance. The admiral amplified the duty of the Allied naval forces, in a message to his captains, as being 'to intercept any supply of men, arms, etc. destined against Greece'. He emphasized that this must

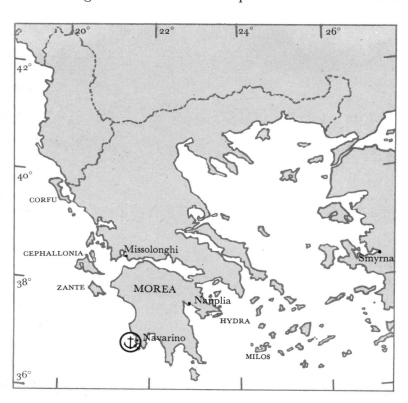

RIGHT: *A general view of the final stages of the action in the Bay of Navarino, painted by Louis Garneray*

LEFT: *Admiral Sir Edward Codrington (1770–1851), the Allied Commander-in-Chief at Navarino. He was a veteran commander, who had served under Howe at the Glorious First of June and commanded the* Orion *at Trafalgar.* RIGHT: *The Allied fleet entering Navarino Bay at the start of the action. The horseshoe formation of the Turkish fleet at the mouth of the harbour can be clearly seen*

be done if possible without fighting, but that it was to be compelled 'if necessary, and when all other means are exchanged, by cannon shot'. He then sailed for Navarino.

There, on 19 September, while he was conducting a 'pacific blockade' and awaiting his allies, he sent word to the Turkish admiral that he would not be allowed to despatch 'men, arms, vessels or warlike stores to any part of Greece or the Greek Islands'.

Codrington's squadron then consisted only of the *Asia*

84 guns, the *Genoa* 76 guns, the *Albion* 74 guns, the *Glasgow* 50 guns and the *Dartmouth* 42 guns. It was therefore scarcely surprising that Ibrahim, who commanded a sizeable fleet, took no notice. On 22 September Turkish ships were seen to weigh anchor, preparing for a descent on Hydra, an eastern island of the Morea then held by patriots. Codrington had been carried to the northward by the current and was unable to interfere, but to his relief de Rigny suddenly appeared with six French ships, in company with three British units, including the *Talbot*

and *Pelican*. The Turks thereupon postponed their sortie, and agreed to negotiate.

A conference took place on 25 September, but, just as the admirals were about to leave, news came that Cochrane, a British officer in Greek service, was active in the Gulf of Patras. Ibrahim insisted on his right to deal with him by force. The demand was refused, Codrington having already informed Cochrane of the situation. Ibrahim had asked further instructions from his Government: pending their receipt, the allies left a token force – two frigates only – off Navarino, the remainder of the fleet dispersing. No sooner had Codrington and de Rigny left than Ibrahim started weighing anchor, but, owing to

the alertness of the frigates, Codrington, returning swiftly, was able to observe his movements.

By 8 October all the Turkish ships were back at Navarino, and two days later Codrington learnt that the Russian squadron was near at hand. It joined him on the 13th, eight ships under Rear-Admiral Count Heiden. The Russians arrived just before de Rigny, who insisted on his need to put in at Zante for provisions. The British and Russians sailed to Navarino in company.

On 17 October, when the Allies were finally united, Codrington sent the *Dartmouth* into the port with a letter, signed by all three admirals, protesting to Ibrahim that his army was devastating the Morea and that they con-

Contemporary prints showing life on board ship at the period of Navarino Bay. TOP: *The interior of a midshipman's berth, based on a sketch by a serving naval officer.* CENTRE: *French seamen in irons.* BOTTOM: *The gunroom of a ship of the line during a heavy sea*

Vice-Admiral the Comte de Rigny (left) and Rear-Admiral Count Heiden (right), who commanded the French and Russian units under Codrington at the Battle of Navarino, which was the most important result of the triple alliance formed to enforce the Turks to grant the demand for Greek independence

Asia 24th of October 1827
in the Port of Navarin

General Order

Before the United Squadrons
remove from the Theatre on which
they have gained so complete a victory,
the Vice Admiral, Commander in Chief,
is desirous of making known to the
whole of the Officers, Seamen, and Marines,
employed in them, the high sense which
he has of their gallant, and steady
conduct on the 20th instant.

He is persuaded that there is no instance
of the Fleet of any one Country shewing
more complete union, of spirit, and of action,
than was exhibited by the Squadrons
of the three allied Powers together in
this bloody and destructive battle. —

He attributes to the bright example set

The French frigate La Provence *lying in Navarino Bay two days after the battle. She was left behind to complete repairs to her mainmast*

sidered him as no longer covered by the law of nations or existing treaties. The letter was never delivered. Ibrahim had disappeared, his second-in-command assuring the Allies that his movements had been kept a profound secret.

The admirals were by now convinced that the only way to make the Turks cease from hostilities by land and sea was to take the combined fleet into Navarino harbour and present their demand 'match in hand'. The *Dartmouth's* captain had been able to observe the disposition of the Turkish-Egyptian fleet which was anchored in a horse-shoe formation with its ends – nearly a mile apart – pointing toward the entrance to the harbour. The transports were behind the men of war. There were three Turkish ships of the line, fifteen frigates, fourteen corvettes and five brigs. The Egyptian contribution was four frigates, three corvettes and four brigs, together with smaller vessels.

Codrington had a total strength of twelve British,

LEFT: *A general order issued by Codrington a few days after the battle, praising the conduct and concerted success of the allied fleet*

seven French and eight Russian ships with which to make the Turks see reason. His task was complicated by the need of keeping the French and Russians apart, and giving each a role consistent with national dignity. His plan was that de Rigny's ships should deal with the Egyptians; his own battleships would oppose the Turkish flagship and larger vessels, and the Russians the rest. On 20 October, a day which Codrington remembered as the eve of Trafalgar, he sailed in from the south-west in two lines, British and French to starboard, Russians to port. At the final approach, the Russians dropped behind the French.

As Codrington drew near the narrow entrance to the harbour, the Turks sent a message saying that Ibrahim had refused permission for the Allies to enter, and that he insisted they should put to sea again. To this Codrington answered that he had not come to receive orders but to give them, and that the first gun fired by the Turks would be the signal for the destruction of their fleet. The shore batteries remained silent, and the fleet sailed in.

Action began even before the big ships had taken up their positions. Seeing the crew of a fire-ship apparently

213

A contemporary cartoonist's view of the action at Navarino Bay

preparing to set her alight, Captain Fellowes of the *Dartmouth* sent a boat to demand that she should either be abandoned, or removed to a safer berth. The Turks fired on the boat, killed and wounded some of the crew, set the fire-ship alight and then abandoned her. The *Dartmouth* sent a second boat to help tow the fire-ship aside, and the officer in charge, Fitzroy, was killed by musketry. The *Dartmouth* then opened with small-arms in support of her men, and the French flagship *Sirène* followed suit, though de Rigny hailed the Turkish *Ihsania* to say he would not use his main armament unless fired upon first. At that moment a Turkish corvette fired two shots. One passed over the *Dartmouth*, the other killed a man aboard the *Sirène*. The French replied, the *Ihsania* instantly opened fire, and battle became general soon after 2.30 pm.

For the first hour, fighting was fierce; then it slackened, as one by one the Turks and Egyptians were silenced. By six o'clock, all was over, and even the Navarino forti-

LEFT: The Battle of Navarino *by Thomas Lang (1759–1857). The* Asia, *Admiral Codrington's flagship, is shown between two Turkish ships of the line*

fications ceased fire. One single frigate and fifteen smaller Turkish and Egyptians were all that escaped serious damage. Of the twenty largest ships, fourteen were sunk or destroyed, and only three were ever worth repairing. The Turkish and Egyptian killed and wounded are not precisely known, but they were certainly between three and four thousand. The Allies had 182 killed and 489 wounded. The British share was 80 killed and 206 wounded; the Russian 59 killed and 159 wounded; the French 43 killed and 144 wounded – some, so they said bitterly, by bad Russian aim. French damage was repaired at Toulon, but as the Russians had no base of their own within reach, they refitted at Malta.

The battle hastened the liberation of Greece, since Turkey was henceforward without a principal fleet, but the war itself dragged on for another two years, the final Treaty being signed in 1829 at Adrianople.

Codrington was recalled for 'explanations'. Not long after the action, he was met by a sporting acquaintance in the street. 'Ah!', said his friend, 'had any good shooting lately?' The admiral was able to say he had had some rather remarkable shooting.

Hampton Roads
1862

The first important naval engagement of the American Civil War, and the first in history between ironclads, with the 'Monitor' and 'Merrimac' at death-grips

THE AGE OF STEAM IN NAVAL WARFARE is sometimes thought to have begun with the duel of the *Monitor* and *Merrimac* in the American Civil War. This is not quite so, for the East India Company's steamer *Diana* was used, under the orders of Captain Frederick Marryat as senior naval officer, in a war in Burma as early as 1824. Lord Cochrane had employed steam in his forays among the Greek Islands in the war of Liberation, and steam had been used in the fleets present in sea operations during the Crimean war. What was newly introduced was steam combined with armour, and this brought about a revolution in shipbuilding: it produced the 'iron-clad'.

The *Merrimac* demands first consideration both as an older vessel than her rival, and because she was in action before the *Monitor*. Rightfully, her name was *Merrimack* (the *Merrimac* being a different ship): in her armoured shape she was re-christened *Virginia* by the Confederates, but she has gone down to history as the *Merrimac* and as such she should perhaps be accepted.

When the Confederates seized the Navy Yard at Norfolk, Virginia, as they did soon after the outbreak of the war, the steam frigate *Merrimac*, built in 1855, was set on fire by the Federalists before they surrendered. The flames were put out, and when a Federal squadron anchored in Hampton Roads, the stretch of water into which runs both the Elizabeth River, giving access to Norfolk, and the James river, the waterway to Richmond, which was at that time the Confederate capital, spies soon reported that the masters of the damaged

Merrimac were preparing a new and terrible kind of warship with which to raise the blockade. The news was true. 'Inequality of numbers', wrote Stephen R. Mallory, Secretary of the Confederate States Navy, 'may be compensated by invulnerability. Not only does economy, but naval success, dictate the wisdom and expediency of fighting with iron against wood.'

The Confederates cut down the *Merrimac* almost to the water's edge, and they built a solid deck over her at this level. Then they erected a huge deck-house, with sloping sides, pierced with portholes for the heavy smooth-bore guns. There were no masts, only a flagstaff, and the funnel passed up through the roof of the deck-house. The flat deck-space, fore and aft, and the sloping sides of the deck-house were intended to be armoured with four inches of iron, but there were no armour plates available. Railway iron was therefore collected and rolled into long narrow strips, which were bolted on to the structure in two layers, laid crosswise. An armoured conning tower, three-sided, was built forward, on the deck-house roof. The bow was armed with a mass of iron, in order to revive the ancient method of attack by ramming.

LEFT: *A reconstruction by the American artist Jo Davidson of the height of the* Monitor-Merrimac *duel*

OVERLEAF: *A contemporary lithograph giving a panoramic view of Hampton Roads during the ironclad duel. It is taken from a drawing made on the spot by a Sergeant from the New York Volunteers*

ABOVE: *The scene in Brooklyn in 1862 at the launching of one of the later monitors, which were built immediately after Hampton Roads*

LEFT: *An early photograph, probably taken before the outbreak of the Civil War, of Commodore Buchanan, who commanded the* Merrimac

Formidable as she was, the *Merrimac* had three serious defects. She had to rely on her original engines, whose unsatisfactory state had been the reason for her being in dockyard hands at the outbreak of war. She was unwieldy – it took her thirty minutes, at her slow best speed, to turn round; and she drew 22 feet of water, restricting her to comparatively deep channels. She was commissioned by Commodore Buchanan, and at noon on 8 March 1862 she started her voyage down the Elizabeth River on her trial trip and her first fighting expedition. Her mission was to destroy the blockaders at Hampton Roads. Not one of her guns had ever been fired, even in practice. Five small gunboats accompanied her.

The Federal ships lay along the north side of Hampton Roads from Newport News to Old Point Comfort, where the Roads open upon Chesapeake Bay. When the *Merrimac* appeared, the *Congress* of 50 guns and the sloop *Cumberland* of 30 guns were at anchor, the seamen's clothes drying in the rigging.

First to observe the smoke of steamers coming down the Elizabeth River was the master of the *Zoave*, an armed tug, which went alongside the *Cumberland*. The officer of the watch sent the *Zoave* to reconnoitre, and the tug, with her 30-pounder gun, fired the first shots at what was described as 'a very big barn, belching forth smoke'. The *Cumberland* and *Congress* cleared for action, shore batteries opened up, and every ship in the Roads hustled into motion.

Buchanan, proceeding very slowly (not much faster than Nelson's divisions at Trafalgar), held his fire. The

Merrimac was soon hit, but the shots rebounded with a clang, and she kept on. Then, at a range of only 500 yards, the *Merrimac*'s bow gun fired at the *Cumberland*, and at once she hit. Soon afterwards her starboard battery blazed away into the *Congress*, and then she ran straight for the *Cumberland*, her ram striking at right-angles to the wooden side. Within a few minutes, with a hole in her big enough for a coach and horses to drive through, the *Cumberland* filled and sank. Then the ironclad turned to finish with the *Congress*. After a steady battering she was forced to surrender. The *Merrimac* set her ablaze, and then turned to deal with the *Minnesota*, another frigate which had been engaging her at some distance.

By this time the sun was going down, so the *Merrimac*, a good day's work done, steamed to the south side of the Roads, and anchored for the night under the Confederate batteries. Buchanan had been wounded, and he transferred command to Lieutenant Jones, giving him orders to deal first next day with the badly damaged *Minnesota*. In the course of the night the blazing *Congress* blew up, scattering Hampton Roads with wreckage, and the *Minnesota* ran aground. The Federals had lost two ships and two hundred men, the Confederates twenty-one men.

Few incidents in naval warfare have been more dramatic than the arrival, on the night of crisis, of the Federal ship *Monitor*. While the *Merrimac* had been brilliantly extemporized from an existing vessel, the *Monitor* was newly built to the designs of a Swedish engineer, John Ericsson. Instead of carrying her ordnance in a fixed-direction battery, she had two large guns mounted in a revolving turret. So low in the water that her deck was nearly awash, all that could be seen of her, turret apart, was a short funnel and the little 'pilot house' from which she was conned. She drew only ten feet of water, so that she was able to anchor and conceal her presence in the lee of the stranded *Minnesota*. In the words of one who first set eyes on her next day, 'she looked like a plank afloat with a can on top of it'. The *Monitor*'s

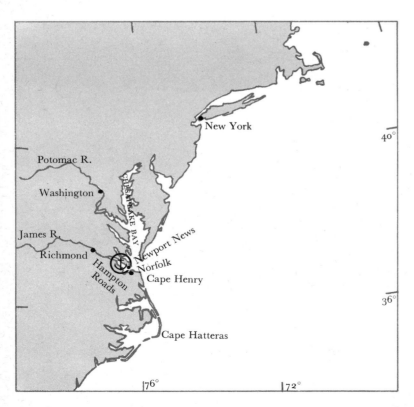

RIGHT: *A coloured lithograph of the Battle of Hampton Roads published in 1889 and designed to illustrate the helplessness of the wooden ship when pitted against the ironclad*

OVERLEAF, LEFT: *A lithograph taken from a French naval officer's painting of the Battle of Hampton Roads*

OVERLEAF, RIGHT: *The gun turret of the* Monitor *showing signs of her struggle with the* Merrimac

engines and boilers were placed aft, and she had been built in a hundred-and-one working days.

Command of the *Monitor* was given to Lieutenant Worden, who was specially promoted captain. She had left New York in tow of a tug on 6 March, and by 4 pm on the day of the Hampton Roads battle she was off Cape Henry, after a passage during which she nearly foundered, though the fact was well concealed. Worden guessed from the distant firing that the *Merrimac* had been in action, and he anchored to the glare from the burning *Congress*.

At 7 o'clock on the morning of 9 March, the *Merrimac*, with her attendant gunboats, was seen to be steaming slowly across the Roads, intent on finishing off the stranded *Minnesota*. Worden at once steamed the *Monitor* into open water, challenging the Confederates to a duel. The little gunboats prudently retreated. Worden was as cool in holding his fire as Buchanan had been the day before, and he allowed the *Merrimac* to shoot first: then he stopped his engines, let his ship drift, and sent an order by speaking tube to the turret. The two 11-inch guns roared out, and the great balls crashed against the sloping plates of the *Merrimac*. The railway iron remained

ABOVE: *A contemporary engraving showing the height of the action at Hampton Roads*

RIGHT: *Two lithographs from a technical description of the Federal ironclad* Monitor. *The first shows, from bow to stern, conning tower, gun turret, funnel and Federal ensign. The second gives detailed plans and dimensions*

unbreached. The dose was repeated at seven-minute intervals, the time the *Monitor* took to re-load.

The Confederate ship, which could fire broadsides at intervals of about fifteen minutes, used her guns well, and made hit after hit, but equally without effect. Diminished draught, due to injury to her funnel, made it difficult for her engines to move her at all. Moreover, while the *Monitor* had plenty of ammunition, the *Merrimac*, which had used up a high proportion of hers the day before, was running short.

Sensibly enough, Jones decided to make use of what shot he had left to finish with the *Minnesota*, against whose wooden sides his guns were sure to be effective; but his pilot was nervous: he confessed later that he was

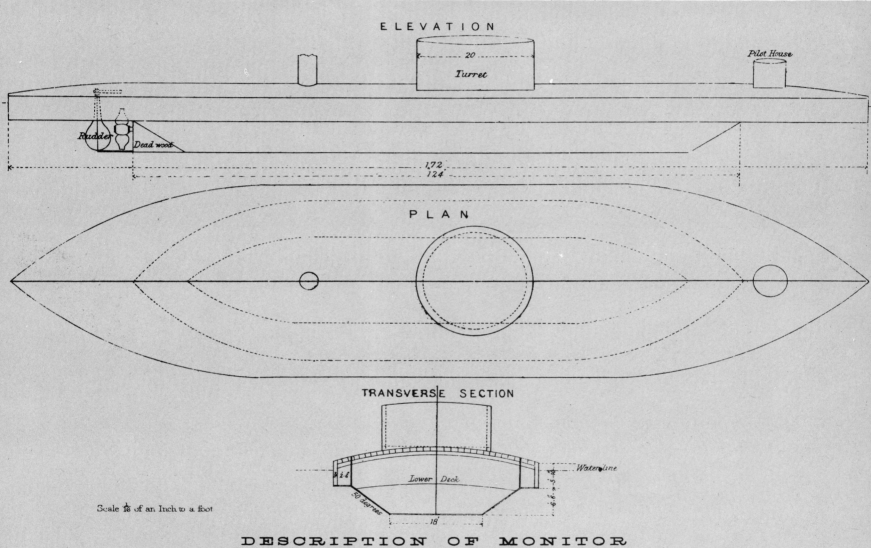

ELEVATION

20

Turret

Pilot House

Rudder

Dead wood

172
124

PLAN

TRANSVERSE SECTION

Waterline

Lower Deck

50 degrees

18'

Scale 1/16 of an Inch to a foot

DESCRIPTION OF MONITOR

"New York Herald," Tuesday, March 11, 1862.

She is a long, wide, and flat-bottomed vessel, with vertical sides and pointed ends, requiring but a very shallow depth of water to float in, though heavily loaded with impregnable armour on her sides, and a bomb-proof deck, on which is placed a shot-proof revolving turret, which contains two heavy guns. She is so low in the water as to afford no target for an enemy; and every thing and every body is below the water-line, with the exception of the persons working the guns, who are protected by the shot-proof turret. The sides of the ship are first formed of plate iron ½ an inch thick, outside of which is attached solid white oak 26 inches thick; outside of this, again, is rolled iron armour 5 inches thick; the bomb-proof deck is supported by heavy braced oak beams, upon which is laid planking 7 inches thick, covered with rolled plate iron 1 inch thick.

The turret consists of rolled plate skeleton 1 inch thick, to which are riveted two thicknesses of 1 inch of rolled iron plates; outside this, again,

are six plates of rolled iron, all firmly bolted together with nuts inside; so that, if a plate is started, it can at once be tightened again. The top is covered with bomb-proof roof, perforated with holes. The lower part of the gun-carriages consists of solid wrought-iron beams. These are planed perfectly true, and are placed parallel in the turret, both of the guns pointing in the same direction. The ports through the side of the turret are only large enough to permit the muzzle of the gun to be thrust through. Inside of them are wrought-iron pendulums, which close them against the enemy as soon as the gun recoils. She is armed with two of the heaviest Dalgreen guns, made to revolve by a pair of steam-engines placed beneath the deck.

The lower vessel is of iron, ½ inch thick, and made in the usual manner. She carries her machinery, coal, &c., aft, and forward the officers, ammunition, and stores. The two partitions of the vessel are separated by a wrought-iron bulkhead. The officers' quarters are very handsome, and are ventilated and lighted by openings from the deck.

Her machinery consists of two horizontal tubular boilers, containing

3,000 square feet of fire surface, and horizontal condensing engines of 40 inch diameter of cylinders, and 22-inch stroke of piston. The propeller is 9 feet in diameter, and 16 feet stroke. It has four blades.

Dimensions.						Ft.	In.
Length of upper vessel	..	..	..	..	..	172	0
Beam of ditto ..	..	..	..	..	..	41	4
Depth of ditto	..	..	..	..	..	5	0
Length of lower vessel	..	..	..	..	..	124	0
Beam of lower vessel at junction with upper	..	..	34	0
Beam of bottom	..	..	..	..	..	18	0
Depth of lower vessel	..	..	..	..	..	6	6
Diameter of turret interior ..	..	..	..	..	20	0
Height of turret	..	..	..	..	..	9	0
Diameter of pilot-house	..	..	..	..	..	6	0
Height above deck	..	..	..	..	..	5	0

Two photographs, the first showing the officers and the second the crew on the deck of the Monitor *a few months after the action at Hampton Roads*

more scared of facing the *Minnesota*'s rapid fire than the *Monitor*'s slow salvoes, and he made a wide detour, running the ship aground. When, after great efforts, the vessel was refloated, the pilot declared he could not take the ship any nearer the *Minnesota* without grounding once again.

Jones then resumed his duel with the *Monitor*, which had been slowly pursuing him, in the delusion that the Confederates were running away. Once more it became a fight at close quarters. The *Merrimac*'s funnel was by now shot-riddled, and smoke from her furnace was pouring low over her casement. Jones tried to ram. Worden, making use of his vessel's superior handiness, turned the movement into a glancing blow, but the Confederates believed that if they had not lost the iron wedge of their ram in sinking the *Cumberland*, they would have sunk the *Monitor*, so the *Cumberland* may not have lived in vain.

Jones next concentrated his fire on the *Monitor*'s conning-tower, and the shift of target away from the turret was successful. Worden was wounded in the head – mortally, so he thought, though like Nelson at the Nile he was mistaken, and he told his second-in-command, Dana Greene, that if the *Monitor* saved the *Minnesota*, he would die happy. In fact, the *Minnesota* was refloated next tide.

By this time it was 2 pm, and although, since she did did not reply to fire, Jones believed he had put his opponent out of action, he could make no use of his apparent advantage. The tide was running out, and the risk of grounding was now serious; the crew was exhausted; the ship was leaking and men were always at the pumps. Jones turned the *Merrimac* in her ponderous fashion, and began to steam towards the Elizabeth River on his way back to Norfolk.

No life had been lost as a result of the armoured duel, and there were few wounded: neither ship had received serious injury. When the *Merrimac* was overhauled, it was found she had ninety-nine indentations in her armour, twenty of them from the *Monitor*. Two guns had been made unserviceable on the first day by shots striking their muzzles.

The battle produced an exaggerated respect for the ram, and a proper appreciation of the revolving turret, which in its way was due recognition for both sides. The later history of the two ships was very different. The *Merrimac* was abandoned and burnt a second time – thoroughly on this occasion – when the Confederates were forced to withdraw from Norfolk shortly after the battle. And at the end of the year the *Monitor* was ordered to Charleston, to support the Federal blockade. She started in tow of a tug, but she was caught in a gale off Cape Hatteras on the last day of her one and only year of existence, and she sank with loss of life. Had she come to grief on her original journey, as she nearly did, a restored *Merrimac* might have made herself master of Hampton Roads, and perhaps of the Potomac. But even such a success could not, in the long run, have affected the issue of the war.

A silver medal struck to commemorate the Federal victory at Hampton Roads, describing the Monitor-Merrimac *engagement in strictly Federal terms*

Mobile

1864

A Civil War victory gained by the Federals under Farragut over the Confederates, in which Farragut showed his mastery of the art of war

IT WAS BEFITTING THAT Franklin Buchanan, commander of the Confederate *Merrimac*, should have done battle with the most outstanding sailor produced by the Civil War – the Southern-born David Farragut, who for almost the whole stretch of the American conflict bore the weight of responsibility of high command in the Union naval forces. Farragut is fit to rank in any gallery of naval heroes, but the circumstances of his life differ sharply from admirals whose careers were built up under the pressure of war, to which Farragut came late.

David Farragut was born in eastern Tennessee, in 1801. His father was of Spanish descent and he had emigrated from Minorca at the time of the Revolution, during which, for a brief period, he had served as a sailing-master in the navy. Farragut was taken to sea at a very early age and served in most parts of the world, including the Pacific. There the *Essex*, in which he was serving as a midshipman, was captured after a gallant defence by an English frigate of much superior fire-power. Farragut was then twelve years old: he did not hear another shot fired in war until he was over sixty, which is

an experience unique in the records of great sea commanders. 'I consider it a great advantage to obtain command young,' he wrote, 'having observed, as a general rule, that persons who come into authority late in life shrink from responsibility, and often break down under its weight.' The history of war illustrates the truth of his words, but his own career proved a glowing exception.

Farragut was not made a commander until the age of forty, which in the peace-time United States navy was not a belated step, and his rise to captain, fourteen years later, brought him the highest rank then obtainable in the service to which he belonged. Shortly after his promotion, Farragut was appointed to the *Brooklyn*. She was one of six steam sloops-of-war recently completed, and the day he took command was the first occasion on which he had trodden the decks of an up-to-date powered vessel. The *Brooklyn* was made of wood. Her batteries – nine-inch smooth-bored Dahlgren guns – were still arranged in broadsides, to which were added one or two pivot-guns which, as their name implies, had a wide traverse. The *Brooklyn*'s class was screw-driven, but had a fully-rigged ship's equipment of sails. Under engines alone she could, at her best, make eight knots.

When the Civil War broke out in 1861, Farragut had been in a somewhat difficult situation. He was on half-pay ashore, living with his wife at Norfolk, Virginia. Though a Southerner by family – his father spent his later life in Louisiana – he had no roots ashore. All his active years had been spent afloat, and he was a loyal servant of

LEFT: *A popular representation of Farragut's victory at Mobile in 1864. It depicts his famous action in climbing the rigging of his flagship, the* Hartford, *in order to direct the battle*

OVERLEAF: The Battle of Mobile Bay *painted by J. O. Davidson in 1886. Farragut's forces can be seen advancing into the bay with the monitors in front. The* Tecumseh *has just been mined and is sinking*

Rear-Admiral David G. Farragut, commander of the Federal West Gulf Blockading Squadron and an outstanding figure in American naval history

the Federal Government. Finding the political climate of Norfolk uncongenial, Farragut moved to New York, and he was soon chosen for active command: not only so, but in admiral's rank.

One of the tasks of the Federal navy, during the whole span of the war, was the blockade of the Gulf of Mexico, from whose ports, and in particular from New Orleans, the Secessionists kept open communication with their many sympathizers in Europe, and from which they exported the cotton which brought them sinews of war. Its navy served the Union well throughout the struggle by capturing important coastal points, and sinking or capturing Confederate commerce-destroyers, which were sometimes officered by Englishmen.

Farragut's most important achievement was his capture of New Orleans, assaulted from seaward in April 1862. Even before the operations began, he had shown outstanding energy and confidence for a man of his age. He used as his flagship the *Hartford*, a ship similar to the *Brooklyn*, and his experience of active service afloat soon caused him to think in terms of the earlier admirals. Again and again his language seems to echo that of Nelson. 'The Flag officer,' he wrote before the assault on New Orleans, 'having heard all the opinions expressed by the different commanders, is of the opinion that whatever is to be done will have to be done quickly . . .' The sentence recalls Nelson before Copenhagen.

Farragut's success was outstanding. First he sailed up the 140 mile estuary of the Mississippi to race past the enemy batteries towards New Orleans: finally, on the night of 24 April, he reached the defending forts. At one moment fire-rafts drifted down on the *Hartford* and set her alight, flames roaring through the open ports and driving men from their guns. 'Don't flinch from the fire, boys!' said Farragut. 'There's a hotter fire than that waiting for those who don't do their duty! Give that rascally tug a shot.'

The tug, which was trying to push the fire-raft more firmly against the *Hartford*, was driven off, and by dawn Farragut was through and on his way to the Louisiana capital. 'It is a strange thought,' he wrote to his wife after his triumph. 'I am here among my relatives and yet no one has dared to say '' I am happy to see you.'' ' As he had often said before, if he had to fight, he would rather it had been against his earlier foes, the British, than against his own people.

Farragut's final and in some ways most remarkable service was his conduct of the operations against Mobile. The port stood on the left bank of the estuary of the Mobile and Alabama rivers, not much more than 150 miles from New Orleans as the crow flies, and second in importance to it as a centre of Confederate maritime activity. Farragut had favoured an attack immediately after his first success, but other Federal preoccupations did not admit of this, and it was chiefly the threat of a new Confederate iron-clad, the *Tennessee*, known to be ready, that decided the attack.

Farragut made a preliminary reconnaissance of the forts on 20 January 1864, and considered that with one supporting iron-clad he could clear the shipping in the bay, and that he could then reduce the forts at leisure, with the help of about 5,000 soldiers.

Six months passed, during which the *Tennessee* was moved to a point where she could threaten an assaulting force. Like the *Merrimac* before her, her strength lay in sloping armoured sides. She had six long-range rifled guns, but she suffered from the weakness of her predecessors in slow speed – six knots at best – and her rudder chains were exposed. She was fitted with a beak for ramming.

Farragut, during these months of waiting, was at work administering the whole force engaged on the blockade. 'I have been down here within two months of five years,' he wrote, in words which again recall Nelson's while on watch off Toulon, 'and recently six months on constant blockade off this port, and my mind on the stretch all the time.' He was depressed, as were so many Federal officers, by the protracted resistance of the South, but he never contemplated even the idea of defeat. 'Any man who is prepared for defeat,' he wrote, 'would be half de-

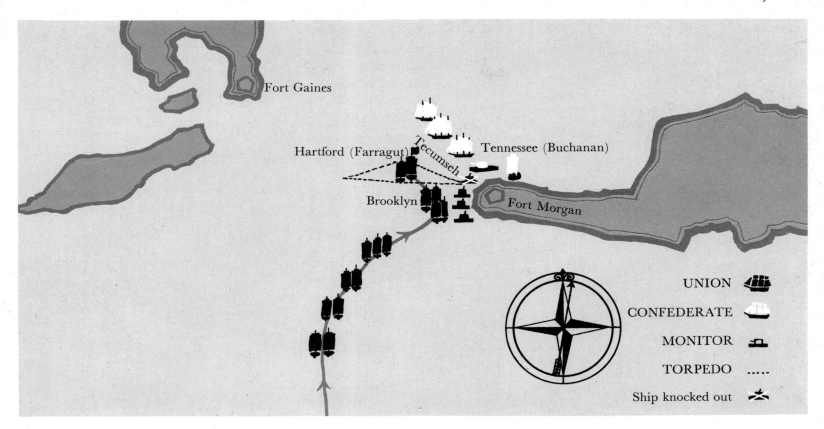

feated before he commenced. I hope for success; shall do all in my power to secure it, and trust to God for the rest.' As for his idea of war: 'Everything has a weak spot, and the first thing I try to do is to find out where it is, and pitch into it with the biggest shell I have, and repeat the dose till it operates.'

At last, in July, iron-clad monitors began to arrive. Four were ear-marked for the attack: two of them, the *Tecumseh* and the *Manhattan*, were sea-going, with a single turret carrying two 15-inch guns, the biggest afloat. The other two were river monitors, the *Winnebago* and *Chickasaw*. They had been built at St Louis for use on the Mississippi. They were of light draught, with four small screws, and they were armed with four 11-inch guns in two turrets.

Besides the *Tennessee* and three wooden gunboats, Mobile's principal defences were Fort Morgan, with 38 heavy guns, Fort Jackson with 27, and Fort St Philip with 21. On an island to the left of the approach was Fort Gaines, and between Fort Gaines and Fort Morgan were obstructions which included mines and fixed torpedoes. Farragut's decision was to advance in columns, the iron-clads in one, the wooden vessels lashed two by two, in the other. The admiral needed a flood tide which would help a crippled vessel past the forts, and if possible a west wind, which would blow the smoke of battle into the eyes of the defenders of Fort Morgan.

On 4 August, the day fixed for an assault, Farragut wrote to his wife, again in words which echo Nelson's: 'I write, and leave this letter for you. I am going to

Mobile in the morning, if God is my leader, as I hope He is, and in Him I place my trust. If He thinks it is the proper place for me to die, I am ready to submit to His will in that, as in all other things . . .'

The *Tecumseh*, the last of his monitors, arrived the same evening as he wrote, when troops were already ashore preparing to invest the forts. About three in the morning Farragut called his servant, to let him know how the wind was. It served. 'Then we will go in the morning,'

From Life on Stone by A. Hoffy.

P.S. Duval Lith. Phila.

PASSED MIDSHIPMAN. U.S. NAVY.

Full Dress.

The Hartford, *Farragut's flagship at Mobile, photographed many years later at Gravesend after she had been re-armed and given a bridge*

said Farragut. At half-past six the column formed, the *Brooklyn,* Farragut's old ship, leading. The flagship followed, with a gunboat, the *Metacomet,* secured to her port side. Fort Morgan's guns opened fire shortly after seven o'clock.

Farragut, in order to have the clearest possible view of the operations, stood in the main rigging of the *Hartford,* which was probably a unique position for a flag officer in battle. Near him were the captain of the *Metacomet,* standing on his wheel-house, and the pilot, who was in the *Hartford's* main-top, so as to see well over the smoke. As the smoke increased and rose higher, so did Farragut climb, till he was close beneath the pilot. The flag-captain, Drayton, became alarmed for the admiral's safety and sent a seaman aloft with a lashing. The seaman remarked that if the admiral *would* stand there, he had better make himself fast. 'I thanked him for his consideration,' said Farragut later, 'and took a turn around and over the shrouds and around my body for fear of being wounded, as shots were flying rather thickly.'

LEFT: A midshipman of the US Navy in the full-dress uniform of the period immediately before the outbreak of the Civil War

The two columns, monitors and wooden vessels, were now nearing the mines and the entrance to the narrow channel, the *Tecumseh* reserving her fire for the *Tennessee.* Then came disaster. Both the *Tecumseh* and the *Brooklyn* pilots began to doubt the line of the safe channel, and both columns were in danger of being thrown into confusion, right under the guns of Fort Morgan. The *Tecumseh* seemed to be making direct for the *Tennessee,* intent on another *Monitor* and *Merrimac* duel, when suddenly she hit a torpedo. Farragut, from his post aloft, saw her lurch and sink, bows foremost, her screws revolving as she disappeared. He stood on.

As the flagship passed the *Brooklyn,* still in perplexity, with her engines at slow and her bows pointed towards the fort, her captain shouted that there were torpedoes ahead. 'Damn the torpedoes,' shouted Farragut from his perch aloft, 'Captain Drayton, go ahead!'

Farragut's decision to hold on was justified up to the hilt. There were indeed torpedoes: they were heard knocking on the *Hartford's* bottom; primers were even heard to snap, but none exploded. The *Hartford* and the other ships went safely through, the *Tennessee* after exchanging shots with the *Hartford* and vainly trying to

ABOVE: *A photograph taken on board a typical Federal gunboat which served against the Southern states in the closing period of the Civil War*

ram, retreating under the guns at Fort Morgan.

Three hours after the fort first opened fire, Buchanan surrendered, after advancing alone to fight the Union ships. He was rammed and blasted until his guns were useless and his ship so battered that he could do nothing else but submit. Mobile was won at a cost to the Union of three hundred and thirty-five men, of whom a hundred and thirteen lay coffined in the bay in the iron hull of the *Tecumseh*.

Farragut had six more years to live. They were full of honour both from his own countrymen and from Europe. His trust in Providence had been as justified as his modest but certain faith in himself. He cannot claim rank as a complete sea commander, since he was denied the experience of fleet actions, but his strategic and tactical grasp, his resolution, and the affection and confidence with which he inspired his fleet, mark him as an admiral in the high tradition.

Farragut's career illuminates certain unchanging elements in sea-power and qualities which, throughout the centuries, have distinguished the greater admirals. First

of these was sheer mastery of his profession; second was the ability to plan, and the patience to wait; third was swift reaction in the face of danger, and the courage to go on. This is an altogether different characteristic from rashness or even from natural courage, for it consists in the ability to weigh possibilities, to gauge the morale as well as the actual strength of the enemy, and in the spirit to sustain one's own side in the face of immediate threat. Nelson showed to what a superb degree he possessed these characteristics at Copenhagen, just as did Farragut at Mobile.

There was a time in Farragut's approach, just before the *Tecumseh* hit the explosive obstruction, and just after she went down, when a lesser man would have hesitated, allowed his advance, which was already unsteady, to degenerate into confusion, and been compelled to retreat. Farragut's 'damn the torpedoes', so Nelsonian in its outlook, so proper in the conduct of a tricky operation, has been well remembered in the history of the American Navy. It is right that this should be so, for Farragut provided a pattern upon which any ambitious sea-officer could model himself. Indeed Admiral Mahan, who wrote the fullest seaman's life of Nelson, was amply justified in devoting a companion appreciation to his distin-

A Federal sloop of war receiving President Abraham Lincoln for an inspection in 1861

guished compatriot, whose service was within the memory of many with whom Mahan himself served.

Farragut was sixty-three at the time of Mobile, and it is interesting to compare his age with that of other admirals in the years of their achievement. Monck was fifty-eight when he fought the Four-Days' Battle, and de Ruyter a year older. Duquesne was sixty-six at the time of his campaign against the great Dutchman. Hawke was fifty-four when he won the day at Quiberon, Suffren two years older at the beginning of his protracted series of battles in the Indian Ocean. Lord Howe was a veteran close upon seventy when he wrested victory at the Glorious First of June, Nelson a stripling just short of forty when he gained his triumph at the Nile. Not a great deal is to

be learnt from the toll of years in the days of sail warfare, except that if a man had 'fire in his belly' it was likely to continue to glow so long as his country had need of his services. Where he was likely to be less resolute as the years passed was where younger men had been known to fail – in the business of that continued watch and ward which wearies ships as well as men, but which seals an enemy's ports and saps his initiative.

That was where Farragut was as eminent as in his leadership in battle.

RIGHT: *The scene on board the* Hartford *at the height of the action, painted by William Heysham Overend*

COMMANDER YEGORIEFF,
OF THE "AURORA."

The "Aurora" was one of the vessels that played a prominent part in the North Sea Incident.

ADMIRAL ROZHDESTVENSKY'S SECOND
IN COMMAND
ADMIRAL FOLKERSAHM (PRISONER)

COMMANDANT BAER,
OF THE "OSLYABIA."

In the earlier reports of the battle the "Oslyabia" was mentioned as one of the vessels that had been sunk by the Japanese.

COMMANDANT SEREBRIAKOFF,
OF THE "BORODINO."

The "Borodino" was one of the most magnificent and newest vessels sunk by Togo in the recent engagement.

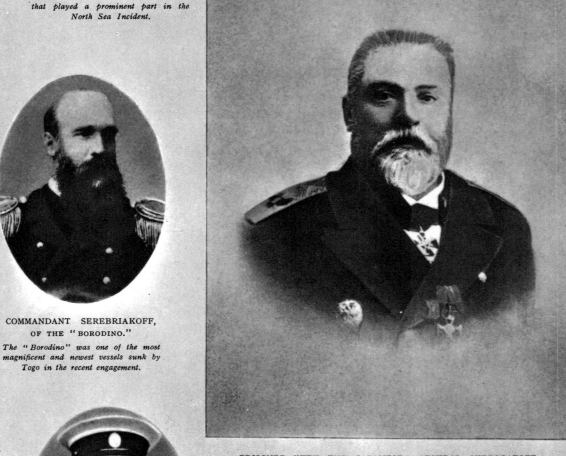

PRISONER WITH THE JAPANESE: ADMIRAL NIEBOGATOFF.

COMMANDANT BUCHVOSTOFF,
OF THE "ALEXANDER III."

The "Alexander III.," the sister ship of the "Borodino," was another of Russia's great losses in the engagement off Tsushima.

COMMANDANT FERSEN,
OF THE "IZUMRUD."

Commandant Fersen is of Scotch descent, his name being a modification of Macpherson.

COMMANDANT TSCHAGIN,
OF THE "ALMAZ"
(ESCAPED TO VLADIVOSTOK).

COMMANDANT IGNATIEFF,
OF THE "KNIAZ SUVAROFF."

Ignatieff was Rozhdestvensky's flag-captain on board the finest vessel of the squadron, now sunk.

Tsushima
1905

In this Japanese strait, the Russian fleet was annihilated by Admiral Togo in the first major fleet action of the present century

THE FIRST FULL-SCALE SEA-BATTLE of the present century, fought between the navies of Japan and Russia, became the holocaust which some students of naval affairs had expected. Russian defeat was total, and it is hard to see what else could have been looked for. There were those who thought that an act of rough justice was done in the Straits of Tsushima in the summer of 1905, but those who were caught up by it had little to do with the train of events which led to their misfortune. They were the victims of high policy and strategic ineptitude.

When war ended between Japan and China in 1895, Japan, an island power with a sea tradition, held possession of much mainland territory, once Chinese, including the Liao-Tung Peninsula and its dockyard at Port Arthur. She intended to keep what she had won, but when the terms of the peace treaty were made known, Russia, the northern neighbour of China along the borders of Manchuria and Mongolia, protested against the cession of Port Arthur, arguing that its permanent occupation by a foreign Power would be a standing threat to the Government at Peking. Germany and France joined in the protest, and the three Powers moved squadrons eastward. Under threat, Japan revised the treaty terms, and restored Port Arthur to China.

Scarcely was the ink dry on the Treaty when Russia

sought and obtained the right to build a railway through Manchuria to the port of Niu-Chwang, and, further, the right to garrison Port Arthur and to use it as a naval base. European statesmen gasped at such bare-faced cynicism, but instead of actively protesting, they themselves joined in a scramble for pickings from China, they watched the continued Russian provocation of Japan unmoved, and they knew nothing of the quiet fervour with which Japan was building up her navy.

In February 1904, Japan felt ready to act. Without a formal declaration of war, her flotillas swooped upon Russian ships lying in the roads outside Port Arthur, and made havoc of them. The Russians were stunned. Even the use of defensive minefields, in which they were ingenious, proved a doubtful blessing, for when Admiral Makharoff, reported to be the best officer in the Russian navy, offered battle on 13 April to Admiral Heimachoro Togo and the main Japanese fleet, the Russian flagship herself hit a mine, and Makharoff sank with her.

The Japanese followed up their early advantage by occupying the heights surrounding the Russian base, and by bombarding ships at anchor. And when, in August, Admiral Witjeft took the Russians to sea a second time, intending to join forces with the squadron at Vladivostock, he was defeated and killed. The Russian Eastern Fleet was no longer effective, and if the Tsar was not to be forced to accept a humiliating peace, he would need to send his Baltic ships round half the world in a bid to restore the balance.

The story of delay, false alarm and complication which followed the Russian decision was a tragi-comedy which the world followed with attention. Command was given to Admiral Rojdestvensky, an officer aged fifty-six, of explosive temperament and with a good record of service years before in operations against the Turks. The core of his fleet were four new battleships, the *Borodino*, *Orel*, *Alexander III* and the flagship *Suvaroff*. With these powerful units, each armed with four 12-inch guns and twelve 6-inch quick-firers, having a nominal speed of 18 knots which the engineers could seldom maintain, went a miscellaneous collection of older battleships, cruisers, torpedo boats, and a fleet-train ranging from transports to hospital ships. It was a procession rather than a unified fleet.

The Tsar inspected the ships at Reval on 9 October. A week later Rojdestvensky was on his way. From the start he was strangely nervous. Reports had credited the Japanese with improvised torpedo craft, which were to lie in wait to attack the Russians at the entrance to the Baltic and in the North Sea. Rojdestvensky actually fired on a Swedish merchantman and a German fishing boat at an early stage in his progress, and an English fishing fleet off the Dogger Bank was appalled to find itself set upon by the might of Russian sea-power. British and Dutch had fought often enough in the old wars off the Dogger, but there had never been such an engagement as this! The Russian gunnery was shocking, but a trawler was sunk, and a number of innocent lives were lost.

When he reached Tangier, watched by a British

LEFT: *A romanticized portrait of Admiral Rojdestvensky*

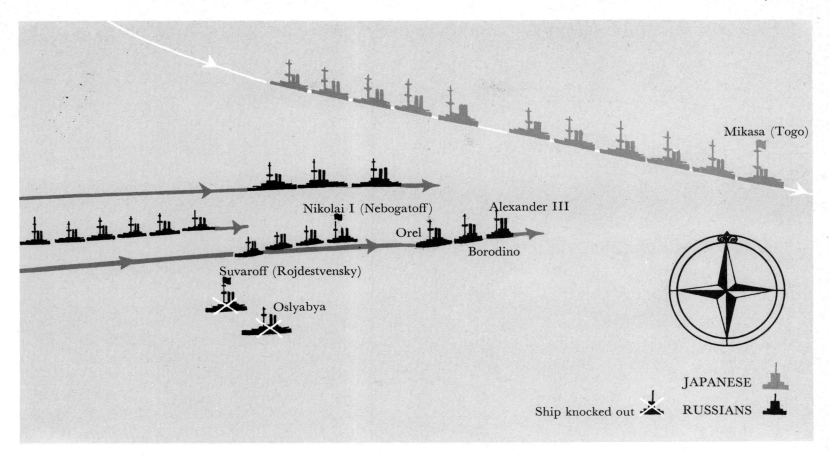

squadron under Lord Charles Beresford, Rojdestvensky divided his force. He himself proceeded round Africa, and he sent a division under Admiral Felkersham into the Mediterranean, with orders to use the route by the Suez Canal.

Rojdestvensky rounded the Cape of Good Hope on 19 December, and then made for Madagascar. On New Year's Day 1905 he anchored off Tamatave, where news arrived that Port Arthur had capitulated. Rojdestvensky's and Felkersham's forces were by now re-united, but the admirals seemed in no hurry to proceed. Their own nearest base was in enemy hands: all they could hope to do was to fight their way through Togo's fleet to Vladivostock. Not many, even of the most cheerful Russians, thought themselves likely to defeat the enemy on passage.

French friendliness was strained to the limit, for it was 25 March before the Russians left Madagascan waters. By 8 April they were off Singapore, keeping well out to sea. Their ships were burning soft coal, and an enormous cloud of smoke trailed from forty miscellaneous vessels, ranging from battleships to colliers.

April and May were spent in the ports of French Indo-China, where Rojdestvensky was given a final reinforcement. Then, on 14 May, he embarked on the final leg of his passage before the inevitable clash with the Japanese. He used the Bashee Channel between Formosa and the Philippines, and headed for Shanghai. There, on 25 May, the fighting ships parted from the auxiliaries, which were

anchored at the mouth of the Yang-tse. In the evening of the same day the admiral made for the Straits of Tsushima which separate the island of that name from Honshiu, the principal home-island of Japan. The weather was bad, with a rising wind and cold rain, which made a blinding haze. This fact cheered the Russians, for they hoped it would baffle the enemy scouts.

While the Russians were making their long voyage, Togo had had ample time to train his squadrons and flotillas, to improve ammunition which had proved defective in earlier battles, and to make the best dispositions possible. He was close to his bases, he knew every aspect of local waters, and he had a hundred reasons for confidence. To the world at large his movements were as mysterious as his country. All that people knew was that Rojdestvensky's chances of victory, whatever might be his nominal strength or even superiority, were slender. Realizing that the Tsushima passage was Rojdestvensky's likeliest route, Togo made Masampo Bay, in South Korea, the main station for his fleet, and it was from there that his attack was planned and mounted.

The Russians had three fast cruisers ahead of the two long columns in which they advanced. At the wing of each column was another cruiser, and two destroyers. Rojdestvensky himself led the stronger, starboard line, in the *Suvaroff*: this contained the four new battleships and four others, eight in all. There were eight ships in the port line, led by Rear-Admiral Nebogatoff in the *Nikokai I*, and the two main columns were followed by four store-

A realistic portrait of Admiral Heimachoro Togo made shortly after the capture of Port Arthur and before the Battle of Tsushima

RIGHT: *The captured Russian battleship* Orel *photographed at Maizura after the battle*

ships, two repair ships and, last of all, two steamers fitted up as hospital ships. On 26 May the clouds began to clear and the sun shone fitfully, but in spite of a fresh south-westerly wind, mist still lay upon the water. Rojdestvensky meant to pass the Straits in daylight. He did not feel confidence in his navigators' skill by night.

Togo had four battleships under his command, the *Mikasa*, his flagship, the *Shikishima*, *Asami* and *Fuki*, the last eight years old. He had some large new cruisers, and he was strong in flotillas. As he knew himself to be superior in speed, his plan was simple. His scouting forces would give him news, by the new wireless telegraphy, of Rojdestvensky's approach. His heavy ships would cross the line of the Russian advance. Cruisers would sweep round the Russian flanks, fall upon the rear, and destroy the auxiliaries. The flotillas would follow up and complete the destruction.

At dawn on 27 May the Japanese *Siano Maru*, an armed liner, almost collided with the Russian hospital ships at the rear of their columns. The *Siano Maru* disappeared into the early morning haze, signalling to Togo away at Masampo. Togo at once slipped from his moorings and headed for the open sea. Simultaneously, his cruiser squadrons closed in upon the reported line of bearing of the enemy. Rojdestvensky drew in his scouts, and closed up his fleet as a precautionary measure.

At 10 am. the Russians saw cruisers on their port beam, and Rojdestvensky formed his fighting ships into line ahead, while the transports moved away to starboard,

under the escort of three cruisers. The Japanese cruisers were commanded by Rear-Admiral Dewa, and they held a course parallel with the Russians at a distance of almost five miles. At 11.20 the Russians opened fire, apparently through the inadvertence of an officer in the *Orel*. Rojdestvensky signalled; 'Ammunition not to be wasted'. Action ceased.

At noon the Russians were due south of Tsushima, and the signal was hoist: 'Change course N. 23° E. for Vladivostock'. It was the anniversary of the Tsar's coronation, and round the bare ward-room tables, officers solemnly drank the Imperial health. At a little before two o'clock Togo came in sight of his opponent, to the south-westward of the island of Okonoshima and to the eastward of Tsushima. He signalled to his fleet: 'The rise or fall of the Empire depends on today's battle. Let every man do his utmost.' He began his attack, exactly as he had intended, by 'crossing the T' in the classical manner, in a slight diagonal and at a range of about 9,500 yards. At the same time, his cruiser squadrons steered for the Russian flanks and rear.

Togo's superiority in speed was such that he was able, once he had crossed Rojdestvensky's bows, to turn and recross. Rojdestvensky then steered a parallel course, and a general engagement took place at a range of between three and five miles. The result was decided by the speed and accuracy of the Japanese fire. 'After the first twenty minutes,' so a Japanese officer reported, 'the Russians seemed suddenly to go all to pieces, and their shooting became wild and almost harmless.'

Just before three o'clock the *Suvaroff* swerved out of the line with her steering disabled, and from then onwards the fight became a massacre. One by one the Russian battleships were put out of action, and by five o'clock they were huddled together in a confused crowd, attacked from the east by Togo himself and from the south by his cruisers. The *Suvaroff* was by now away to the westward, disabled and burning, though with her flag still flying. Rojdestvensky had been wounded twice and his flag-captain killed. His last order to Nebogatoff had been to try to get through to Vladivostock with at least part of the fleet. But as the sun went down, so did any remaining Russian hopes. They had been beaten by the

LEFT TOP: *A photograph taken from the* Asahi *showing the* Nikokai *under Rear-Admiral Nebogatoff surrendering to the Japanese*

LEFT CENTRE: *Admiral Togo's fleet on the scene of the engagement off Tsushima Island*

LEFT BOTTOM: *A painting by Norman Wilkinson showing the massive Russian fleet destroyed at Tsushima*

Two Russian warships captured at Tsushima photographed in July 1905 after they had been repaired and commissioned as part of the Japanese fleet

big ships, and there were still the torpedo boats, which during the night wrought further havoc.

All next day, destruction continued. Rojdestvensky, with a few of his officers, had transferred to a destroyer, but she was met by a Japanese flotilla and was captured during the afternoon of the 28th. The only Russian ships which ever reached Vladivostock were one small cruiser, the *Almaz*, and two destroyers. It was a story beside which that of the Armada of Philip II of Spain seemed almost like a victory.

As a result of the battle the Japanese revived the old practice of incorporating some of their best captures, repaired and restored, into their own fleet. Their own loss was confined entirely to torpedo craft, and even damage to their larger units was negligible. No victory had ever been more humiliating, in spite of much individual Russian valour, or more complete. An Eastern Power had proved that she could man and train a fleet equal to anything afloat. During the course of the next thirty-five years Japan was to continue to build up her naval power until, in due time, she was able to challenge even the might and efficiency of the United States.

Battleship Guns in Two World Wars

15. *Blast bags or breeches* 16. *Slide locking lever* 17. *Barbette* 18. *Training gear* 19. *Loading arm* 20. *Turret rollers* 21. *Lower roller path* 22. *Training rack* 23. *Gun-loading cage* 24. *Alternative shell-loading gear* 25. *Training shaft* 26. *Telescopic rammer* 27. *Waiting position* 28. *Walking pipe space* 29. *Main or trunk cage* 30. *Turret trunk* 31. *Cordite cases* 32. *Magazine* 33. *Cordite supply scuttle* 34. *Cordite handing room* 35. *Practice projectiles* 36. *High explosive projectiles* 37. *Lifting and traversing gear for supply of shells* 38. *Shell bogie* 39. *Shell room* 40. *Alternative hand gear* 41. *Shell room*

RIGHT: Key for 14-inch Gun Turret

1. *Ventilation ducts* 2. *Range-finder sighting-head* 3. *Turret locking-bolt control* 4. *Gun-loading cage* 5. *Gun-loading cage rammer and cage control* 6. *Gun-loading rammer* 7. *Range-finder* 8. *Gun wash-out tank* 9. *Navigating cabinet* 10. *Barbette armour* 11. *Turret locking-bolt* 12. *Elevating cylinder ram* 13. *Gun well* 14. *Gun-loading cage hoist* 15. *Gun-loading rammer chain casing* 16. *Barbette armour* 17. *Turntable rollers* 18. *Armour chock* 19. *Central ammunition hoist winches* 20. *Striking-down tube* 21. *Final drive of training rack* 22. *Top of central ammunition hoist* 23. *Training rack* 24. *Training gear shaft* 25. *Bridge trays* 26. *Hydraulic exhaust pipes in turret* 27. *Gun-loading hoist* 28. *Rammer from central hoist to traverser* 29. *Gun-loading rammer chain casing* 30. *Striking-down control standard* 31. *Training gear space* 32. *Training gear worm wheel and friction clutch casing* 33. *Hydraulic exhaust pipes in turret* 34. *Hydraulic supply pipes in turret* 35. *Ventilation ducts* 36. *Hydraulic supply pipes in turret* 37. *Striking-down tube* 38. *Central ammunition hoist* 39. *Control on turret for shell-ring drive and rammers* 40. *Shell-ring rammers* 41. *Shell-ring drive engine control* 42. *Revolving shell-ring* 43. *Shell-ring support* 44. *Control for cordite rammer* 45. *Cordite rammer and hopper* 46. *Cordite charge bogie* 47. *Hydraulic exhaust from turret*

The 14-inch guns (right) fitted on 'King George V' Class battleships, which fought in the Second World War, had a greater effective range than the 15-inch guns (left) fitted on 'Queen Elizabeth' Class battleships, which served in the First World War

LEFT: Key for 15-inch Gun Turret

1. *15 ft. coincidence type range-finder* 2. *Gun-layer's periscope* 3. *Local-control cabinet* 4. *Officer's look-out periscope* 5. *Turret 8-inch armour* 6. *Range-finder training wheel* 7. *Gun-loading cage hoist lever* 8. *Rammer lever* 9. *Guides for loading cage* 10. *Breech handling* 11. *Lock* 12. *Floor of gun-house* 13. *Recoil cylinders* 14. *Elevating wheel*

Coronel and the
Falkland Islands
1914

*Off Coronel, a crack German squadron under Admiral von Spee sank two British cruisers,
which were avenged off the Falkland Islands a few weeks later*

SUPERIOR TRAINING, SUPERIOR GUNNERY, including weight of metal, speed, good tactics, these were the factors which told in the earlier armoured sea-fights. It was so off Coronel, in the first dire reverse suffered by the British at the hands of the Imperial German Navy.

The first world war opened with the virtual disappearance of German shipping from the broad oceans. There was one exception, the crack squadron commanded by Graf von Spee. His ships consisted of the heavy cruisers *Scharnhorst* and *Gneisenau*, and the light cruisers *Emden*, *Leipzig* and *Nürnberg*: one other cruiser, the *Dresden*, later joined him from the Atlantic. Before the outbreak of war von Spee had been based at Tsing-Tau, north of Shanghai, but with Japan on the same side as Britain, he had prudently disappeared into the Pacific, one of his ships, the *Emden*, later causing alarm and damage off the coasts of India. Spee himself, with his main force, appeared off Samoa – which was well prepared to receive him – and then vanished into the blue.

One day, so the Admiralty in London believed, the German squadron would break into the Atlantic and raid the trade-routes. If possible, Spee must be destroyed before he could do it, and Rear-Admiral Sir Christopher Cradock was probably the man to do it.

Hardly had the war opened when the new German

battle-cruiser *Goeben* and the light cruiser *Breslau* were allowed to reach Constantinople by way of the Dardanelles. The event had been a shock to naval and lay opinion alike, and the ships affected the course of history, for it was they that brought Turkey into the war on the side of Germany. No such calamity, it was felt, must ever happen again. Spee's account must be settled before he could do harm on anything approaching the *Goeben*'s scale.

To face Spee, Cradock had the cruisers *Good Hope* and *Monmouth*, the light cruiser *Glasgow*, and an armed liner, the *Otranto*. The Admiralty ordered him to base himself on the Falklands, and they informed him that an old battleship, the *Canopus*, would shortly join him. She did so, but she was slow and unreliably powered, useful to fall back upon if pressed, but an uncertain asset to an admiral whose orders matched his wish to 'destroy the German cruisers'.

Cradock and his squadron passed through the Straits of Magellan in October 1914, and course was then set up the Chilean coast to look for the Germans. The *Glasgow*, Cradock's fastest ship, was sent ahead, and the aged *Canopus* escorted the squadron's colliers at her best speed.

During the last days of the month the *Glasgow*, while off Coronel, picked up cipher wireless messages which she suspected to be from a German cruiser, probably the *Leipzig*. Graf Spee learnt of the *Glasgow*'s presence in his neighbourhood, and he decided to steam south, in the hope of cutting her off. In the early hours of 1 November there occurred the odd situation that Admirals Spee and

LEFT: *A painting by W. L. Wyllie showing the German flagship,* Scharnhorst *sinking rapidly. In the background is her sister ship the* Gneisenau, *which continued longer in action*

253

TOP: *HMS* Glasgow, *a light cruiser launched in 1909, and the only British ship present both at Coronel on 1 November and the Falkland Islands on 8 December*

BOTTOM: *The German cruiser* Nürnberg *which served at both Coronel and the Falklands. She was sunk on 8 December by HMS* Kent

LEFT TOP: *Rear-Admiral Sir Christopher Cradock commanded the British squadron at Coronel and was killed in action against von Spee*

BOTTOM LEFT: *A German medal struck to commemorate the gallantry of Admiral von Spee at Coronel and the Falkland Islands. With him are his sons, Heinrich, who served on the* Gneisenau *and Otto, who served on the* Nürnberg. *Both were killed in action.*

Cradock were steaming towards one another, both under the impression that only a solitary enemy cruiser was likely to be encountered.

At 2.30 pm., in a strong south-easterly wind and a high sea, Cradock ordered a line of search. There were to be intervals of fifteen miles between ships, which were to proceed at ten knots. Some two hours later the *Glasgow* reported smoke to the north east, away towards the Chilean coast. Then she reported two large ships and a smaller one, and Cradock realized that he was approaching Spee. The German admiral altered course towards the *Glasgow*.

When Cradock discovered the enemy strength he found that the *Leipzig* was in company with the *Scharnhorst* and *Gneisenau*. The *Dresden* was then about twelve miles behind the squadron, invisible, and the *Nürnberg* still further away. It was some time before Spee was aware that he was face to face with Cradock, and six o'clock before he identified all four British ships.

Cradock formed line ahead, *Good Hope*, *Monmouth*, *Glasgow* and *Otranto*, and he steered a course which, had his speed been greater, would have crossed Spee's bows and brought his ships between the Germans and the land, thus silhouetting them against the declining sun. Countering the movement, Spee altered course to port and increased speed, the *Scharnhorst* drawing ahead of her own squadron. The lines were now about twelve miles apart, the ships' courses gradually converging. One of Cradock's last messages was to the *Canopus*, some 250 miles away, telling her that he was about to attack.

Cradock's action has been criticized, with the wisdom of hindsight, by most historians, perhaps with little sense of the actual occasion. Cradock's two bigger ships were inferior in armament to Spee's – he had two 9·2-inch guns in the *Good Hope*, and sixteen 6-inch. The *Monmouth* had fourteen 6-inch, while Spee's flagship and her principal consort had eight 8·2-inch apiece, and six 5·9-inch, the German guns in each case being better placed for use in a rough sea. Further, the *Scharnhorst* had recently won the Kaiser's prize for shooting, and the Germans were a highly trained active service squadron, while Cradock had mainly reservists. Nevertheless, the Royal Navy had not known serious reverse in an action on any scale since the eighteenth century; it had a tradition of facing odds stretching back to the Spanish Armada, and Cradock would have marked the case of the *Goeben*, for he was a thoughtful man.

While it is unlikely that the British admiral considered that he could defeat Spee, he had no reason to doubt that he could damage him, and damage should have led to destruction. Spee had no available base, and if his speed were reduced, the *Canopus* could be at hand within twenty-four hours, and her 12-inch guns could have been decisive. Night was falling, and if Spee was not attacked at

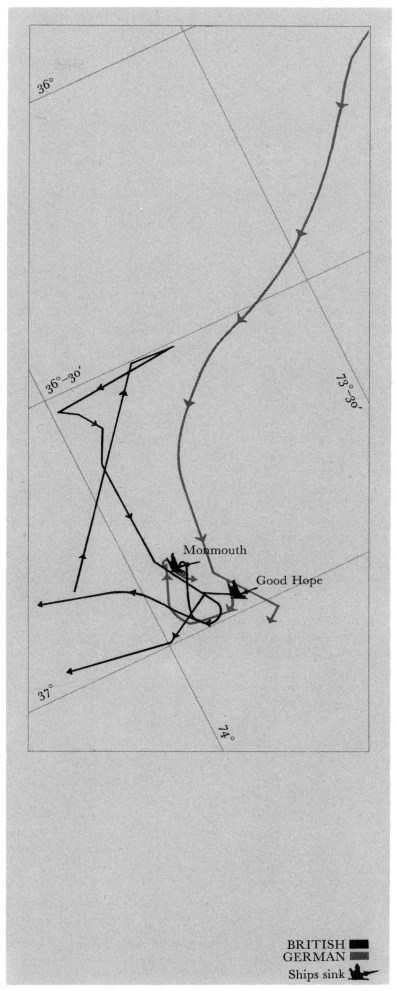

BRITISH ■
GERMAN ■
Ships sink ⚓

once, he could scarcely be shadowed. He could have blown out of the water any shadowers close enough to be effective in the local conditions. Finally, if the Germans, now at last discovered, eluded Cradock, there was nothing to stop them getting into the Atlantic, which was the very thing that Cradock was there to prevent.

In the hour before sunset the two squadrons steamed southward, gradually lessening the range. The evening was stormy and the ships were rolling heavily, seas breaking over the bows. The clouds were clearer to westward, where the sun was going down in a red glow. By 7 pm. it was on the horizon. Just as it set, Spee opened fire, at a range of nearly seven miles. Action soon became general except for the unprotected *Otranto*, which drew away to starboard of the *Glasgow*, since her guns would have been ineffective.

The battle lasted about an hour. Good gunnery told at once, and at the third salvo the *Scharnhorst* found Cradock's range. The British ships were silhouetted sharply against the light on the western horizon, while the Germans appeared like vague shadows against the loom of the land. The *Good Hope*'s larger guns were knocked out early in the fight, one of them before it had fired, and within five minutes the *Monmouth* had been badly hit by the *Gneisenau*. The *Leipzig* and *Dresden* were concentrating on the *Glasgow*, and converging courses were shortening the range each moment. By 7.40 the *Monmouth* was down

RIGHT: *Picking up survivors from the* Gneisenau, *photographed from the* Invincible, *Admiral Sturdee's flagship, by Paymaster Sub-Lieutenant A. D. Duckworth. HMS* Inflexible *is in the background*

TOP: *HMS* Good Hope, *Admiral Cradock's flagship, sunk at Coronel with all hands*

BOTTOM: *Admiral Sturdee's flagship at the Battle of the Falkland Islands, HMS* Invincible, *which was later sunk at Jutland in 1916*

by the head and on fire aft. The *Good Hope* had turned towards the Germans, on fire amidships, possibly with the idea of using her torpedoes. The end came at 7.50 when, with her guns still firing, she suddenly blew up. There was no prospect of the rescue of survivors from the icy sea.

The British then scattered, the *Monmouth*, gravely damaged and listing heavily, keeping away northward, the *Glasgow* and *Otranto*, followed by the victorious Germans, steaming west. They were soon swallowed up in the darkness, justifying belief that, when night fell, shadowing became difficult if not impossible.

At 9 pm. Spee heard gunfire to the north of him, and he altered course to investigate. The stricken *Monmouth*, her guns useless, had run into the *Nürnberg*, still behind the rest of her squadron. The *Nürnberg* fired a salvo into the British ship, from which there was no reply. The Germans ceased fire, expecting the British to surrender. They did no such thing. Further salvoes heeled the *Monmouth* over and she sank, carrying all her officers and men to the bottom, but with her flag still flying.

British reaction to the German success was swift. Lord Fisher had just taken office as First Sea Lord. He ordered two battle cruisers under Admiral Sturdee to the Falklands. They arrived, the *Invincible*, *Inflexible* and supporting cruisers, on 7 December, and began coaling. Spee arrived off the islands with his squadron the very next day, intending to destroy the wireless station. He was greeted by the guns of the old *Canopus*, which had been moored as guardship in the inner harbour at Port Stanley. Her active presence gave the battle-cruisers just the necessary time to make ready for sea, and Graf Spee was pursued and destroyed, after a most gallant defence.

The *Glasgow* took part in both actions. 'Throughout the engagement off Coronel,' wrote her captain, 'perfect discipline and coolness prevailed under the trying circumstance of receiving a considerable volume of fire without being able to make adequate return. The men behaved exactly as though at battle practice; there were no signs of wild fire, and when the target was invisible the gunlayers ceased firing of their own accord. The spirit of officers and ship's company is entirely unimpaired by the serious reverse in which they took part . . .' They had not long to wait for their own turn to come.

Graf Spee's conduct throughout the two battles in which he was engaged showed him a leader of the highest quality, and his personality won the respect of both sides. When, after Coronel, he was made much of by the German colony at Valparaiso, he spoke no word of triumph over the dead, and he said of the flowers which were offered him: 'They will do for my funeral'.

It is also due to the memory of Cradock to record that he was a thoughtful student of war, with a varied and honourable record of active service. Although he failed completely in his object of damaging a superior enemy, his example of fortitude had its effect, and the words which he wrote as a captain that, in his own belief, 'our personnel (after a few hard knocks) will prove as good as ever', were shown to be true in the years to come, when the Service he loved fought its long and arduous campaigns against the Imperial German Navy, and later against that of Hitler's Reich.

Admiral Fisher, photographed in his cabin on board HMS Renown *in about 1900. As First Sea Lord in 1914, his rapid action in sending the* Invincible *and the* Inflexible *to the defence of the Falkland Islands was responsible for the defeat of Graf von Spee*

HMS Dreadnought, 1906

LAUNCHED: *10 February 1906*
TRIALS: *3 October 1906*
LENGTH (OVERALL): *526 feet*
DISPLACEMENT (FULL LOAD): C *20,700 tons*
GUNS: *10 × 12-inch*
      10 × 12-pounders
TORPEDOES: *5 tubes submerged*
          4 broadside
          1 astern
SPEED: *21·6 knots*

The new First Sea Lord (in 1904), Sir John Fisher, conceived the idea of the Dreadnought, *the first all big gun battleship, which had twice as many 12-inch guns as any other battleship then afloat. Built in a remarkably short time in Portsmouth Dockyard, she was the most admired and controversial battleship of her day and gave her name to the generation of capital ships that followed her. Her advent made obsolete the largest fleet of battleships in the world, and enabled Germany to start building at something like parity.*

An unusual feature of the Dreadnought *was the reversal of the crew's and officers' quarters, which put the men aft and the officers foreward to bring the latter nearer the conning tower in this long ship—though the men thought that this was to spare the officers from the vibration caused by the new machinery. (She was, in fact, singularly free from vibration.)*

The Dreadnought *began her career as flagship of the Home Fleet from 1907 to 1912, then became flagship of the Fourth Battle Squadron from 1912 to 1916, distinguishing herself during the First World War by ramming and sinking U.29 on 18 March 1915. After the Lowestoft raid in 1916, at the urgent request of the local municipal authorities, she was sent to the Thames estuary as flagship of the Third Battle Squadron (King Edward VII's). In 1919 she was in reserve, and in 1920 she was sold.*

Key to the *Dreadnought* Cross-Section

1. *12-inch gun turrets*	16. *Wardroom*	
2. *12-pounder guns*	17. *Officers' cabin*	
3. *Barbettes*	18. *Offices*	
4. *Cordite trays*	19. *Offices and stores*	
5. *Control tower*	20. *Stores*	
6. *Conning tower*	21. *Magazine*	
7. *Transmitting room*	22. *Shell room*	
8. *Engineers*	23. *Seamen's mess*	
9. *Boilers*	24. *Royal Marines' mess*	
10. *Engine room*	25. *Stokers' mess*	
11. *Fuel tanks*	26. *Rudder*	
12. *Flues*	27. *Propellers*	
13. *Air trunks*	28. *After control*	
14. *Navigating bridge*	29. *Torpedoes*	
15. *Boats*	30. *Capstan gear*	
	31. *Chain locker*	

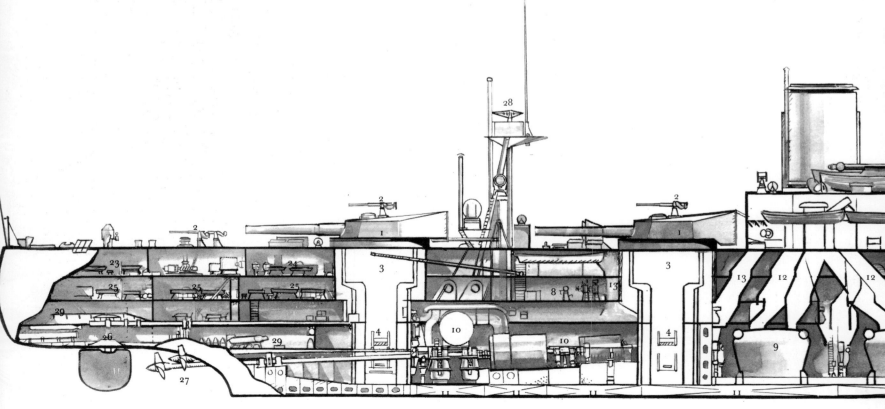

Jutland

1916

In this greatest naval battle of the First World War, the Imperial German Navy proved its skill and fighting qualities, but Britain retained control at sea

THE BRITISH, AND POSSIBLY MOST OF the German public, had expected a full scale sea-battle early in the First World War, perhaps during the opening days. They had nearly two years to wait, and when the time came, the result seemed inconclusive and, for the Grand Fleet, disappointing. The Germans claimed a tactical victory, since with inferior forces they inflicted higher losses than they sustained. The British soon realized that the broad strategic picture was unchanged. They retained their predominance at sea, and they knew that if ever they were to be defeated, it would not be by means of the German High Seas Fleet. In fact, the German High Command before long turned to another mode of warfare, unrestricted attack by submarine, and there they came within measure of success.

The Germans had learnt two valuable lessons from earlier and lesser surface engagements. The first, which was the result of an action in the Heligoland Bight in August 1914, was that they faced in Vice-Admiral Sir David Beatty a battle-cruiser leader willing to use his great ships almost like a cavalry general. The second, resulting from an action off the Dogger Bank in the following year, when they lost the *Blücher*, was the need for better protection of their ships' magazines. Essential steps were taken.

LEFT: *The last moments of the battle cruiser HMS* Queen Mary, *blown up during Beatty's opening action against the German battle cruiser force*

In the face of a British fleet superior in numbers, German strategy was to trap part of it, probably the battle-cruiser force, and to destroy it before Admiral Sir John Jellicoe, the British Commander-in-Chief, could appear in strength. This was the plan when Scheer took charge of the German fleet early in 1916, and was pressed to justify the navy's existence in view of the sacrifices of the German army before Verdun.

Scheer devised two operations. One was to have as its immediate object the bombardment of an east coast port in Britain, such as had been made before. This would be a task for Vice-Admiral von Hipper's battle-cruisers, while submarines would be stationed off the Grand Fleet's bases, and Scheer would act as cover. The help of Zeppelin airships would be involved, and favourable weather conditions would be necessary. The other plan was to stage a raid by Hipper on British shipping off the Danish coasts, again with Scheer in support and with submarines lying in wait.

On 15 May submarines took up their allotted stations for the first plan, but bad weather grounded the airships until 30 May, by which time the submarines were almost due to return. Hipper was therefore ordered to proceed to the Skager Rak and show himself off the Norwegian coast, so that his presence would be reported, Scheer staying discreetly out of sight off the coast of Jutland.

The British Admiralty had information that something big was in train, and Jellicoe sailed secretly on the night of 30 May. As airship reconnaissance had been impos-

sible, Scheer, when he set out, was in ignorance of the size of the total force he was likely to meet. But, as he himself had successfully deceived the British into the belief that he was still in the river Jade, Jellicoe was ignorant of the fact that the entire High Seas Fleet was out in support of Hipper.

The battle which followed is one of the most complicated in history. This is scarcely surprising, since it began with a double deception and continued under such weather conditions that, while some two hundred and fifty ships of all types were involved, – a hundred and fifty under Jellicoe's control, a hundred and one under Scheer's – it was a rare moment when more than a few ships at a time could follow the movements of their own main forces, or catch more than an uncertain glimpse of the enemy. Radar had not yet been invented, and there can be no better illustration of prevailing conditions than the fact that a Zeppelin flew high over the field of battle, totally unaware of the struggle beneath her.

Jutland was one of the last big-scale battles in naval war in which the gun was paramount, for although airships, seaplanes, submarines, mines and torpedoes were all at or near the scene of encounter, none played a major role,

and the British seaplane carrier *Engadine*, pioneer of a class of ship which was to become all-important in the future, was actually used to tow a damaged cruiser!

Action was precipitated by an incident which occurred when Scheer was still forty miles south of Hipper, and Jellicoe more than fifty miles north of Beatty. Hipper's light cruisers went to investigate a neutral steamer. They were surprised in their search by Beatty's scouts. Beatty had with him six battle-cruisers, the *Lion*, *Princess Royal*, *Queen Mary*, *Tiger*, *New Zealand* and *Indefatigable*, supported by four new battleships under Sir Hugh Evan-Thomas, the *Barham*, *Warspite*, *Malaya* and *Valiant*.

Beatty turned in pursuit without waiting to see whether Evan-Thomas had understood his signals, which were obscured by smoke, and by the time the battleships followed him, the interval between Beatty and his support had been much increased. Led south at high speed by Hipper with the *Lutzow*, *Derfflinger*, *Seydlitz*, *Moltke* and *von der Tann*, Beatty rushed into the trap prepared for him by Scheer.

Weather conditions gave readings on the British instru-

OVERLEAF, LEFT: *Beatty's flagship, HMS* Lion, *photographed in action from the German battle cruiser* Derfflinger

LEFT: *Admiral Jellicoe making his way up to the bridge of HMS* Iron Duke, *his flagship at Jutland*

OVERLEAF, RIGHT: *The last of HMS* Invincible *which sank in the earlier stages of the battle after her magazines exploded*

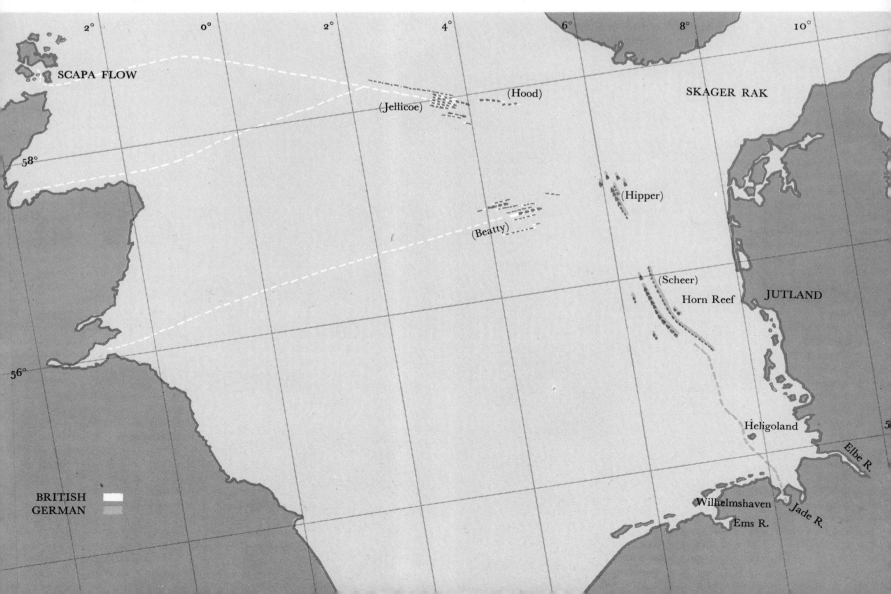

LEFT: *Admiral Beatty, Commander of the British battle cruiser force at Jutland. He succeeded Admiral Jellicoe as Commander-in-Chief soon after the battle.* RIGHT: *Admiral von Scheer, Commander-in-Chief of the German High Seas Fleet at Jutland*

ments much in excess of the true range, and Beatty withheld his fire longer than necessary. When he opened fire, his early salvoes fell far beyond Hipper, while his own ships showed clearly against the western sky. Beatty suffered heavily during his run south. The *Indefatigable* and *Queen Mary* were blown up in quick succession, and Beatty's flagship narrowly escaped the same fate. The armoured roof of one of the *Lion*'s turrets, struck by a heavy shell, 'folded back like an open sardine tin', as one of her officers noted, and the ship was saved only by the dying act of the Major of marines, who gave the order to flood the turret's magazines.

'There seems to be something wrong with our bloody ships today!' exclaimed Beatty to his flag-captain. There was indeed, but the admiral remained unshaken in his intention to pursue, and if possible destroy the enemy. By this time Evan-Thomas, cutting corners, was in full support, and records show that the Germans were hit hard and often, though the damage they suffered was not disastrous. The most serious was the result of a flotilla torpedo attack which achieved a hit on the *Seydlitz*, and forced Hipper to turn away.

At 4.33 Beatty received a signal from Commodore Goodenough saying he had sighted the enemy's main fleet. Beatty turned towards the reported position. Two minutes later the long line of Scheer's battleships were in view from the *Lion*, at a distance of twelve miles. Realizing the nature of the trap, Beatty made a turn to the northward towards Jellicoe, using the respite given him

by the torpedo attack on Hipper. It was now Beatty's responsibility to see that the main fleets met under conditions favourable to Jellicoe, which meant that Hipper must be prevented from sighting the Grand Fleet and warning Scheer of the trap into which he was steaming. Evan-Thomas, following Beatty's turn, came under concentrated fire from both Scheer and Hipper and received damage, though all his ships were able to stay in the line.

While the battle-cruisers were engaged, Jellicoe's fleet had been moving south in six columns abreast. In order to make proper use of his fire power, Jellicoe would need to manoeuvre into line ahead. On which flank should he deploy? Much rested on his decision, but he was in ignorance of the position and course of the Germans.

At Trafalgar, Nelson's approach had been made at a walking pace, the enemy always in full sight. At Jutland, Jellicoe and Scheer neared one another unseen, at a combined speed of between forty and fifty knots, the exact composition of the enemy being as yet unknown.

When Jellicoe and Beatty joined forces, Beatty had just broken off a second action, during the course of which he had pushed across Hipper's bows and forced him to retire under cover of Scheer's guns. Hipper ordered a destroyer attack, but this was baulked by the sudden appearance of advanced units of the Grand Fleet. When the British forces met, the combined errors in reckoning of Jellicoe's flagship *Iron Duke* and Beatty's *Lion* amounted to eleven miles; moreover, since Beatty had temporarily lost visual contact with the enemy, all he could report, at 6.14 pm., was, 'Enemy battle fleet bearing south east'. Jellicoe thereupon gave the order to form line of battle on the port wing on a course south-east-by-east, so keeping between the enemy and their coast.

When Jellicoe's movement was completed, an immense line of battleships stretched to the horizon, by far the most powerful naval armament the world had yet seen. Scheer held on, soon to find himself swept by the guns of the entire British Fleet. He had run straight into the trap, and there seemed no escape from destruction. 'The arc stretching from north to east was a sea of fire', he reported later. By this time four out of Hipper's five battle-cruisers were badly damaged, and at the first possible moment Hipper shifted his flag from the *Lutzow* to the *Moltke*.

The German Commander-in-Chief, with disaster facing him, saved himself by a manoeuvre which was reckoned so difficult, and which was so well screened by torpedo attacks and smoke screens put up by his destroyer flotillas, that no one on the British side knew exactly what had happened until the war was over. This was a complete

RIGHT: *Admiral Jellicoe's personal message to his officers and men after the Battle of Jutland*

Admiral Jellicoes Message to the Fleet.

I desire to express to the Flag Officers, Captains, Officers and Men of the Grand Fleet my very high appreciation of the manner in which the ships were fought on May 31st 1916

At this stage, when full information is not available, it is not possible to enter into details, but quite sufficient is already known to enable me to state definitely that the glorious traditions handed down to us by generations of gallant seamen were most worthily upheld.

Weather conditions of a highly unfavourable nature robbed the Fleet of that complete victory which I know was expected by all ranks, which is necessary for the Safety of the Empire & which will yet be ours.

Our losses were heavy and we miss many most gallant comrades but, although it is very difficult to obtain accurate information as to the enemy losses, I have no doubt that we shall find that they are certainly not less than our own. Sufficient information has already been received by me for me to make that statement with confidence.

I hope to be able to give the Fleet fuller information on this point at an early date, but do not wish to delay the issue of this expression of my keen appreciation of the work of the Fleet, and my confidence in future complete victory.

I cannot close without stating that the wonderful fortitude of the wounded has filled me with the greatest admiration. I am more proud than ever to have the honour of commanding a fleet manned by such officers and men

(Signed) J. R. Jellicoe

Admiral, Commander in Chief

Extract from a letter written on 31 May 1917, the first anniversary of the Battle of Jutland, from Admiral Beatty to his wife.

"Grand Fleet

It hardly seems a year since that terrible day when we might have accomplished so much and our failure to do so has cost us dear, when those great ships and gallant lives were lost. As time goes by, one realises more clearly the opportunity that was missed, an opportunity that will never recur, and what would have been easy then will be infinitely more difficult in the future. Fate is not over-generous in the matter of giving opportunities, and if you miss one you never get another. However, I console myself with the thought that the Battle Cruiser Fleet did all that it could have done, and that next time, if Fate is kind and gives us a next time, the Battle Fleet will have their chance."

and simultaneous turn about on the part of every German battleship. The movement, which Scheer had practised against the exact situation in which he now found himself, was made at the very moment when defeat seemed inevitable.

Having escaped once, Scheer twice changed course later in the day in order to evade Jellicoe's fleet as it continued south-easterly on its majestic progress, being saved a second time by his 'battle-turn'. His second great moment of danger caused him to order his destroyers to attack under a smoke screen, and the already scarred battle-cruisers received the desperate signal, 'Charge the enemy. Ram. Ships are to attack without regard to consequences!'

Scheer's withdrawal was made good by 7.20, and although Jellicoe had altered course to the west to avoid torpedoes, Beatty kept touch and reported the German position. At 8.17 Hipper's battle-cruisers once again came in sight, and Beatty opened fire at 10,000 yards. Before the Germans could retire the *Derfflinger*'s last undamaged turret had been put out of action, and, for the first time since the battle opened, the *Princess Royal* had ranges free from the *Lion*'s smoke. Beatty's ships had fired the first British big-gun salvoes in the battle, and they fired the last.

At dusk, Jellicoe took up night stations. He wished to keep his divisions in a tight formation in order to avoid the possibility of his big ships mistaking one another for the enemy. His main concern was now to prevent Scheer breaking through to the east and so escaping home. Beatty was stationed in the van. The battleships were formed in the centre in three columns abreast; light cruisers and flotillas brought up the rear.

Three choices lay before Scheer as he strove to regain the security of the German minefields: a south-westerly route to the Ems: southerly to Heligoland and Wilhelmshaven; south-east for Horn Reef and the Elbe. To attempt to return to the Baltic by way of the Skager Rak would have been to invite destruction.

Jellicoe, despite some evidence that Scheer would use the Horn Reef channel, decided that the Germans would proceed south, though he despatched a minelayer to block the south-easterly channel. This was the way Scheer took, and although he lost one ship to the *Abdiel*'s mines, he succeeded in cutting through the rear of Jellicoe's fleet during the hours of darkness, and withdrew without disaster.

Fierce fighting occurred during the night among the flotillas, but by extraordinary mischance, Jellicoe was not informed that the enemy had been engaged. It was only when dawn broke that he knew the full extent of his lost opportunity, and as he turned north for home he found himself in command of a battlefield empty but for rafts and wreckage.

War is fought with other weapons besides explosives, and the Germans, first to reach port, were first with news which came as a staggering blow to British pride. Incontestible British losses were three battle-cruisers, for in addition to the *Queen Mary* and *Indefatigable* of Beatty's squadron, the *Invincible*, ahead of Jellicoe's main force, had been sunk by the oncoming German battle-fleet. Three cruisers were also sunk, and eight destroyers.

German losses were revealed more slowly: one battleship, one battle-cruiser, four light cruisers and four destroyers. What was not known until long afterwards was that although twenty-six of Jellicoe's battleships were unscathed, only six of Scheer's escaped without damage, which in some cases was serious. The cost in lives was more disproportionate than that in ships: 6,000 British, 2,500 Germans. Many Germans were saved from their stricken vessels, while in the three British battle-cruisers scarcely anyone survived.

Jellicoe, as Churchill remarked, was the only man who could have lost the war in an afternoon. Since the fate of the Allies depended, in the last resort, on the maintenance of British sea-power, he had far more at stake than Scheer, and he was taking no chances. He was fighting a battle on an unparalleled scale. He was hampered by uncertain visibility, bad signalling, too-centralized control, continuous smoke, and faults in ship design. He was not to know that the High Seas Fleet would never again give him such an opportunity as had eluded him, but this was so, and Beatty, his successor, had no better fortune.

No naval battle in history has resulted in more controversy than Jutland. The literature is acrimonious, partisan, and still increasing. Nothing can disguise the truth of the fact that there were three moments at which Jellicoe might possibly have contrived decision: after he first deployed the Grand Fleet; when Scheer ran into him a second time; finally, when he considered and rejected the advice, which he received a little before midnight, that the likely passage by which the enemy would return was the Horn Reef. 'Three times is a lot,' was the Churchillian comment. He added: 'The ponderous, poignant responsibilities borne successfully, if not triumphantly, by Sir John Jellicoe during two years of faithful command, constitute unanswerable claims to the lasting respect of the nation. But the Royal Navy must find in other personalities and other episodes the golden links which carried forward through the Great War the audacious and conquering traditions of the past . . .'

Although this is true, it remains to say that Jellicoe offered a pattern of the scientific naval officer to those who served in his command. No leader has inspired more affection among those closest to him.

The Pursuit of the Bismarck
1941

The 'Bismarck', the most powerful battleship afloat, was pursued and sunk in the Atlantic after having sunk the British battle-cruiser, 'Hood'

IN THE EARLY SUMMER OF 1941, after the Second World War had been in progress for the better part of two years, Great Britain and her self-governing dominions found themselves without effective Allies. France was defeated, and Britain's small army had been driven from the Continent by the most efficient and mobile conqueror since Napoleon. Her cities faced aerial assault by night, and her Navy was stretched to the limit – theoretically, far beyond it. America was sympathetic but neutral, and Stalin, then partial to Hitler's conquering Germany, had boasted that he would pull no British chestnuts out of the fire.

At sea, Britain's commitments were world-wide, yet her lifeline, the Atlantic, was in immediate danger of severance by submarine blockade. As if all this misfortune were not enough, it was known in May that the *Bismarck*, the most powerful man-of-war yet built in Europe, was preparing for her first sortie. If she could break out into the Atlantic, she could devastate shipping, and the ports of the French west coast would be open to receive her when her mission was fulfilled.

The *Bismarck*, flying the flag of Admiral Lütjens, sailed from the Baltic on 18 May, in company with the heavy cruiser *Prinz Eugen*. Their departure was confirmed by air reconnaissance, and it was believed that their destination was westerly, and that they would approach the Atlantic

trade routes by way of the Denmark Straits, which divide Greenland from Iceland.

The British cruisers *Norfolk* and *Suffolk* were on patrol in that area, and the Germans were sighted by both ships on 23 May, the *Norfolk* coming under fire at a range of six-and-a-half miles and disengaging under cover of smoke. Her captain's report was picked up by Admiral Tovey, who was then commanding the British Home Fleet. He was then 600 miles to the south-east. Admiral Holland, who was nearer, turned towards the position at full speed. Holland's flag was in the battle-cruiser *Hood*, a twenty-five year old ship, but one whose power and equipment was thought sufficient to enable her to face anything afloat. With her was the battleship *Prince of Wales*, recently completed and not yet fully worked up.

As the British capital ships were good for not more than 28 knots and the Germans were rated at 30, surprise was essential to bring about an action, and Holland relied for guidance on Admiral Wake Walker's two cruisers. At the critical stage in Holland's approach, the *Norfolk* and *Suffolk* temporarily lost touch with the Germans in a snow-storm. Believing that this was because the enemy had altered course to south-east, Holland himself altered from a westerly intercepting course to due north, reducing speed to 25 knots.

At 2.47 am. on 24 May the *Suffolk* regained contact, and the *Bismarck*'s position and speed could then be plotted. Speed in the two big British ships was increased to 28 knots, and by 4.30 am. visibility was up to twelve

LEFT: *Survivors from the* Bismarck *being rescued from the Atlantic by the British cruiser* Dorsetshire *on 27 May 1941*

273

miles. The *Prince of Wales*'s reconnaissance aircraft prepared to take off to give Holland the exact enemy position, but the pilot found his fuel contaminated by sea water, and the machine was jettisoned.

Holland meant to concentrate the fire of both his ships on the *Bismarck*, leaving the *Prinz Eugen* to the *Norfolk* and *Suffolk*, but when the enemy came in sight at 5.35 am. and action started eighteen minutes later, the relative positions favoured the Germans. At a range of about thirteen miles they were too fine on the *Hood*'s starboard bow for her two after-turrets to come into action, while to the *Bismarck* the British were slightly before the beam and were therefore exposed to their full broadside. Instead of being able to open fire with the *Hood*'s eight 15-inch guns and the ten 14-inch guns of the *Prince of Wales*, Holland had only the four forward 15-inch guns of the *Hood* and five forward 14-inch guns of the *Prince of Wales* usable, since one of the *Prince of Wales*'s six forward guns was defective. Lütjens had the full use of eight 15-inch guns in the *Bismarck* and eight 8-inch guns in the *Prinz Eugen*.

Fire was opened simultaneously, at about 26,500 yards, by all four ships, Lütjens concentrating on the *Hood*, which was leading the British. Holland had ordered both his ships to concentrate on the left hand German, assuming her to be the *Bismarck*. This was not so. Fortunately the gunnery officer of the *Prince of Wales* altered target on his own responsibility.

With both German ships concentrating on the *Hood*, she was soon hit, the *Prinz Eugen*'s 8-inch guns causing a fire near the British flagship's main-mast which spread forward and blazed high above the upper deck. At 5.55 Holland ordered a 20-degree turn away from the enemy. This would have brought the full broadsides of both his ships to bear; but in the act of turning a salvo fell round the *Hood*, flame leapt hundreds of feet, and her mighty form dissolved into a vast column of smoke, out of which her bow and stern rose steeply as she broke amidships and disappeared beneath the sea. Plunging shells had exploded her magazines, and the 'might, majesty, dominion and power' which the ship represented had gone the same way as three others of her ill-fated type at Jutland, a quarter of a century before.

The Germans were now free to concentrate on the *Prince of Wales*. She was soon in trouble. A 15-inch shell hit her compass-platform and killed or wounded every man there except Captain Leach. Within a few minutes she was hit six further times, two shells falling on the

RIGHT: *The* Bismarck *in action against HMS* Hood *in the early hours of 24 May. The* Hood *was soon heavily damaged in a joint attack by the* Bismarck *and the* Prinz Eugen *and sank in flames after her magazines exploded*

TOP: *An aircraft of the RAF Coastal Command discovered the presence of the German battleship* Bismarck *in Dobric Fjord on 21 May, shortly before she began her first and last sortie into the Atlantic.*
BOTTOM: *The* Bismarck *photographed in Norwegian waters from the cruiser* Prinz Eugen, *immediately before her Atlantic sortie*

water-line aft, admitting 500 tons of water. Gun after gun broke down, and the builder's foreman, who was on board, did invaluable work putting right defects. Even so, the ship's forward salvoes averaged only three instead of five guns, while the *Bismarck* seemed quite undamaged.

Captain Leach wisely decided to break off the engagement until reinforcements could be summoned, but even as he turned away under cover of smoke, the ship's after turret jammed. Yet one of the final salvoes from the *Prince of Wales* made three hits. The damage slightly reduced the *Bismarck*'s speed, and caused a leak of oil fuel which was enough to decide Lütjens to abandon his Atlantic mission.

The *Prince of Wales* now joined the *Norfolk* and *Suffolk* in the work of shadowing. The Germans steered south-west, sometimes attempting to shake the British off. Admiral Tovey with his main fleet, some 300 miles away by this time, was steaming at high speed to intercept, the earliest time at which this could occur being calculated as at 7 am. on 25 May.

At 1.20 pm. on 24 May the *Suffolk* reported that the Germans had reduced speed and had altered course south-east. British prospects brightened. Admiral Somerville with his Gibraltar force was summoned north, and every available ship was ordered to close. As it was not yet certain whether the *Bismarck* had been damaged, or was merely husbanding her fuel, airmen from the carrier *Victorious*, which was with Admiral Tovey, were called upon to try to reduce her speed.

At 10 pm. on the day the *Hood* was sunk, nine aircraft took off from the carrier in appalling weather, the flight-deck rising and falling some fifty feet. They were manned by pilots on passage to Malta who had never before flown off the deck of a ship! At 11.27 they obtained radar contact. Attacks were pressed home against heavy anti-aircraft fire under the worst possible conditions. One torpedo hit amidships, but it did no serious damage. Two shadowing aircraft were lost.

Shortly before this air attack, the *Bismarck* had turned to engage her surface shadowers, in order to allow the *Prinz Eugen* to break away independently to the south-west. The battleship then resumed her own southerly course. The next episode occurred in the early hours of 25 May, when the *Suffolk*, which had for so long been following the *Bismarck* on her radar, lost touch, perhaps through over-confidence.

General opinion inclined to the view that Lütjens must have turned to the west, and he was hunted in that direction: actually he had altered course south-east, making for St Nazaire. The next period, which lasted for no less than thirty-one-and-a-half hours, was one of mounting perplexity. False reports that the *Bismarck* had turned north-east and was breaking back the way she had

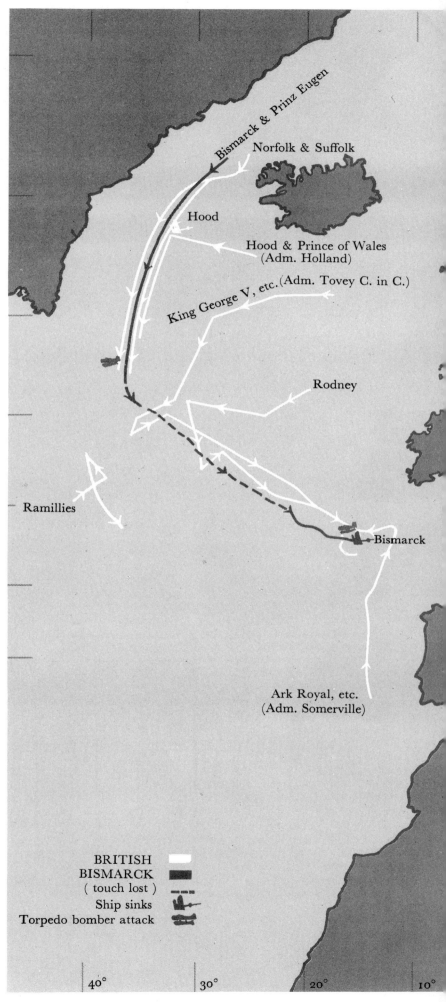

BRITISH
BISMARCK
(touch lost)
Ship sinks
Torpedo bomber attack

come caused Admiral Tovey to reverse course, thus losing precious distance.

The next episode occurred at 10.30 am. on 26 May, when Lütjens was re-sighted by a Catalina aircraft of the Royal Air Force Coastal Command. The aircraft came under heavy fire, but her crew managed to send a report that the battleship was some 690 miles north-west from Brest, making a speed which would bring her within the protection of U-boat patrols and the Luftwaffe's bombers, within twenty-four hours.

By this time, many of the searchers were running short of fuel, two ships, one of them the *Prince of Wales*, having to return to port on this account. Admiral Somerville seemed now to be in the best position to intercept, and his aircraft, flown from the *Ark Royal*, soon found a ship and attacked her, in very poor visibility. She proved to be the British cruiser *Sheffield*, then twenty miles north of the enemy, and it was therefore fortunate that the airmen's aim was poor. Later strikes, also made in bad weather conditions at about 8.45 pm. were more successful. Two torpedoes hit. One, right aft, wrecked the *Bismarck*'s steering gear and jammed her rudders. This damage sealed her fate, though it was some hours before the matter was apparent.

During the night of 26 May five destroyers under Captain Philip Vian, which had been detached from a convoy, gained contact with the enemy, and carried out torpedo attacks which were beaten off by radar-controlled fire from the *Bismarck*'s main batteries. But Vian's ships shadowed throughout the night, and they delivered the *Bismarck* next day to her destruction. At 8.46 on the morning of 27 May the *King George V*, Admiral Tovey's flag-ship, opened fire, almost simultaneously with the *Bismarck*, at a range of 16,000 yards. With Tovey was HMS *Rodney*, and the British Commander-in-Chief allowed the *Rodney*'s captain open order and permission to fire as he found best. Gunfire continued until 10.15, when the *Bismarck* had been reduced to what appeared to be a flaming shambles.

Although the German salvoes had ceased, the *Bismarck*'s construction proved to be as astonishing as her

LEFT TOP: *The rival commanders, Admiral of the Fleet Lord Tovey and Admiral Lütjens, who went down with the* Bismarck

LEFT CENTRE: *The German cruiser* Prinz Eugen *which, with the* Bismarck, *was responsible for the sinking of HMS* Hood *on 24 May. On the evening of the same day she broke away from the* Bismarck *and escaped undamaged*

LEFT BOTTOM: *HMS* Hood, *a battle cruiser launched in 1918 and in her day the largest warship in the world*

Geheime Kommandosache

Marinenachrichtendienst

Eingegangen	Weiter an	Tag	Uhrzeit	durch	
27/5 0114	HOS, HSA	27/5	0115	*[handwritten]*	Gef. *[handwritten]* Gel *[handwritten]*
von MWY durch *Peter*					Üb:
Verzögerungsvermerk	*[handwritten]*		*[handwritten]*		

Fernschreiben von _____

[handwritten marginal notes]

```
                +KR  MWY     02289    27/5  0100=

                  MBZ  TM    2=   KR   1 SKL=

                                  KR   2 SKL=

          GLTD  KR   1 SKL=    KR   2 SKL=    KR GR NORD=

          --GKDOS-- GEHEIM GESCHL FT 0036 KKN

          2357/18.-

          KR  KR  FUEHRER  DES  DEUTSCHEN  REICHES, ADOLF

          HITLER.-

          WIR KAEMPFEN  BIS  ZUM  LETZTEN  IM  GLAUBEN  AN

          SIE  MEIN   FUEHRER,  UND  IM  FELSENFESTEN

          VERTRAUEN  AUF  DEUTSCHLANDS  SIEG=

                                          FLOTTENCHEF+
```

ABOVE AND OVERLEAF: *Signals exchanged between Admiral Lütjens and Hitler as the attack on the* Bismarck *increased in intensity:*

26 May 1941 23.57 hours

To the Führer of the German Reich, Adolf Hitler: We shall fight to the end with faith in you, my Führer and with inflexible confidence in Germany's victory. Fleet Commander

Geheime Kommandosache

Marinenachrichtendienst

Eingegangen	Weiter an	Tag	Uhrzeit	durch	
27/5 0245					
von MWY durch Peter				bekannt	
Verzögerungsvermerk				3 ... Lage	
Fernschreiben von					

+KR MWY 02304   27/5 024==

MBZ: TM 2=   KR 1 SKL=

KR 2 SKL=

--GKDOS-- GEHEIM GESCHL FT 0223 FFL 0153.-
KR KR FLOTTE W SIEBEN NULL FUER FLOTTENCHEF.-
ICH DANKE IHNEN IM NAMEN DES GANZEN DEUTSCHEN
VOLKES= ADOLF HITLER.-
AN DIE BESATZUNG SCHLACHTSCHIFF BISMARCK:
GANZ DEUTSCHLAND IST BEI EUCH. WAS NOCH
GESCHEHEN KANN WIRD GETAN. EURE
PFLICHTERFUELLUNG WIRD UNSER VOLK IM KAMPFE
UM SEIN DASEIN STAERKEN=
ADOLF HITLER+

Hitler's reply to Admiral Lütjens's signal:

27 May 1941 01.53 hours

To Fleet Commander: I thank you in the name of the whole German nation. Adolf Hitler

To the ship's company of Battleship *Bismarck*: The whole of Germany is with you. Everything possible is being done. Your devotion to duty will strengthen our people in its battle for existence. Adolf Hitler

The End of the Bismarck, *a reconstruction of the scene painted by Charles E. Turner.* HMS Dorsetshire *can be seen in the background*

power of offence, which was equivalent to that of a fleet in earlier days of steam warfare. Despite the hammering to which she had been subjected, some of her 110 survivors reported that her belt armour remained unpierced, and that no shell or torpedo had penetrated her engine rooms. Most of her machinery was intact when the turbine-engineer-officer was ordered to blow the explosive charges in the sea valves, and the two torpedoes fired by the cruiser *Dorsetshire* merely speeded her disappearance and did not cause it.

Most of the current types of naval vessel, apart from the submarine, were engaged in the pursuit of the *Bismarck*. She was shadowed by cruisers and she was passed over, with shattering results, to a battle-cruiser and a battleship. After contact had been lost, it was an aircraft

which re-discovered her, and crucial damage was done by sea-borne air attack. Night shadowing was maintained by destroyers, and the gunfire of battleships decided the *Bismarck*'s fate. She had been fought to the last with the greatest gallantry, and the *Prinz Eugen* lived to survive many another day.

In the First World War, two powerful German ships had affected the whole issue by being allowed to enter Turkish waters. The British intended to make sure that no comparable episode occurred in the second conflict, but it took the whole of their available resources, together with the loss of their finest looking ship and nearly all her gallant company, to ensure that the *Bismarck* and her consort did not increase the existing menace to the Atlantic life-line.

Midway
1942

The American counter to Pearl Harbour, in which the Japanese advance in the Pacific was halted by skilful action and courage of a very high order

JUST AS THE PACIFIC DWARFS any other ocean, so the sea fighting in which the Americans and Japanese engaged after the attack on Pearl Harbour in December 1941 – reminiscent, in its factor of surprise, of that on Port Arthur in 1904 – made earlier maritime campaigns seem, by comparison, miniature. Distances, forces deployed, potentialities, all were immense, and the element of air power was so predominant in the decisive naval battle fought during the first year, that surface and even submarine-and-surface contact became secondary.

The ease with which the Japanese made their vast conquests bred a desire to establish a defensive perimeter behind which to consolidate their gains. Over-estimating their own capacity for sustaining war, and disregarding the almost limitless resources of America, the Japanese decided to thrust still further outwards – plans which took in the Aleutian Islands, Midway, Samoa, Fiji, New Caledonia and Port Moresby.

Their first failure was at Port Moresby; their second, mounted against Midway Island, 1,200 miles west north-west of Hawaii, began at the end of May 1942. The American counter, much helped by having broken the enemy code, was to hurry the carriers *Enterprise* and *Hornet*, under Admiral Spruance, to Pearl Harbour, where Admiral Fletcher's damaged *Yorktown* was repaired at high speed. By the end of the month the

three carriers, with eight cruisers and fourteen destroyers, were steaming towards Midway, all under Admiral Fletcher's command. Fourteen submarines were disposed west and north of Midway, general control of operations coming under the Commander-in-Chief US Pacific Fleet, Admiral Nimitz at Pearl Harbour. The value of Midway itself to the Japanese would not have been high, since it afforded only a shallow harbour and a small airfield, but it would deprive America of an advanced base useful for the submarines which were already harassing Japanese supply-lines.

Admiral Yamamoto was sent to sea with the strongest force he could muster, nine battleships including the new *Yamato* flying his flag, four carriers, cruisers and destroyers, and transports with some 2,000 troops.

On 3 June Admiral Fletcher took up a position some 200 miles north-north-west of the island, ready to meet the threat. The Japanese approached in three groups. To the northward was Vice-Admiral Nagumo with all four carriers, two battleships, cruisers and destroyers. His task was to overcome Midway's shore-based aircraft and any opposition from carrier-borne planes if they should be in the neighbourhood – their presence was not expected. From west-south-west came the transports, which had sailed escorted from the Marianas, ready to assault the island when air opposition had been overcome. Admiral Yamamoto's battle fleet was in support, powerful enough to destroy most surface forces and to exploit success. Submarines were stationed at the approaches to Midway,

and on a line west of Hawaii, ready to report American movements.

First to be spotted was the Japanese convoy, which was seen by a flying boat at 9 am. on 3 June. Nine Flying Fortresses went up from Midway to attack, but all their bombs missed, and a night attack by torpedo-carrying Catalinas scored only a small success: but Yamamoto now knew that the Americans had been alerted, though he still hoped to reach Midway without meeting more than local opposition.

By dawn on 4 June the Japanese carrier force had reached a position 200 miles north of Midway without detection. From there they launched a hundred bombers, escorted by fifty fighters. Admiral Fletcher at this time was about 200 miles east-north-east of the Japanese, also still undetected. Shortly afterwards, the Midway air patrols sighted the approaching strike and later the carriers, and battle was fairly joined.

First, fifteen Flying Fortresses which had been sent against the assault force were diverted towards the carriers: then all Midway aircraft were flown off, fighters to meet the striking force, torpedo-aircraft and dive-bombers to attack the carriers. All suffered heavy loss. The fighters brought down some Japanese, but not enough to prevent the Midway installations from being well bombed. The aircraft attacking the carriers, lacking fighter protection, were virtually annihilated. Flying Fortresses dropped over a hundred bombs from 20,000 feet without scoring one hit, and the situation seemed all in favour of the Japanese.

There then began a series of strokes and counter-strokes which serve to illustrate the term 'the fortunes of war'. The Japanese at last discovered the presence of the American carriers, and they altered course to the north-eastward to close the enemy, ranging every available aircraft. The Americans, meanwhile, with earlier news, sent a hundred planes at 8 am. from the *Enterprise* and *Hornet*, *Yorktown*'s being held in reserve.

Assuming that the Japanese were still approaching

LEFT: *As the primer-man pulls the releasing lever, the gun captain kicks the pedal which closes the breech of this 16-inch gun, in Lieutenant-Commander Dwight C. Shepler's painting*

RIGHT TOP: *Vice-Admiral Chuichi Nagumo, Commander of the First Carrier Striking Force, who led the Japanese carriers into the Battle of Midway*

RIGHT CENTRE: *Admiral Isoroku Yamamoto, Commander-in-Chief of the Japanese Combined Fleet 1939–43, an inspiring leader who planned the attack on Pearl Harbour in 1941*

RIGHT BOTTOM: *Admiral Frank Jack Fletcher, the American tactical commander who repulsed the Japanese assault on Midway Island*

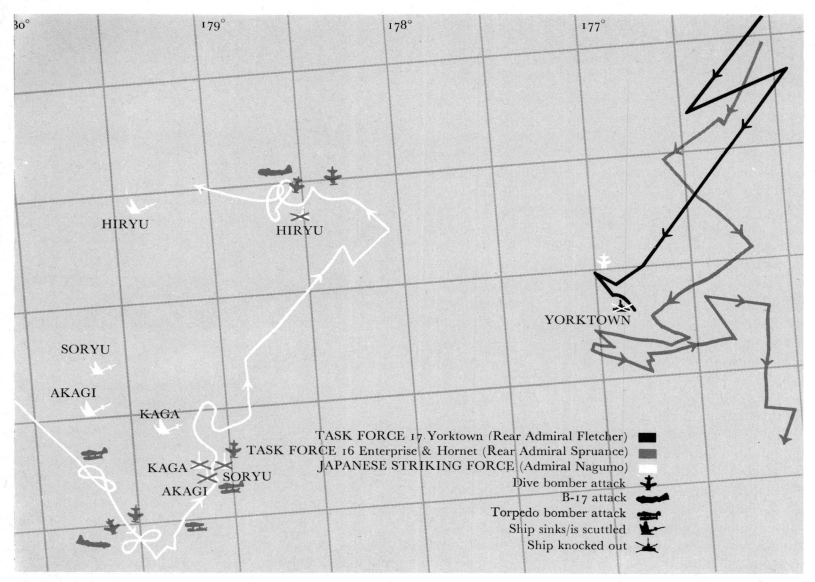

The action on 4 June 1942

TASK FORCE 17 Yorktown (Rear Admiral Fletcher)
TASK FORCE 16 Enterprise & Hornet (Rear Admiral Spruance)
JAPANESE STRIKING FORCE (Admiral Nagumo)
Dive bomber attack
B-17 attack
Torpedo bomber attack
Ship sinks/is scuttled
Ship knocked out

HIRYU
HIRYU
YORKTOWN
SORYU
AKAGI
KAGA
KAGA
SORYU
AKAGI

ALEUTIAN ISLANDS
MIDWAY ISLAND
Pearl Harbour
HAWAII
Equator
SAMOA
Port Moresby
FIJI
NEW CALEDONIA

Midway, and without knowing their change of course, the Americans found the estimated enemy position to be empty sea. The *Hornet*'s dive-bombers and fighters thereupon turned south, found nothing, and either reached Midway or ran out of fuel south of it. The same ship's torpedo-aircraft discovered the enemy by chance, attacked, and were all shot down.

The *Enterprise*'s dive-bombers also found the Japanese, but their fighters and torpedo-aircraft reached them first, the fighters patrolling high overhead waiting for the dive-bombers, until fuel shortage forced them to return: when, therefore, the torpedo-aircraft and dive-bombers went in together from different directions at about 10 am., they would have been without fighter protection

RIGHT: *A Japanese carrier circles in an attempt to avoid attacks by US bombers*

OVERLEAF: *A Japanese torpedo strikes the USS* Yorktown *in the later stages of the battle ; she was finished off by a submarine while in tow*

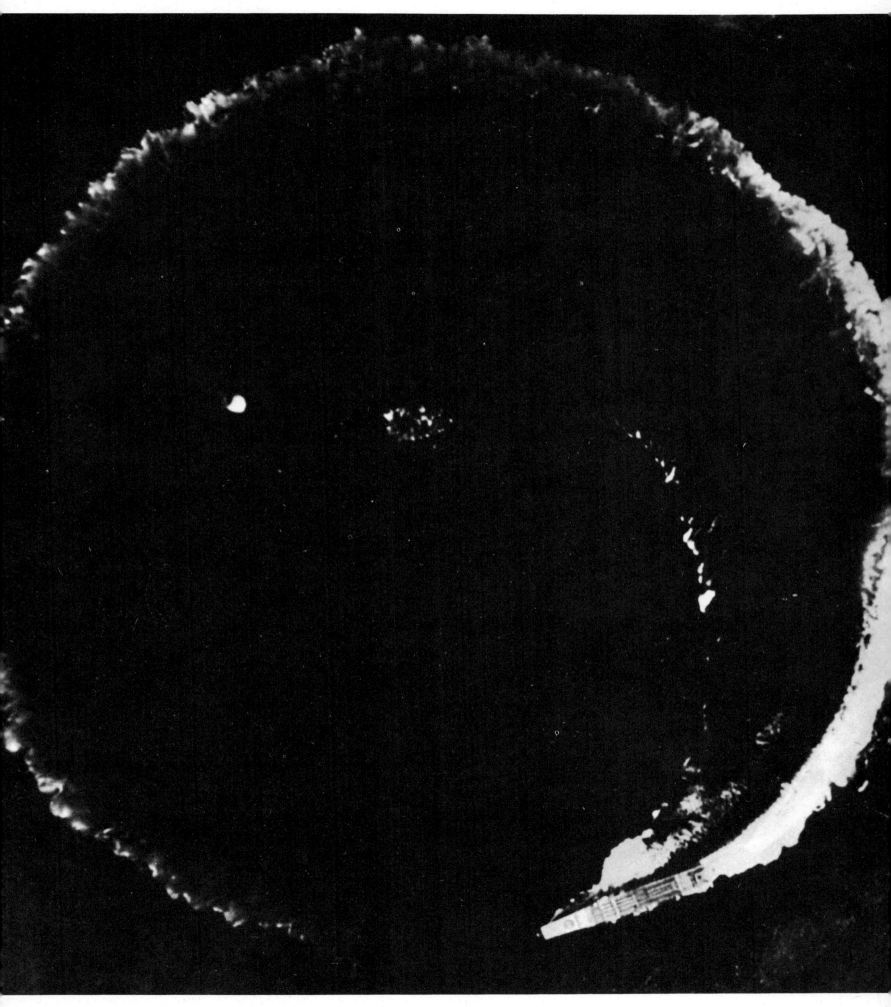

USS Yorktown, *bow on, listing to port after being hit by Japanese torpedoes; a destroyer stands by to remove survivors*

altogether had it not been for a further chance which brought the whole *Yorktown* strike, launched about an hour later than the others, to the same position at the same time.

It was the dive-bombers that did the damage. The Japanese patrols attacked mainly the torpedo-aircraft, which were considered both more dangerous and more vulnerable, and despite anything the *Yorktown* fighters could do, twenty out of twenty-six torpedo aircraft were shot down, with no hits recorded. But in the resulting mêlée the dive-bombers were unopposed, and they delivered such blows as virtually won the battle. The carrier *Kaga* was hit by four bombs, the *Soryu* by three and the *Akagi* by two. Uncontrollable fires broke out in all three ships, and soon all lay stopped. During the afternoon the *Soryu* was hit with three torpedoes by an American submarine and at dusk she went down. The *Kaga* and *Akagi* had little longer to live.

A Japanese attack on the American carriers arrived soon after noon, and it was concentrated on the *Yorktown*. Three bombs hit, though the attackers were shot down. Damage to an already patched ship was severe, though she could still steam at 19 knots. But soon afterwards she was attacked again from the one remaining Japanese carrier, the *Hiryu*. Two torpedoes hit, and the *Yorktown* became a derelict: while in tow she was finished off by an enemy submarine. Before nightfall the *Hiryu* herself had been hit by six bombs, and sank next day. Although the Americans did not yet realize it, they had won a great victory with a force far inferior in numbers to the enemy. They had halted Japanese expansion, and had robbed the enemy of two-thirds of its big carriers.

All was not quite over. Admiral Yamamoto, realizing the size of the disaster to his carriers, had already signalled for a general retirement, but he ordered a surface bombardment of Midway, partly as a face-saver, partly

A close-up view of the Japanese cruiser Mogame, *with her superstructure wrecked and burning, and her turrets useless after attack by US planes*

to cover his withdrawal. Four heavy cruisers which had been escorting the transports were detailed for the task, but in trying to avoid an American submarine, two of them, the *Mogame* and *Mikuma*, collided. The operation was abandoned, and the cruisers turned for home, the *Mogame* leaving a trail of oil fuel.

On 6 June the American carriers *Enterprise* and *Hornet*, which were now in pursuit of the Japanese, found and hammered the damaged cruisers. The *Mikuma* was sunk, but the *Mogame*, in spite of her oil leak, managed to struggle 2,000 miles to Truk.

The Americans, now nearing the end of their fuel, returned to Pearl Harbour, and to the well-earned congratulations of Admiral Nimitz. The battle was the beginning of the turning of the tide of Japanese success. There would be American set-backs in the future, but from now onwards confidence in final victory had unassailable evidence behind it.

88.   Combined training is needed by land based aircraft and Fleet units to provide for better exchange of information and coordination of attack. The superior operations of the unit of B-17's under Lieut. Colonel W. C. Sweeney, U.S.A. of 431st Bombardment Squadron show the benefit of prolonged experience with naval forces which this squadron had obtained during coordinated patrol operations. All units require more training in sending clear, complete and accurate reports that will give a commander all the information he needs to know, completely correct, without repeated questioning.

89.   Correct information is still one of the hardest things for a commander to get in action. It is especially difficult in such a battle of many battles as this one was, spread over a vast sea area. Training, suitable tracking aircraft, and some of the other steps mentioned in the foregoing paragraphs should alleviate this difficulty. It is considered that Commanders of Task Force SIXTEEN and SEVENTEEN and Naval Air Station Midway showed sound judgment and decision in correctly interpreting the many confused situations that came up during the action.

90.   The performance of officers and men was of the highest order not only at Midway and afloat but equally so among those at Oahu not privileged to be in the front line of battle. I am proud to report that the cooperative devotion to duty of all those involved was so marked that, despite the necessarily decisive part played by our three carriers, this defeat of the Japanese Arms and ambitions was truly a victory of the United States' armed forces and not of the Navy alone.

The concluding paragraphs of his report on the Battle of Midway by Admiral Chester W. Nimitz, the US Commander-in-Chief

Leyte Gulf
1944

American sea-power in the Pacific gradually pressed the Japanese back to their home waters, and this victory ensured the re-conquest of the Philippines

JAPANESE EXPANSION was corroded inch by inch, and it is arguable that their High Command, by adopting the same principle as their ally Hitler in refusing voluntarily to yield ground once gained, did much to lose themselves the war. Certainly Russia and the Western Allies, America and Great Britain, learnt from the hard experience of being thrust back, and plucked advantage from the shorter communications which were compensation for withdrawal.

By the autumn of 1944, when Anglo-American forces were firmly lodged in Continental Europe, the American navy in the Far East felt itself strong enough to mount an assault on the Philippine Islands. Defence was a cardinal matter for Japan. Not only would American reconquest of Luzon, the northernmost island, be a direct threat to the Japanese home islands, but their supply route by the South China sea was vital to the future course of the war. It was their oil-pipe, and already their navy and their industries generally were beginning to feel an acute shortage in this commodity, essential to warfare at sea. American submarines had already sunk so many tankers as not only to prohibit the building up of fuel stocks in Japan, but also to make it difficult at times to find oilers for the Fleet Train. This tended to limit the navy's mobility when embarked on a distant operation, and affected the question of its base.

The prelude to the battle of Leyte Gulf, one of the most intricate sea battles ever fought, may be said to have taken place at the end of August 1944, when for the first

time American air strikes were extended to the Philippine Group. Carriers struck at the lonely islands of Chichi Jima and Iwo Jima – the first of which was only 500 nautical miles from Tokyo – and against Mindanao, the largest southern island of the Philippines. Following up their success, surface forces closed the coast, and on 10 September annihilated a convoy of thirty-two small cargo ships. Shortly afterwards, lodgements were made in the Palau islands, east of Mindanao, and at Ulithi Atoll. Ulithi, 850 miles east of Leyte Gulf, to which the main attack was to be directed, was to serve as the principal forward base until the Americans had gained a firm foothold in the Philippines.

On 15 September, five days after the opening success against the convoy, it was decided to by-pass Mindanao altogether. Leyte would be attacked, with carrier-borne support, in October, the Fleet having already had useful experience in this type of operation both in the Mediterranean and Pacific. Four divisions would be employed, supported by Admiral Kincaid with battleships, cruisers, destroyers and escort carriers. In the meanwhile strikes by the big Fleet carriers under Admiral Halsey flew many sorties over Formosa, from which island land-based Japanese aircraft were able to operate over Luzon. The Japanese had some success in counter-attack, but they believed American damage to be higher than it was,

RIGHT: *A US carrier in the Pacific awaits its returning fighter-planes after a Japanese air strike, painted by Lieutenant Richard A. Genders*

and in six days the Japanese lost well over 600 aircraft at a cost of 90 American.

On 17 October Admiral Kincaid's advanced units landed commandos on Suluan Island in Leyte Gulf, and on the following day on Dinagat and Homonhon, two islands about 45 miles to seaward of the main beaches of Leyte Island itself. At 10 am. on 20 October, after heavy bombardment, the main assault went in and, for once, local resistance was soon overcome. But by this time, the Japanese navy had reacted in strength.

The admiral whose task was to destroy Kincaid was Kurita. He made his approach from a fuelling base at North Borneo, but by the time he was ready to sail, the Americans had already made good their landing. Even so, if he annihilated Kincaid's fleet, the American position would be serious if not desperate, particularly if Kurita were able to destroy the supply and supporting ships. Kurita was in great strength. He had two mammoth battleships, the *Yamato* and *Mushashi*, three older battleships, *Nagato*, *Kongo* and *Haruna*, twelve heavy cruisers including the *Atago* in which he flew his flag, and nineteen destroyers. Kurita would approach Leyte Gulf through the Mindora Straits and the Situyan Sea to the San Bernardino Straits: there he would turn south, headed for Leyte Gulf. A detached force under Admiral Nishimura would at the same time approach Leyte from the south. Air support would be land-based, for such carrier strength as Japan still possessed would be with Admiral Ozawa, whose Fleet was ordered to sail from Japan.

The battle soon resolved itself into a struggle for the security of the Philippine landings and the survival of Kincaid's force, for Admiral Halsey, who was working under Admiral Nimitz (Kincaid being in General MacArthur's sphere) had been drawn with his entire Fleet to the north by the magnet of Admiral Ozawa. His directions, although covering the operations in which Kincaid was concerned, contained the sentence: 'In case opportunity for destruction of a major portion of the enemy fleet offer or can be created, such destruction becomes the primary task'. And Halsey believed that the main threat was from Ozawa.

First blood was drawn by American submarines. Kurita was shadowed and two cruisers were hit, including the flagship *Atago*, which was sunk. Then the *Takao* was damaged and the *Mayo* sunk. Kurita transferred to a destroyer, and later to the big *Yamato*, and he pushed on, as planned, towards Leyte. Acting on the submarines' reports, Halsey had at first moved in towards the Philippines in three groups whose movements were aimed at Leyte, at the San Bernardino Straits and at Luzon. Carrier-borne attacks were also made on Kurita, who lost the *Mushashi* to air attack. But Halsey was worried by the absence of Japanese carriers, and believing Kurita to have been crippled and to have turned tail, he reconcentrated his forces and turned north, to meet a possible carrier threat. He informed Kincaid of his movements, and added his opinion that Kurita had been badly damaged, and was possibly in retreat.

In actual fact, the situation was as follows: Ozawa's northern force, one large and three light carriers, two battleships, three cruisers and ten destroyers, was indeed approaching from Japan, but it was short of aircraft and shorter still of trained pilots. The real threat was coming from Kurita, who despite attacks and damage was heading at twenty knots for the San Bernardino Straits with four battleships, six heavy and two light cruisers, and ten destroyers. Nishimura was also approaching with surface forces including two battleships, and against this double threat Kincaid had six battleships (old and equipped for bombardment rather than for fleet action, and with much of its ammunition expended), eight cruisers, and some thirty destroyers. His escort carriers, unarmoured and small, were intended and armed for troop and convoy support, not for Fleet action.

Throughout the night of 24-25 October, while Halsey was standing away from Leyte to meet Ozawa, Kurita was nearing the vital area of the invasion. Admiral Kincaid's dispositions had been based on the assumption that main attack would come from the south, from the Surigao Straits up which Nishimura would be approaching, and he saw no need to look over his shoulder. Nishimura duly appeared, was attacked and destroyed, as was a second independent force under Admiral Shima. One of the ships sunk was the cruiser *Mogami*, which had been fortunate to survive Midway.

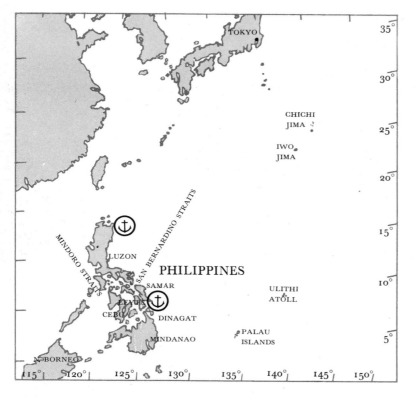

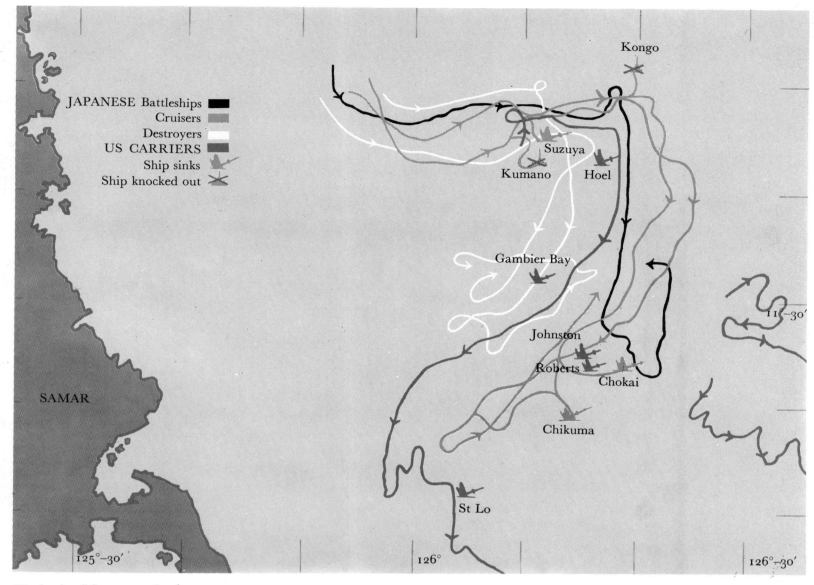

The battle off Samar, 25 October 1944

At dawn on 25 October, when the Leyte covering forces were dealing with Nishimura and Shima and Halsey was 300 miles away looking for Ozawa, Kurita was steaming down the east side of Samar towards Leyte, his presence unsuspected. He had passed through the San Bernardino Strait in darkness and had every prospect not merely of surprising Kincaid, but of inflicting such a defeat as might have jeopardized the whole invasion.

At 6.45 am. Kurita sighted Kincaid's northern group of escort carriers. They were operating about forty miles to seaward, chiefly to provide support for the troops ashore. The carriers were in three groups: the northern and central groups contained six, the southern, about 120 miles away, only four. The northern carriers, now in immediate danger, were under Rear-Admiral C. A. F. Sprague, the central under Rear-Admiral Stump, and the southern under Admiral T. L. Sprague, who was in general command under Kincaid.

Although he had surprised the Americans, Kurita was himself surprised, for he did not expect to meet any carriers so far from the Gulf itself. He concluded that Kincaid's force must be part of Halsey's main Fleet. For their part the escort carriers, believing themselves well protected to the northward by forces which had in actual fact by then concentrated on Halsey, had no patrols in the direction of Kurita's approach, and the first thing they knew of the enemy was at 7 am., when the Japanese battleships opened fire. It was a very rare instance of the older type of capital ship being in visual range of a carrier, and, theoretically, the life of even a heavy carrier in the face of gunfire of battleship calibre should have been very short indeed.

Rear-Admiral C. A. F. Sprague, helped by the reckless courage of his light surface escorts and by his airmen, retreated eastward, into the wind, flying off everything on board. Then the carriers hauled gradually round to the south and south-west, under smoke, and from 7.30 onwards the escort – seven small ships, all short of torpedoes – pressed home an attack in face of intense fire.

The defence was brilliantly successful. The cruiser *Kumano* was damaged, and Kurita's order of battle was temporarily disorganized. Three of the escorts were sunk, but Kurita paused to take stock.

His indecision lost him the day, for there came upon him an amazing series of attacks from Avengers and Hellcats from all three carrier groups, the first to arrive being Stump's. The aircraft went in with everything they had; torpedoes were short and the bombs were unsuitable for attacks on ships – some aircraft indeed had nothing more effective than machine guns. But boldness worked: two of Kurita's cruisers were crippled and had to be sunk, and the admiral became convinced he was in the presence of a strong carrier force. By 9.20 am., after two hours of gunfire, during which he had only succeeded in sinking one 18-knot carrier, the *Gambier Bay*, he recalled his forces and stood to northward. In so doing, he lost one further cruiser from what was little more than an improvised air attack, and he intercepted a message in plain language ordering aircraft to land and refuel on an airstrip at Leyte. With visions of attacks by shore-based squadrons, Kurita decided, soon after midday, to withdraw from the area.

25 October 1944 was certainly the escort carriers' busy day, for not only had they to meet the gunfire of battleships and cruisers, but at 8 am., when affairs with the northern group were critical, the Japanese air commander at Manila decided to send in suicide attacks by land-based aircraft. This was the Kamikaze (Divine Wind) Corps, Kamikaze being the name given to the typhoon of the year 1281 which destroyed two fleets from Korea and South China sent by Kublai Khan against Japan.

Four of five Kamikaze struck at the southern group and two carriers were hit. Both survived, though one was still further damaged by a submarine torpedo a few moments later. It was then the turn of the northern group, which had just escaped from Kurita. Three ships were hit and one, the *St Lo*, was sunk. But the ordeal was now over at

LEFT: *Firemen urge on their boilers in the engine-room of this US battleship, as the bridge signals for full speed to evade Japanese planes, in Lieutenant-Commander Dwight C. Shepler's water-colour painting*

RIGHT TOP: *Admiral William F. Halsey, commander of the American aircraft carrier fleet at Leyte Gulf*

RIGHT CENTRE: *Admiral Takeo Kurita, commander of the Japanese Second Fleet, charged with the task of destroying the US fleet under Admiral Kincaid, which was covering the landings on Leyte and the neighbouring islands*

RIGHT BOTTOM: *Vice-Admiral Jisaburo Ozawa, who commanded the force which sailed from Japan to support Admiral Kurita and was destroyed by aircraft from Admiral Halsey's carriers*

The US carrier Gambier Bay *(sunk shortly after this photograph was taken) bracketed by shells from a Japanese cruiser, which can be seen on the horizon towards the right of the picture*

last, supplies to the landings proceeded normally, and the final phase of the battle was the annihilation of Ozawa's carriers by Halsey's aircraft and further damage to the retreating Kurita.

The last scene of all in the Leyte battle again brought further trials and successes for the escort carriers. The most damaged groups, those of the two Admirals Sprague, had now to retire to Ulithi to repair, leaving Stump's group to support the land operations. At about noon on 26 October, six further Kamikaze made for Stump. Four were shot down, but one hit the *Suwanee*. Damage was grave and casualties heavy, but the ship was saved.

The same day, the group scored its final success. The Japanese had landed about 2,000 men on the west coast of Leyte, to reinforce the hard-pressed defenders. They had been brought from Mindanao in four transports, escorted by the light cruiser *Kinu* and a destroyer.

As the ships returned they were spotted between Leyte

and Cebu islands. The carriers sent every available aircraft against them, and although all torpedoes and heavy bombs had been expended the day before, with such weapons as they still possessed – rockets and small bombs – the American pilots achieved a near-annihilation. Two transports out of four were sunk, and both the men of war.

The battles concerned with the landings at Leyte Gulf were by no means the last big-scale naval operations in the war with Japan, but they marked the end of serious carrier opposition on the part of the enemy and they showed how even a weakly equipped air striking force could hold at bay the strongest battleships, when unsupported by their own aircraft. The carrier had undisputedly become the capital ship, and the whole scale and scope of maritime warfare was so remote from that of the oared galleys of Lepanto as to belong to another world – less picturesque, infinitely faster, infinitely more destructive.

The Development
of the Warship

THE THREE PAGES WHICH FOLLOW illustrate the gradual change of design in the warships of the nations whose battles have been described in the foregoing pages.

At the start of the period covered by this book the galley, which dated back to the days of Actium, Salamis and beyond, was giving place to sail, and battles would soon be decided by the broadsides of ships of the line.

For nearly three centuries the warship changed very little in essentials, the refinements occurring mostly in armament and size. By Nelson's day the man-of-war had achieved all of which sail was capable, and the time was ripe for some revolutionary innovations.

These were found in the invention of steam power and the introduction of the ironclad, which first appeared in combination at the Battle of Hampton Roads in 1862. Thereafter development was rapid, through the early monitors and the dreadnoughts of the First World War to the submarines and aircraft carriers of the Second.

In the latest phase the heavily gunned battleship has lost its mastery, and has given way in turn to the aircraft carrier, the new capital ship, whose air striking force commanded the sea at the end of the Second World War. And now the aircraft carrier's dominion is shared by the nuclear submarine, the warship of the future.

A Venetian galley of the type which took part in the Battle of Lepanto, 1571. (*Length*: up to 150 feet; *speed*: *c* 10 knots; *armament*: up to 10 heavy, 12–14 lighter guns)

An English galleon of the type which served under Howard of Effingham against the Spanish Armada, 1588. (*Length*: *c* 100 feet; *speed*: *c* 7 knots; *armament*: up to *c* 55 guns)

The *Amelia*, Marten Tromp's flagship at the Battle of the Downs, 1639. (*Built*: Rotterdam; *launched*: 1637; *speed*: *c* 7 knots; *armament*: 56 guns)

The *Amarante*, a Swedish ship of the time of the Battle of the Sound, 1658. (*Built*: Stockholm; *launched*: 1653; *length*: 125 feet; *speed*: *c* 7 knots; *armament*: 38–52 guns)

The *Monk*, a British ship which took part in the Four-Days' Battle, 1666. (*Built*: Portsmouth; *launched*: 1659; *length*: 108 feet; *speed*: *c* 8 knots; *armament*: 52–60 guns)

A French ship of the time of Duquesne's and de Ruyter's encounters off Sicily, 1676. (*Armament*: 80 guns)

The *Royal Katherine*, Sir George Rooke's flagship at the Battle of Malaga, 1704. (*Built*: Woolwich; *launched*: 1664; *length*: 124 feet; *speed*: *c* 9 knots; *armament*: 84–90 guns)

The *Royal George*, Sir Edward Hawke's flagship at the Battle of Quiberon Bay, 1759. (*Built*: Woolwich; *launched*: 1756; *length*: 178 feet; *speed*: *c* 9 knots; *armament*: 100 guns)

The *Bonhomme Richard*, formerly the *Duc de Duras*, a French East Indiaman, Paul Jones's flagship at the Battle of Flamborough Head, 1779. (*Rebuilt*: 1778; *length*: *c* 150 feet; *speed*: *c* 9 knots; *armament*: 42 guns)

The *Ville de Paris*, the Comte de Grasse's flagship at the Battle of Chesapeake Bay, 1781. (*Launched*: 1764; *length*: 187 feet; *speed*: *c* 9 knots; *armament*: 104 guns)

The *Artésien*, one of the ships which fought in Suffren's squadron during his operations in the East Indies, 1782–3. (*Built*: Brest *launched*: 1765; *length*: 155 feet; *speed*: *c* 9 knots; *armament*: 64 guns)

The *Queen Charlotte*, Lord Howe's flagship at the Battle of the Glorious First of June, 1794. (*Built*: Chatham; *launched*: 1790; *length*: 190 feet; *speed*: 10 knots; *armament*: 100 guns)

The *Vanguard*, Nelson's flagship at the Battle of the Nile, 1798. (*Built*: Deptford; *launched*: 1787; *length*: 168 feet; *speed*: *c* 9 knots; *armament*: 74 guns)

A Danish raft battery of the type which played a prominent part in the defence of Copenhagen against the British in 1801. (*Armament*: 24 guns)

The *Victory*, Nelson's flagship at the Battle of Trafalgar, 1805. (*Built*: Chatham; *launched*: 1765; *length*: 186 feet; *speed*: 10 knots; *armament*: 100 guns)

The frigate *Amphion*, Hoste's flagship at the Battle of Lissa, 1811. (*Built*: Bett's Yard, Mistley Thorn; *launched*: 1798; *length*: 144 feet; *speed*: *c* 10 knots; *armament*: 32 guns)

The brig *Detroit*, Barclay's flagship at the Battle of Lake Erie, 1813. (*Built*: Malden, Canada; *launched*: 1813; *speed*: *c* 9 knots; *armament*: 19 guns)

The *Asia*, Codrington's flagship at the Battle of Navarino, 1827. (*Built*: Bombay; *launched*: 1824; *length*: 196 feet; *speed*: *c* 9 knots; *armament*: 84 guns)

301

The Confederate ironclad *Merrimac*, commanded by Commodore Buchanan at the Battle of Hampton Roads, 1862. (*Rebuilt*: Norfolk, Virginia, 1862; *length*: 281 feet; *speed*: *c* 6 knots; *armament*: 2 × 12 inch, 8 × 11 inch guns)

The Federal steam sloop-of-war *Hartford*, Farragut's flagship at the Battle of Mobile, 1864. (*Built*: Boston; *launched*: 1858; *length*: 225 feet; *speed*: 9 knots; *armament*: 12 × 9 inch, 1 × 8 inch, 1 × 60 pounder, 1 × 20 pounder guns)

The battleship *Mikasa*, Admiral Togo's flagship at the Battle of Tsushima, 1905. (*Built by*: Vickers; *completed*: 1902; *length*: 415 feet; *speed*: 18 knots; *armament*: 4 × 12 inch, 14 × 6 inch, 20 × 12 pounder guns, 4 torpedo tubes)

The heavy cruiser, *Scharnhorst*, Graf von Spee's flagship at the Battles of Coronel and the Falkland Islands, 1914. (*Built by*: Blohm and Voss, Hamburg; *completed*: 1907; *length*: 449¾ feet; *speed*: 22½ knots; *armament*: 8 × 8·2 inch, 6 × 6 inch, 20 × 24 pounder guns, 4 torpedo tubes)

The battleship *Iron Duke*, Jellicoe's flagship at the Battle of Jutland, 1916. (*Built*: Portsmouth; *completed*: 1914; *length*: 580 feet; *speed*: 20 knots; *armament*: 10 × 13·5 inch, 12 × 6 inch guns, 4 torpedo tubes)

The aircraft carrier *Ark Royal*, Admiral Somerville's flagship in the Pursuit of the *Bismarck*, 1941. (*Built by*: Cammell Laird; *completed*: 1938; *length*: 685 feet; *speed*: 30 knots; *armament*: 16 × 4·5 inch guns; *aircraft*: 60)